TEXE MARRS BOOK OF NEW AGE CULTS AND RELIGIONS

NEW AGE
CULTS & RELIGIONS

LTP Living Truth Publishers

New Age Cults and Religions
Second Edition 1996

Scripture quotations are from the King James Version of The
Holy Bible.

Cover design: Texe Marrs

Printed in the United States of America

Library of Congress Catalog Card Number 91-62569

ISBN 0-9620086-8-0

DEDICATION

I dedicate this book to my wife, Wanda, who has made many sacrifices and worked diligently side-by-side with me to see this important work through to successful completion.

contents

Unmasking the New Age Cults and Religions

Dangerous new cults and strange religious groups and churches are stalking the citizens of America. That is the subject I explore in *New Age Cults and Religions.* Four years in the making and based on exhaustive research and extensive documentation, this is the first complete, authoritative reference guide to the proliferating cults and sects of the fastest growing religious, political, and social movement on earth today: *The New Age Religion.*

Few Christians today understand the gravity and serious nature of the menace which confronts us. Most do not understand that frightening New Age cults and religions have deeply infiltrated and now seriously impact our society. For example, groups such as *The Pacific Institute* and *The Forum* (formerly *est*) and others regularly conduct New Age seminars and training courses for such huge corporations as AT&T, Southern Edison, General Motors, and Lockheed Aerospace, as well as governmental agencies as varied as the National Aeronautics and Space Administration (NASA), the U.S. Department of Labor, and the military services.

The Silva Method, which trains people to contact spirit guides, has now been used in public schools in Buffalo, New York, while the techniques and principles taught by a false "bible" of the New Age, *A Course in Miracles,* are being applied by city governments in Houston, Minneapolis, and New York City. Meanwhile, witches and goddess advocates from the *Church of Wicca* have been invited to make presentations at public libraries in San Jose, California.

One New Age "church," the Swedenborgian *Church of the New Jerusalem,* has been accepted for full membership in the National Council of Churches. The New Age foundation called the *Esalen Institute* sponsored the trip to the United States of top Soviet politician Boris Yeltsin, while Sri Chinmoy, leader of a major New Age religious "peace" organization, was honored with an audience in Moscow by Russian president Mikhail Gorbachev. Chinmoy is also the spiritual mentor and guru for three-time Olympic champion Carl Lewis, dubbed the "world's fastest human."

Covering over 100 of the major cults and religious sects, *New Age Cults and Religions* explains:

* Why New Age cults and religions are extremely dangerous--spiritually and psychologically--and how they are able to lure and attract people of all ages and backgrounds--even men and women brought up by conservative parents, and raised to attend fundamentalist and evangelical churches.

* How these groups use such insidious methods and techniques as mind control, brainwashing, love-bombing, and esteem attacks to wear down and win over potential recruits.

* Why and how the New Age cults and religions employ such popular propagandistic tools as campaigns to protect the environment, save the whales, end world hunger, or inaugurate world peace to draw new converts and build up membership.

* The deceptive nature of these groups, including their effective but cynical and misleading use of Christian terminology, their twisting of Biblical scriptures, their calling

on the name of "Jesus," and the performing of false "miracles" and "signs and wonders" by cult leaders.

* Why more "Jim Jones" type mass suicide and massacre incidents are not only likely but inevitable in the near future.

New Age Cults and Religions also gives readers an inside look at the many false "Christs" and messiahs pushed by New Age cults and religious groups. You'll discover the unholy "bibles" of the New Age--for example, the mysterious 2,097-page *Book of Urantia*, the *Book of OAHSPE*, the *Book of Mormon*, and the *Keys of Enoch*.

Moreover, you'll discover that many of the more insidious cults promote a bizarre form of "Christianity," complete with reincarnated "Christs," strange apparitions of long dead saints and biblical prophets, and "new scriptures" such as "The Jesus Letters," dictated by entities from an unknown spiritual realm.

New Age Cults and Religions breaks through the hazy fog and clouds of false teachings and doctrines spread today by cults and new religious groups dedicated to the overthrow of traditional Christian tenets. Shining a spotlight on the hidden, inner workings of these groups, this book shows clearly just how powerful and seductive, yet unholy and cruel, are their goals and practices. Here are just a few of the topics covered in this reference sourcebook:

* The *Tara Center* and *Share International*--twin organizations headquartered in North Hollywood, California and London, England, led by an articulate Englishman, Benjamin Creme. Creme is the self-styled "John the Baptist" forerunner for the "Lord Maitreya," a shadowy New Age "Christ" whom Creme insists is already on earth today: "Our brother walks among us!"

* *Findhorn*, in Scotland, a nature community that has been called the "Vatican of the New Age movement."

* *Transcendental Meditation*, a Hindu religious group led by the Indian guru Maharishi Mahesh Yogi. Maharishi not only owns a university in Fairfield, Iowa but he is now busy overseeing the multimillion dollar construction of 20 "heavenly cities"--New Age communities--in strategic sites near key cities throughout North America.

* *The Church Universal and Triumphant* (CUT), founded by its personable and magnetic leader Elizabeth Clare Prophet. Prophet's community in Montana is furiously building underground bunkers and shelters in preparation for the World War III that, Prophet prophesies, is sure to come soon. CUT members, numbering as many as 300,000 worldwide, believe both in "Jesus" and a superior being they call "Count St. Germain."

* *Scientology*, a tremendously successful religious cult founded by the late, enigmatic L. Ron Hubbard. Hubbard's book *Dianetics* was a smash #1 *New York Times* bestseller, and his science fiction novels are also breaking sales records. How many know that Hubbard began as an initiate and disciple of the infamous British Satanist Aleister Crowley, who called himself "the Beast, 666?" How many know that Scientology has fostered the worship of the black goddess Kali? Do you know the hidden meaning of the word "Dianetics" coined by L. Ron Hubbard?

* *The UFO societies and organizations*--are they satanic, or are they on to something genuine and staggeringly real? *New Age Cults and Religions* provides the answers as it explores the newer UFO cults, peopled by UFO cultists who say they are communicating with extraterrestrials claiming to be bearers of the glad tidings of a New Age World Religion and a coming One World Order.

* *The Order of the Golden Dawn*, with a reputed 40,000 membership, led by an occultist who has ominously proclaimed that the New Age can only be brought into being through

"blood, disruption, chaos, and pain." Guess who's targeted for this violence and suffering?

* *The Mormons*, a religion with an incredible 6 million international followers. Discover why this is an unchristian religion and why its elders are now rapidly changing its temple rituals and doctrines to conform to the unity rules of the coming New Age World Religion, in which Mormonism is already playing a significant role.

* The *Sufi Moslems* of the U.S.A., a religious group started by a man who claims to have received his instructions from an apparition who identified "herself" as "Mother Mary."

* The *Messianic Church of Yahweh* (MCY), a New Age religious cult based on a belief in crystal and other occult powers. MCY was the brainchild of Randall Baer, a brilliant man who was miraculously converted to *true Christianity* and vowed to expose the New Age movement. Shortly afterwards, Randall Baer died under bizarre circumstances. The police report simply states that his car veered off a rocky 300-foot cliff into a valley far below. Was this an *accident*? If not, *who killed Randall Baer?*

* *Ramtha*, a 35,000-year old warrior spirit channeled by an attractive blonde Seattle woman, JZ Knight. Knight's followers include TV actress Linda Evans (*Dynasty's* "Crystal"). With the millions brought in by the "sage wisdom" of Ramtha, Ms. Knight has been able to afford an incredibly plush lifestyle. Rich beyond our wildest dreams, JZ Knight's stable of Arabian thoroughbred horses are comfortably housed in a barn with expensive crystal chandeliers hanging from the rafters.

* *Theosophy*, an occultic group so evil that even Elvis Presley, raised in a Christian home, was lured into its deceptive "secret doctrine."

* The *Temple of Set* and the *Church of Satan*, two decidedly satanic religious groups. The Church of Satan, founded by showman Anton LaVey, has in the past attracted into its fold celebrities ranging from actress Jayne Mansfield to singer and actor Sammy Davis, Jr. The Temple of Set, headed by Dr. Michael Aquino, has conducted mysterious ritual services in the same castle in Germany where Nazi Gestapo chief Heinrich Himmler once held midnight occultic pagan initiation ceremonies for his elite SS troops.

Pray That Eyes Will Be Opened

It is my fervent prayer that after you have read this important book exposing the unholy and threatening New Age cults and religions, you will share it with others. Our Lord four years ago gave me a commission to go forth--unafraid and trusting in His power--and unmask the New Age, including its many octopus-like tentacles. That is why I wrote *New Age Cults and Religions.*

Today, so many unwitting people are ignorant of the devices of the New Age and of its hidden goals. Let us together pray that this book will open up the eyes of thousands, letting them know that even as the Adversary works through a vast network of cults and religions, ultimately God's Will shall prevail. He *is* indeed Lord of all!

Texe Marrs
Austin, Texas

PART 1

THE NEW AGE EXPLOSION

The first and cardinal rule in the New Age is simply this: "Believe in any god and in anything, but do not claim that your god, or your belief, is exclusive."

The New Spiritual Revolution Sweeps Across America

"The hard pink light of an autumn afternoon streams through the windows, illuminating a young woman with a mane of tight black curls and an expression that borders on the beatitude. She is explaining her vision of a cosmic destiny for mankind, a New Age of existence peopled by superior beings." Her vision is of a world in which there is no suffering, only laughter and smiles. "It is a flow that cannot be resisted or ignored," Kim Perene says. "One day we are all going to wake up, and it will be all around us."

Kim Perene is a 24-year old secretary and New Age believer recently interviewed in the Lifestyle section of the *Atlanta Journal* by staff writer Alan Sverdlik. Ms. Perene's view is shared by millions across America and tens of millions across the globe. The ranks of New Age believers is huge and ever growing. Now well past the glittery and sensationalist fad stage of crystals, spirit channeling, and UFOs--though intense interest in such phenomena continues--the New Age has entered what I call its *hardcore doctrinal phase*.

During this more durable period of New Age growth, the

role of New Age cults and religious sects is becoming increasingly dominant. In addition, many churches and religions fostered by New Age thinking and spirituality are finding more and more disciples and initiates. Moreover, as I will demonstrate, thousands of New Age cults, religions, sects, organizations, groups, and churches are now coalescing, cooperatively joining and linking themselves into one gigantic religious brotherhood.

Setting aside individual differences and doctrinal nuances, the New Age leadership is today proposing that since "all is one," it is fitting that a New World Religion be forged out of the disparate units which make up the New Age movement as a whole. In the coming era, then, what we will no doubt see is an emphasis on the common characteristics and shared beliefs of all in the New Age. The many New Age cults and religions will hold hands and, regrettably, uniformly take sides against Christianity. The New Age groups will become a united, adversarial group in opposition to long cherished traditions fostered by the Judeo-Christian ethic. In fact, this process is already far advanced.

Just a few years ago, when my bestselling book, *Dark Secrets of the New Age*, was first published, there were a number of Christian pastors and other leaders who confessed to me that they simply did not believe that such a thing as "the New Age" even existed. Today, few deny that there is an incredible, ongoing transformation taking place in American society. The evidence of this surrounds us on every front.

In the *Los Angeles Times* last year was the report that an estimated 30,000 New Agers had filled the Los Angeles Airport Hilton Convention Center for a three-day long Whole Life Expo. Claiming to "vibrate a lot of positive energy" this event has been held in Southern California each year since 1983. The most recent expo featured 200 speakers and nearly 300 exhibit booths. Long lines of people paid up to $33 per workshop plus $17 a day for general admission. Participants found a smorgasbord of New Age techniques, practices, religions, and messages to chose from. For example, on one hand there were seminar presentations concerning mystical ways to attract money, while, at a number of Expo exhibition booths, subliminal tapes were on sale which promised to reveal the "positive and miraculous power of prosperity consciousness." "Get your first million here today," one display sign announced.

The theme of this particular expo was "Healing Mother Earth," and a panel of Hollywood celebrities was on hand to promote the New Age view concerning holistic healing and ecological concerns. There were also electronic devices being demonstrated--brain machines which hold out the promise of altering brain waves to send a person into an eternal form of electronic bliss. The pitch was that through glorious alterations in brain chemistry, an exalted state of cosmic consciousness can be achieved. Presto!--god-like powers.

Across the United States many such expos, conventions, and grand galas are being presented. But this is only the froth, the foam atop a smashing series of oceanic waves that are pelting and blasting away at the shoreline of American society. "The main fight, make no mistake," said theologian Neal Sperre in 1961 in his book *Christology and Personality*, "is between the Christian faith and its inner classical meaning and the new orientalized versions." As Sperre went on to say, "the supernatural, personalistic, classical Christian faith is now being undermined by an ultimately impersonal, or transpersonal faith. Winds are blowing gale-strong out of the east."

These statements are not hyperbole and the problem is not being over-dramatized. The New Age Movement is a herculean accomplishment by powerful spiritual forces firmly opposed to Biblical Christianity. As Barbara Marx Hubbard, a leading New Age visionary, has proclaimed: "A New Order is being born that will be as different from what exists now as the Renaissance was from the Middle Ages." Hubbard believes that humanity is genetically "pre-programmed for New Age enlightenment" and she has warned that those of us who are not ready for the New Age religion will be destroyed in a cataclysmic conclusion to the current age of traditional Christianity.

The Cult Explosion

Perhaps the most frightening thing about the New Age is its use of unchristian cults and aberrant religions and sects to promote its goals. The upsurge of cults in the United States began in the late-60s and became a highly visible social phenomenon by the mid-70s. Many studies have been conducted, thousands of media reports and articles published, expert testimonies given in legal cases, and legislative hearings held in an attempt to deal with the destructive and harmful cults which are now dangerously influencing millions of lives. The scary thing today is that many of the New Age and occultic cults and religions now prosperous and growing were, only a few years ago, considered unhealthy and ridiculous. But in recent years, many have undergone a whitewashing in the public mind-view and their far out teachings are being unquestionably accepted.

For example, once upon a time it was generally considered absurd, outrageous, and certainly unwise for a person to embrace such cult groups as Scientology, Hare Krishna, Eckankar, the Moonies, or one of the multitude of Hindu gurus. Not so today. Logic has been turned on end so that in the current era, even the most dangerous cults are readily afforded an aura of respectability.

Believe me, many of the groups described in this book are not harmless. Though there is disagreement as to the relative danger of each of the cults and religions, there is no dispute that at least *some* of these groups can be hideously life threatening.

Recently, I had occasion to read the book *Combatting Cults Mind Control,* by Steven Hassan. Hassan is a brilliant man who himself managed to escape from the clutches of a controversial New Age cult. Today, he is a full-time worker in exposing cult techniques. He writes in his book that there are people today involved in cults who are being "systematically lied to, physically abused, encouraged to lose contact with family and friends, and induced to work at jobs which offer them little or no significant opportunities for personal or professional growth."

Hassan also says that what he has learned about many of the cults conjures up "an image of totalitarianism from George Orwell's *Nineteen Eighty-Four*." He goes on to add that while the world at large may not as yet have become the nightmare reality that Orwell depicted--a place where state "thought police" maintain complete control of people's mental and emotional lives and where it is a crime to act and think independently or even to fall in love, nevertheless:

> In an increasing number of organizations in our world, *Nineteen Eighty-Four* has come true: Basic respect for the individual simply doesn't exist, and people are gradually led to think and behave in very similar ways through a process of mind control.

Because of this unseemly and torturous process, says Hassan, "they lose the ability to act on their own and are often exploited for the sake of the group's economic or political ends . . . whether religious or secular in its apparent orientation."

Therefore, we should not take these cults lightly. I believe strongly that individuals who become caught up in New Age cults and religions may well find, eventually, that they are not only imperiled in a spiritual sense, but that their physical well-being is also at stake. Many of the cults listed in this book deprive their disciples and initiates of basic nutritional needs. Some prescribe a rigid vegetarian diet or require their members to use a regimen of unsafe and unhealthy herbs and other natural substances that are extremely harmful and damaging to the body. Yet, members of the cults rarely question the necessity for such strict and excessive dietary restrictions. Obedience to the leadership and the need to develop harmonious and close relationships with other peer members in the group prevent the individual from using his or her full mental capabilities and evaluative thinking process.

Please understand, I am not saying that *every* group, *every* cult, *every* religious sect and organization listed in this book constitutes a present danger to their members' health and welfare. I only point out that some do. And while the others may not endanger the *physical* body, certainly they have placed in jeopardy the *spiritual* health and moral reasoning capacity of the men and women under their discipleship. This, in fact, is an even greater and more significant reason to avoid the New Age cults and religions, as well as the popular New Age environmental, political, economic, social, educational, and related organizations and groups.

All influence their members to develop and defend a worldview totally contradictory and even sometimes hateful of true Christianity. Jesus once told us not to fear he who could kill the body, but rather fear only he who can kill the soul. We should realize, therefore, that the most dangerous aspect of the New Age is the spiritual damage that it may cause the individual. This is a harm that may well endure for an eternity.

The Octopus-Like Tentacles of the New Age

Many people are unwittingly drawn into the New Age because of its insidious, yet subtle, infiltration of so many areas of our daily lives. For example, the New Age is now freely and with little organized opposition being taught in the business world, with seminars and workshops conducted on-premises in America's largest corporations. Our children are being introduced to New Age practices and theories in schools. Nightly we view television "entertainment" that is jam-packed with New Age plots, and the secular book world is literally eaten up with New Age themes in both the fiction and non-fiction categories of books.

Unfortunately, many people whose first experience with the New Age is by one of these methods often soon develops an insatiable appetite to learn more about the New Age. This is because of the seductiveness and lure of the New Age message. It so often comes disguised as an exciting new way to enhance or empower the self while, in reality, the New Age simply represents another feeble attempt of the Adversary to pollute Christianity, promote immorality, and foster unethical attitudes.

The frightening situation today is that, whether in the corporate work place, in our schools, or in any of hundreds of other forums, New Age cults and religious groups are being invited in. Often they come cloaked in a disguise other than that of a religion. The leaders of the New Age well know that the American ethic dictates that religion and dogma be excluded from the workplace and from our public schools. Therefore, these messengers of deception must hide the true nature of their mission.

Tens of Thousands of Entry Points

As one prominent New Age authority has stated, "There are tens of thousands of entry points" into the New Age. Indeed, there are so many New Age cults and religious groups active today that entire directories have been published to list them. Examples include *Network: the First Report and Directory, The National New Age Yellow Pages*, and *The New Age Catalog*. Moreover, new groups spring up almost daily.

Some of the groups discussed in this book are being paid large sums of money by industry and government to bring their programs into the workplace. For example, in 1986 representatives of IBM, AT&T, and General Motors gathered in New Mexico to discuss how occultic techniques and Hindu mysticism might help their executives become more competitive in an increasingly challenging world marketplace. Meanwhile, New Age subjects from est to firewalking are being explored by top management. At Stanford

University's much respected Graduate School of Business, a seminar on "Creativity in Business" includes such activities as meditation, chanting, dream work, the use of Tarot Cards, and discussion of New Age capitalism. Although these incidents were widely reported in the secular press, including the vaunted *New York Times*, and also exposed in Christian magazines such as *Eternity*, the inroads of the New Age into the business community have continued to blossom. Today a large part of the funding for New Age cults and religions come from our business community.

Funding also comes from governmental agencies. For example, NASA, our nation's space agency, paid Werner Erhard, founder of the New Age group est and the newer The Forum, the sum of $40,000 to personally travel to NASA's space center and teach managers there his New Age thinking techniques.

Moreover, our education system is fast becoming almost an adjunct of the New Age Movement. As Dave Hunt, in his book, *Peace, Prosperity and the Coming Holocaust*, writes:

> The New Age Movement does its most strategic work in the public schools. It is teaching our children that they are gods, and that the only authority they need to follow is the "Inner Light" of their "Higher Self." New Age educators are deliberately trying to bring about a transformation of thinking, morals, worldview, and personal identity in the public schools of America.

It should be noted that such phrases as "Higher Self" or "Inner Light" are New Age terms for *deity*.

It is a well-known fact that since the 60s, New Age groups have pushed New Age concepts and practices for application in our schools. For example, the Association for Humanistic Psychology suggested over a decade ago that public school teachers incorporate the following activities into their daily routine. As you read this, you should understand that the recommendations of this New Age group have since been duly complied with by thousands of school districts across America and Canada:

> THE STUDENT WILL: Do yoga each morning before class; interpret their astrological charts; send messages via ESP; mind project; astral project; heal their own illnesses; speak with their Higher Selves and receive information necessary for joyful living; lift energies from the power chakra to the heart chakra (Buddhist and Hindu concepts); practice skills necessary for color healing; hold an image of themselves as being perfect; receive advice from their personal (spirit) guides; merge minds with others in the class to experience a collective consciousness of the group.

New Age organizations and religions ranging from Transcendental Meditation and the Silva Method to the Church of Wicca have brought their techniques and methodology into schoolrooms. However, fearing retribution by Christian fundamentalists, these techniques are often covered up by the use of innocuous phrases, titles, and names to describe them. For example, occult forms of meditation are rarely called *meditation*: instead such destructive and mind-warping techniques in the classroom are cloaked in such deceptive language as "centering," "focusing," "magic time," "visualizing," "think time," "creativity," "mind play," "visioning," "guided imagery," "guided fantasy," and so forth.

It is clear that the New Age has graduated from the Gee Whiz, Golly Gee, Shirley MacLaine faddism stage into a bright new era of respectability and acceptance in which it is influencing every segment of our lives. New Age cults and religions are ascending to center stage, and increasingly their unchristian values are being enthusiastically accepted by the movers-and-shakers of society. The American way of life is being drastically revised and debilitated. What is even more astonishing is that the thousands of New Age cults and religious groups, as well as the multitude of New Age groups in political, economic, educational, and other arenas, are now networking together and making an astonishingly successful attempt at forming a World Religion of Unity.

Unity is made possible because New Age believers easily cross over from cult to cult and from group to group. Not too long ago I did a study on why people enter the New Age Movement and why people become involved in New Age cults and religions. In speaking to over 150 New Age believers involved in cults, I discovered that a full 131 had been active in at least four other cults in the previous three year period. In other words, over a period of about three years the typical New Age believer involves himself or herself in a total of *five cult groups*.

My findings are confirmed by many other researchers. For example, Geoffry Ahern, in his book *Sun at Midnight*, reported that he had interviewed 18 men and women involved in the New Age cult founded by Rudolf Steiner called Anthroposophy. He found that 12 of the 18 had previous experience and involvement in other cults prior to entering the realm of Anthroposophy. Another researcher has found that cult members stay in a cult an average of only 90 days before, for one reason or another, they drift on, inevitably to become linked up with yet another cult or religious faction. It is apparent that these people have few spiritual bearings for they seem to be like unanchored ships in a storm, tossed by the tempest of the sea and carried away with every wind of doctrine and every sleight of hand by the gurus.

The one trait prevalent among almost all those who are involved in New Age cults and religions is that they are seekers of spiritual experience. In other words, they do not desire to simply have a *surface* knowledge or a *shallow* faith, their heartfelt desire is to *know*, to become immersed in "truth." They are, therefore, sitting ducks for the New Age elite who declare forthrightly that theirs is not a religion but an all-encompassing *spiritual movement*. In a recent issue of *Back to Godhood* magazine, published by the Hare Krishna movement (known officially as the *International Society of*

Krishna Consciousness), the Hindu god Krishna was quoted from the Hindu scriptures, the *Gita*, as saying that the seeker must "abandon all varieties of religion and surrender unto me."

This is a prime example of how the New Age promotes universal spiritual values and requires *surrender* of the new recruit's logical reasoning and critical thinking faculties. The appeal is not to logic nor to what is ultimate Truth. Certainly the appeal is not to a sound mind; but instead, the New Age cults strive to arouse and massage one's emotions. Their expertise lies in the ability of their leadership to dredge up experiential feelings, desires, and deeply felt longings and instincts in the fresh and vulnerable new disciple.

God As You Understand Him: The New Age Deity

The first and cardinal rule in the New Age is simply this: "Believe in *any* god and in *anything*, but do not claim that *your* god, or *your* belief, is exclusive." That is, as long as you accept that all is one and that your religion is no better than the next person's, then you qualify to be a New Ager. It does not matter whether you worship a Hindu guru, your own Higher Self, the group, or a pagan deity from ancient Rome, Greece, or Babylon.

Indeed, the second, unyielding rule of all New Age cults and religions is simply this: *God is what or whom you personally wish him (or her) to be.* This is also the same rule so vigorously enforced by Alcoholics Anonymous (AA). Indeed, AA can certainly be classified as a New Age cult based on its occultic origins and its rejection of biblical Christianity. As his many biographies reveal, AA's founder, Bill Wilson despised evangelical Christianity. Along with friends Aldous Huxley and Gerald Heard, he opened himself up to demonic contact by taking such hallucinogenic drugs as LSD. Eventually he died of debilitating emphysema-- Wilson was a three pack a day cigarette smoker.

Actually, AA is perhaps the *ideal* New Age religion in that it denies being a religion at all while proudly boasting that it is a *spiritual movement*. There is even a Fundamentalists Anonymous to help people "escape" from such evangelical fundamentalist Christian churches as the Assemblies of God, Pentecostals, Southern Baptists, and so forth.

Moreover, AA has as one of its essential 12 steps the goal of turning over one's life--that is *surrendering*--to "God as you understand Him." It is not at all accidental that this universalist doctrine is exactly the same as that of the Hindus and their cousins, the Hare Krishnas, who quote Krishna as they tell their disciples "Abandon all varieties of religion and just surrender unto Me." The question really becomes, who is the *"Me?"* To *whom* must the individual surrender his reason, his intellect and--quite frankly--his soul?

That is the question of questions, but the answer is not to be found in the literature of Alcoholics Anonymous or any of the other New Age cults and religions. While these groups offer us a wide range of different "gods" and "Christs" to be worshipped and adored, most are in agreement that it really just does not matter *which* god or *which* Christ one serves. To choose a *particular* god means that you are involved with religion, but in the New Age, imbued as it is with a doublespeak form of language deception; spirituality is in, religion is out. A "spiritual person," it is taught, simply picks and chooses among the available deities--or he can even create his own.

A New World Religion is Promoted

However, because contradictions in the New Age are not uncommon, we should not be at all surprised that many in the New Age, while insisting that we abandon all varieties of "religion," go on to the absurd conclusion that while abandoning all varieties of religion, we should boldly go forth to establish a *New World Religion*. This is to be a unified religion which combines all of the spiritual aspects known to and practiced by man. Thus, we find a growing *unity movement* among the various New Age groups and sects and a monumental, almost superhuman effort to establish a New World Religion. This new world religious system, its leaders have proclaimed, is to be one that accepts all religions while denying that any is superior. In other words, the only acceptable religion will be a New World Religion that is syncretic, unified, and fused from a conglomeration of all the other spiritual ideas in existence on the face of planet earth.

Amusingly, or sadly, whichever is your perspective on the matter, the proponents and advocates of this New World Religion deny that it is a "religion" since it does not have an exclusive basis but is universalist; it is not separative but is accepting and tolerant of all other faiths. Thus, the New Age is *the* religion of all religions and yet it is claimed not to be a religion.

As Brad Steiger, UFO expert and New Age channeler, writes in his book *The Fellowship*, the new "evolving religion . . . will be structured to serve the spirit of the Oneness." He adds, "Even the word 'religion' will not be used anymore . . . Drop the term 'religion' and use the term 'spirituality.'"

This seemingly contradictory effort by the New Age to promote spirituality while denouncing separatist religions becomes more understandable once we comprehend that the real goal of the New Age is to extinguish true, biblical Christianity. Since Christianity stands alone and is distinct from all other faiths, the clarion call of the New Age cults and religions is for mankind to rid itself of distinctions and separativeness and come together as *one spiritual entity*. Separate, exclusive religions are prohibited; a unified New World Religion is the goal.

Truths of the New World Religion

This drive for a New World Religion has been reported in a number of authoritative sources. For example, in a Long Beach, California *Press-Telegram* newspaper (July 7, 1990), the religion page carried a feature article with this headline: "New World Religion Combines Eastern, Western Ideals." In the article, reporter Dana Drake wrote: "A New World Religion is abroad. It is nameless as yet, but it is a synthesis of the Eastern and Western approaches of God and is based upon six truths." The first truth, said Drake, involves the existence of God as both transcendent and immanent; that is, God is both outside of us and yet is within every person. A second truth, said Drake, is that God is greater than the whole yet present in each part. This, she explained, comes from the *Baghavad Gita*, the Hindu scriptures, in which the god Krishna is quoted as exclaiming, "Having pervaded this whole universe with a fragment of myself, I remain."

Another "truth," or belief, of the New World Religion is the *denial of Christ as the God of the Bible*. Instead, as Drake suggested, in the New World Religion, Christ is simply the eldest of a great family of brothers. What's more, each of us is treading the Path of Evolution, eventually to become divine in our own right. This Path of Evolution involves beliefs of both reincarnation and karma, the methods by which man becomes a perfect deity.

Yet another belief or truth in this New World Religion, Drake reports, is the coming of a *World Teacher* or *Savior* who upon his appearance will bring new revelation to man. This is not referring to the Jesus Christ of the Bible, but to a different "Savior"--one far, far different. In the New World Religion, for example, Buddha, who taught that God is light and showed the way to illumination, is as much in favor as is the Jesus of the Bible for "All are men made perfect." Yes, we are all simply part of the whole. But some are more advanced on the Path of Evolution, because another "truth" of the New Age World Religion is that those of us who become enlightened and perfect become members of the elite spiritual hierarchy known as the White Brotherhood.

Astara, a religious group covered in this book, is an exemplar of this New World Religion. In one of its publications, Astara insists that its teachings are a "compliment to *any* religion." Furthermore, Astara is said to be perfect "for those who profess no specific faith (for) it is a compendium of them all." In Astara's guidelines we find this statement describing their membership: "Here, in a common wave of souls seeking Light, are to be found Christians, Jews, Hindus, Buddhists, and the adherent of many other faiths as well as the non-member of any." "If your needs and goals run parallel to these," the publication continues, "then you are indeed a New Age Seeker--and Astara may very well be the ideal channel, arriving in your life at the ideal moment." (From the publication *If You Are A Seeker...*).

A New Religion Called "Networking"

If a group, cult, church, or organization will simply profess that all belief systems are essentially the same, and that at the core of each is a common basis for understanding and cooperation, that group thereby makes itself an eligible and desirable participant in the overall New World Religion. This is why so many of the New Age cults and religions described in this book are now working closely together, weaving their universal teachings into a mosaic of views acceptable to all. Theirs' is what one of their leaders, Marilyn Ferguson, in her book *The Aquarian Conspiracy*, has called an "open conspiracy."

Another leader, Jose Arguelles, who masterminded the worldwide Harmonic Convergence of August, 1987, in an interview in *Magical Blend* magazine frankly stated, "We are almost at the completion stage of bringing all the thousands of New Age groups, organizations, and churches together."

Ken Keyes, yet another New Age leader whose group is also featured in this book, has declared: "We are at the final world stage of putting it all together. It is a New Religion called 'Networking' . . . The New Age Wave is now entering social change."

The future of the New Age cults and religions is that of a growing unity amidst diversity. Indeed, one New Age group promoting this goal is an organization appropriately named the *Unity-and-Diversity Council.*

In recognizing that each of their groups, cults, or religions is part of the whole--only one unit in the cafeteria-style spiritual conglomeration that makes up the New World Religion, each New Age cult leader nevertheless clings doggedly to his own special variety of teachings, and, of course, to his own closely held financial assets. Yet, while most people involved in the New Age freely acknowledge and recognize that they are all part and parcel of a consolidated spiritual movement--even a New World Religion--most deny that they are "religious!"

A prime example of this inconsistency is the wording of the official petition for incorporation of the Theosophical Society, published in founder Helena Blavatsky's *The Key to Theosophy.* The author states: "The petitioner (the Theosophical Society) is not a religious body. I report this negative finding for the reason that the word 'theosophical' contained in petitioner's names conveys a possible religious implication . . . Merely to teach a religion . . . is not . . . religious work."

In other words, the Theosophical Society maintains that it is not a religion but rather, its purpose is "Merely to teach a religion." This is, of course, pure nonsense; it is doublespeak. A group formed to *teach a religion* is indisputably a religious body. But this is an obvious fact that the Theosophical Society and most other New Age groups, vociferously deny.

Yet, there are some New Age leaders who readily admit their intentions to work toward a New World Religion. Lola Davis, in her book *Toward A World Religion for the New Age* writes, "An increasing number of people are . . . preparing mankind for a World Religion that's compatible with the New Age."

What is the New Age?

Up to now I have discussed the New Age Movement and its multifaceted cult organizational arrangement without completely defining the term "New Age." In my book *Dark Secrets of the New Age* I noted that one important way to grasp the significance and meaning of the New Age is revealed in its vocabulary. I observed, for example, that when New Age representatives use such familiar Christian terms as God, Christ, Messiah, the Second Coming, born again, salvation, angel, heaven and hell, and the Kingdom of God, their meanings are radically different from those expressed in the Word of God. Below I have taken the liberty of listing several key terms familiar to Christianity which are also common in the New Age. But I have taken the further step of revealing the esoteric, or hidden and occultic New Age meaning of each.

God: An impersonal energy force, immanent in all things. To the New Age, "God" can be referred to either as she or he, mother or father, god or goddess. Most New Age teachers hold that Mother Earth, the sun, the moon, and the stars--indeed all of nature--can be worshipped as "God."

Christ: A reincarnated avatar, messiah, or messenger sent from the "hierarchy" (see *Angels* below) to give the living on earth spiritually advanced revelation. The New Age contends that Buddha, Mohammed, Confucius, Jesus, and many others were "Christ," but many contend that one greater than all of them will soon come to usher in the New Age. To the Christian, this coming New Age "Christ" is, in fact, the Antichrist.

Angels: Frequently called Ascended Masters, Masters of Wisdom, Ancient Masters, spirit guides, inner guides, spirit counselors, one's Higher Self, the Self, Superbeings, aeons, muses, or walk-ins. Collectively called the "hierarchy." Whichever term is used, the discerning Christian will recognize these shadowy entities not as "angels," but as demons.

Born Again (Rebirth): Personal or planetary trans-formation and healing. The point at which a New Age believer "lets go" and allows his Higher Self or Inner Guide (translated: demon) to guide and direct his life. Some New Agers describe this as *Kundalini*, a Hindu term meaning "serpent power," a moment of instant rebirth when the recipient is said to be transformed by a flash of light, receiving the benefit of higher consciousness as well as greater spiritual awareness and wisdom. Such a rebirth is said to convey "Christ Consciousness" on the individual.

The Second Coming: The New Age assigns two definitions to this phrase, each of which subverts the true meaning of the Second Coming of Jesus prophesied in the Bible. first, it is claimed that at the Second Coming a New Age believer achieves "Christ Consciousness," an exalted, mystical, higher state in which he is spiritually transformed into a divine being. This phrase also can mean the appearance on earth of the New Age Messiah, or "Christ," and his hierarchy of demons from the spirit world.

Heaven/Kingdom of God: The terms heaven and Kingdom of God are often indistinguishable to the New Ager. Each refers to a spiritually cleansed and purified earth in which mankind has achieved "Christ Consciousness" and has become akin to godkind. The New Age, or Aquarian Age, is expected to be the era when heaven and the Kingdom of God are realized on earth. The reincarnated "Christ" (the Antichrist) is to reign over the New Age kingdom, bringing in a One World Religion and consolidating all nations into one monolithic government.

Hell: New Agers deny the existence of a hell and a judgment. They also deny that sin and evil exist. God is alleged to be beyond good and evil, neither of which is a relevant term to the New Age. Evil is simply an illusion. The beliefs in reincarnation and karma reinforce the New Age's rejection of the reality of hell, strengthening the false teaching that man is inevitably evolving into godhood.

Practices, Techniques, and Doctrines of the New Age

Understanding the special definitions assigned Christian words and phrases by New Age leaders, we see the subtle deceit and confusion employed.

The New Age can therefore be defined as a religious system composed of a large variety of cults, groups, organizations, and other entities, whether or not that group or entity admits that it is in fact New Age. The exact practices, techniques, and doctrines of the various groups within the New Age vary considerably. For example, a particular group may emphasize one or more of the following:

Eastern Mysticism
Visualization
Another "Jesus"
Witchcraft
Lucifer worship
Ascended Masters
Man is God Doctrine
Numerology
Reflexology
Dragons
Lord Maitreya
Networking
Reincarnation
Paganism
Anti-semitism
Sun God worship
Psychic Powers
Holistic Health
Shamanism
Human Potential
Crystal Powers
Parapsychology

Mystery Teachings
Globalism
Universalism
Atlantis and other "lost worlds"
Signs and Wonders
Goddess Worship
Hypnosis
Divination
Wizards
Swastikas and other Occult
    Symbols
Karma
An Occult Hierarchy
Nature worship
The Jewish Kabbala
Vegetarianism
Yoga
Altered States of
    Consciousness
Magic
The Perennial Philosophy
Tarot Cards

Spirit Channeling	Trance States
Psychic Forces	Astrology
Seances and Mediums	Rune Stones
Color Therapy	Aryan/Aquarian race theory
Mandalas	Mantras
Initiations	Jungian Archetypes

New Age vs. True Christianity: A Contrast

All of these indications of New Age influence and teachings are labeled by the Bible either as abominations or they are clearly understood to be acts or behaviors of a dangerous nature prohibited to man by God. In effect, a vast number of the practices and teachings of the New Age are *expressly forbidden in the Bible*. For example, *enchantments and sorcery* are prohibited in Leviticus 19:26; II Chronicles 33:6; Isaiah 47:8-11; Daniel 1:20; Deuteronomy 18:10-12; II Kings 17:17; and Jeremiah 27:8. *Spirit channeling*, or conjuration of spirits from a realm beyond our physical senses, is shown to be an abomination and a sin in many passages, including Deuteronomy 18:11; Isaiah 8:19; I Samuel 28:1-25; and I Chronicles 10:13-14. Likewise, *astrology*, the divination of the supposed influence of the stars upon human affairs and terrestrial events, is seen to be a hoax and an unholy pseudoscience in such Biblical passages as Isaiah 47:12-15; Jeremiah 10:2; Daniel 5:7-15; and Deuteronomy 18:10-14.

For another example, we note that *polytheism*, the worship of many gods, and the false teaching that we can worship a god of our own understanding, are clearly seen to be lies once we read Exodus 20:3, which says we are to have no other gods before the God of the Bible. This is one of God's commandments.

In respect to the New Age teaching that man should trust in his own intuition, his Higher Self, and that *he himself is an evolving god,* we read this admonition in Proverbs 28:26: "He that trusteth in his own heart is a fool . . ."

Moreover, both the New Age doctrine of *reincarnation* and the theory that man can become a god are seen to be merely tricks of the Adversary that have ancient origins, as reported in the third chapter of Genesis. There, the serpent suggests to Eve that regardless of what God told her, she would surely not die if she ate the forbidden fruit; rather, the serpent said, if she would *disobey God* and eat the fruit, her eyes would be opened and she would be *like God.*

There Is Only One "I AM"

One of the New Age religious groups covered in this book calls itself "I Am." In itself this is certainly a blasphemous statement, and in Isaiah 47 we see God's judgment on such a blasphemous belief. According to that passage, the person who declares and says in his heart "I am and there is none other beside me" will, in spite of his or her many sorceries and great demonically inspired power, eventually be destroyed. And to those who would claim that they themselves are divine we have merely but to read Ezekiel 28:1-2:

> The Word of the Lord came again unto me, saying, son of man, say unto the prince of Tyrus, Thus saith the Lord God; Because thine heart is lifted up, and thou hast said, I am a God, I sit in the seat of God, in the midst of the seas; yet thou art a man, and not God . . .

I would like to emphasize the importance of the verse above. What the Lord Himself stated through Ezekiel is substantially this: that the man who says "I am a god" deceives himself for he is *only* a man, a fact which will no doubt be borne out in due time. For, when we continue in

Ezekiel, in the same chapter (28) we see that this Prince of Tyrus, who erroneously believed himself to be divine, came under the judgment of God. God ruled that the "terrible of the nations" would draw their swords against this ruler and his nation so that they should be brought "down to the pit" and should die there. The Prince of Tyrus was to be slain by his enemies as a fitting penalty for his blasphemy and rebellion.

In Ezekiel, the Lord made a stunning and revealing declaration that should certainly be heeded by those in the New Age cults and religions who are tempted to say "I am God." The Lord asked this question: "Will thou yet say before him that slayeth thee, I am God? But thou shalt be a man, and no God, in the hand of him that slayeth thee. Thou shalt die the deaths of the uncircumcised by the hands of strangers: for I have spoken it, saith the Lord God" (Ezekiel 28:9-10).

Should Not A People Seek Unto Their God?

In addition to the "I am God" doctrine, another unholy practice common to most New Age groups is that of spirit channeling, or communication with spirits from beyond. Once again the Bible has the answer to whether this is a healthy and safe practice. Isaiah 8:19, 22 records:

> And when they shall say unto you, Seek unto those who are mediums, and unto wizards that peep, and that mutter: should not a people seek unto their God? Should they seek on behalf of the living to the dead? ... And they shall look unto the earth; and behold trouble and darkness, dimness of anguish; and they shall be driven to darkness.

The consequences of seeking after spirit channellers, mediums, sorcerers, wizards, and the like are dire: "... they shall be driven to darkness."

The Nature of Jesus

Then we get to the subject of the nature of Christ Jesus. The Bible makes absolute, flat-out statements that Jesus is fully and wholly God, Paul declaring that in Him is all the fullness of the Godhead bodily (see Colossians 2:9-10). Yet, most New Age groups deny that Jesus is wholly God, contending that He was simply a perfected man, only one in a succession of Christs, and so forth. An example comes from Annie Besant, former head of Theosophy, who in her book, *Esoteric Christianity*, claimed that Christ was not God but was simply a man who perfected himself and came to give the Mystery Teachings to us. Besant asserts that another being actually had inhabited the body of Jesus:

> That Mighty One who had used the body of Jesus as His vehicle, and whose guardian care extends over the whole evolution of the fifth root race of humanity, gave unto the strong hands of the Holy Disciple who had surrendered to Him his body the care of the infant church. Perfecting his human evolution, Jesus became one of the Masters of Wisdom ... He was the Hierophant in the Christian Mysteries, the direct teacher of the initiates. He is the inspiration that kept alive the Gnosis in the church ...

What Besant is proclaiming here is that there is a Mighty One, whom she declines to name, who merely used the body of Jesus as his vehicle. Yet, the first chapter of the Gospel of John tells us quite forthrightly that Jesus came in the flesh *as God* and that there is no other God but Him. It reveals that He was the Word that was made flesh, the Word that was *with* God from the beginning, and *also* that Jesus is God. Jesus, therefore, did not "perfect His human evolution," He did not become one of the "Masters of Wisdom." The only half-truth we can find in Annie Besant's statement is that Jesus did in fact take Christianity under His special charge, though not in the sense that Besant implies.

The New Age Revival of Gnosticism

It is interesting that New Agers such as Besant would mention "Gnosis in the church." For in essence, the New Age is a revival of the gnosticism that was prevalent in the days of Paul and the early apostles. This is even admitted by many New Age elitists who boast that they are gnostics and what they have come to do is bring people to "know" their divinity through a process of *Gnosis*. For example, in *Omni* magazine recently, author Christopher Lash penned an article, "Soul of a New Age," in which he stated:

> The influence of the gnostic tradition on New Age thought is unmistakable. The transpersonal (New Age) psychologist Ken Wilber, described by an admirer as the "Einstein of Consciousness," draws heavily on gnosticism in books like *The Atman Project* (1980) and *Up From Eden* (1983). A summary of his cosmology reveals the extent of his indebtedness to gnostic mythology: "Human life is moving *up* from Eden, not down. The fall...was nothing less than the involuntary descent of God into matter--the creation of the universe itself... The universe is involved in the mighty drama of awakening and reunion ... Salvation represents a progression ... to awareness of our prior union with God."

Lash also notes that another prominent New Ager, Robert Anton Wilson, author of *The Cosmic Trigger: Final Secret of the Illuminati*, traces the history of New Age thinking all the way back to the Rosicrucians, the Renaissance magic societies, medieval witchcraft, the Knights Templar, etc., to Gnosticism, and hence back to the Greek Mystery religions and the Egyptian cults. Lash concludes that:

> The New Age movement is best understood... as the 20th century revival of an ancient religious

tradition, gnosticism; but it is a form of gnosticism considerably adulterated by other influences and mixed up with imagery derived from science fiction-- flying saucers, extraterrestrial intervention in human history, escape from the earth to a new home in space . . .

Where second century gnostics imagine the Savior as a spirit mysteriously made flesh, their 20th century descendants conceive him as a visitor from another solar system. Both believe, moreover, that visitors from space built Stonehenge, the pyramids, and the lost civilizations of Lemuria and Atlantis.

While *Omni* magazine's Lash correctly identifies the gnostic influences of the New Age religion, he fails to note that the gnostics believed that Christ did not actually come in the flesh but was more on the form of a "phantom." The New Age updates this view to declare that all of us can become phantoms once we achieve the perfect spirit state, thereby rejecting all matter, including our bodies. At that point, like Jesus, we may ourselves become "Christs," partakers of the Cosmic Consciousness, also called Christ Consciousness, attained through our tapping into and linking up with the divine. The divine, naturally, is simply the earth, the stars, the galaxy, and everything contained therein. So in essence, we arrive back to the pantheistic view that man is part of the All, the All is God, and therefore, man is his own God and is the creator of his own universe, having created it with his own magical thoughts and inner conceptions.

An Impersonal Force as God

If man is the creator of his own universe, then, of course, there can be no personal God, and this is exactly the teaching of the New Age. Dorothy Thomas, founder and director of the Keyes Institute, which bills itself as a "Human Potential Center," alludes to this cardinal New Age teaching when she writes in a recent newsletter:

> I feel a great depth of gratitude to that which I call 'God.' Maslow defined God not as a person, but as a force, a principle, a gestalt-quality of the whole of Being, an integrating power that expresses the unity and therefore the meaningness of the cosmos, the dimension of depth. I love what unfolds in that place of surrender to the will of THAT...

Clearly, Thomas' definition of God, shared by human potential psychologist Abraham Maslow, would deny the personal God of the Bible. The New Age God, the Divine Intelligence, is not a personality but is defined by such terms as *a Force, a Principle, a Quality, an Integrating Power, an Expression of Unity, the Divine Intelligence, The Presence*, or *a Dimension of Depth*. Finally, Thomas expresses the ultimate rejection of the true God when she exclaims that she is more than willing to surrender to the will of "THAT." So we see God being relegated in the New Age to being a THAT.

This is certainly a great departure from the Mighty and Holy God of the Bible who sits in heaven overseeing the minute affairs of men and ruling and reigning in all things according to His Supreme Will. This God came in the flesh as Jesus. He is the only way to heaven (see John 10:9; and John 5:39-40). This same Jesus who is God Almighty warned that in the last days many false cults would arise (Matthew 24:5). His prophesy is now being fulfilled by the multitude of the New Age cults and religions that are a plague upon our land.

"But the Lord is the true God, he is the living God... The gods that have not made the heavens and the earth, even they shall perish..." (Jer. 10:10-11).

New Age vs. True Christianity: 12 Vital Differences

It is unquestionable that the doctrines and teachings of the New Age diverse sharply with those of biblical Christianity. On pages 46 through 48, I provide a chart outlining 12 vital differences between the New Age cults and religions and biblical Christianity. There are many more than 12, of course, but most of these 12 are so crucial that the huge chasm and gulf between true Christianity and the New Age religion stands out visibly and in sharp contrast.

The Best Book on Cults

In a recent issue of *The Discerner*, an outstanding Christian newsletter published periodically by Religion Analysis Service, a Minnesota-based Christian group with over 40 years experience analyzing and exposing cults, cult expert Ewald Eiscle wrote an article entitled "Recognizing Occultism or Heresy." In it he related the following:

> We are often asked which is the best book on cults . . . The answer is always the same. If a Christian knows the Word of God, he has not only the answer to the cultist or recruiter for the cults, but he also has the Sword of the Spirit with which to attack as well as defend. Knowledge of the Word should be the highest priority for a believer.

Ewald Eisele is absolutely correct. It is my intent in *New Age Cults and Religions* to enable Christian believers to understand the false teachings of the New Age and its deceptions, and encourage them to go out and boldly witness in love, compassion, and wisdom to those deceived by the New Age. But the best book by far exposing the cults is the Holy Bible. The cultist may indeed ridicule and reject the Bible, God's Word, but as Eisele wisely remarks, "He will

New Age vs. True Christianity
A Contrast

New Age Teaching

1. "God" is the creation and creator, the All-in-One. He/She/It is the Divine Intelligence and the Creative Force.

2. God and the Holy Spirit are impersonal: a presence, a vibration, an energy force, universal law, Universal Mind, Cosmic Consciousness, Divine Presence, Eternal Reality, Real Presence, Creative Force, Cosmic One, etc.

3. Each human being is endowed with a spark of divinity. An illumined, or enlightened, person is beyond such moral distinctions as "good" or "bad."

4. Jesus did not die for the sins of the world. His shedding of blood, though tragic, is irrelevant to man's spiritual needs today. No atonement. Christianity is a "bloody religion."

Bible Teaching

1. God is separate from, greater than, and Master of His creation (Acts 17:28; Col. 1:16-17; I Cor. 4:7; Gen. 1:1; Isa. 48:11-12).

2. God is "Personal." Though a spirit, He is infinite, is eternally transcendent (external to man) and worthy of our worship. (John 1; 16:13-14; Rev. 4:11).

3. Humanity is fallen, born in bondage to sin, and in need of redemption. Satan is real and evil exists. Man can become free of the condemnation of sin through Jesus Christ. (Rom. 3:23; John 3:16-19, 8:44; Jer. 17:5-9; Eph. 2:8-9; Rev. 20).

4. Jesus died on the cross as a sin sacrifice. Through His blood we are saved and through His resurrection we are assured of eternal life and victory over death. (Heb. 9:22; Matt. 26-28; John 3:16; Rom 3:23; Gal. 1:1-5; 2 Cor. 5:21; Eph 2:8-9).

5. Jesus was *a* god, *a* Christ, *a* perfect Master, *a* man who earned his divinity, *a* perfected man, *a* messenger of God, *a* prophet of God; He was as much God as are all of us.

6. Man must take responsibility for his problems and forgive himself. There is no one outside of man to whom we must plead for forgiveness, no one outside of ourselves who *can* forgive us.

7. Man must endure many life cycles (reincarnation) until his karma is cleansed, pure spirit is achieved, and union with "God" is attained.

8. Through good works and/or enlightenment, man can aspire to divinity and union with "God" (all that is). This is the universal law.

9. Eating meat produces negative karma in a person. Meat is forbidden and the (enlightened) superior spiritual being does not eat meat (vegetarianism).

5. Jesus is, was, and forever shall be God Almighty, the one true God; and there is no other besides Him. Jesus created all things. He, the Father, and the Holy Spirit are eternally One. They cannot be separated--ever. There is but *one* Godhead. Jesus is the only Christ. (1 John 2:20-25; Heb. 1:8; Col. 1:14-19, 2:9-10).

6. A loving God can forgive our sins and cleanse us. He offers man the free gift of salvation. (1 Peter 1; 1 John 1:2-6, 3:16; James 4:6-11).

7. Man has only one physical life on earth. Upon death, man returns to God, the Creator, who is our Judge. Those saved escape condemnation and receive eternal life. (John 3:16; Heb. 9:27).

8. Man is not saved by Law or through his good works. Nor can man become enlightened through his own efforts. Eternal life and heaven are free gifts given by a loving, personal God to those who accept His grace and are thus born again. (Gal. 3:1-4, 2:16; Titus 3:5; John 3:3).

9. God blesses all things He has created for man to eat, including meat. (Col. 2:16; I Tim. 4:3).

Bible Teaching (continued)

10. There is only one mediator between man and God—Christ Jesus. Communication with spirit guides and entities is an occult practice called necromancy. It is an abomination to God. Such spirits are unclean and not of God. (Deut. 18:10-12; I Tim. 4:1; Isa. 8:19; I Sam. 28:1-25; I Chr. 10:13-14).

11. The Bible is authoritative, powerful, and able to guide man in every aspect of his life, producing joy and satisfaction in the reader who knows Christ as Lord. (Rev. 22:18-19; John 5:39; Acts 17:2, 11; 18:28; Rom. 15:4; 16:26; II Pet. 1:21).

12. God is the great I AM--transcendent to His creation, magnificent, glorious, King of kings. Man is made to serve God. Someday, every knee will bow and every tongue confess that Jesus Christ is Lord. (Phillip. 5:2-13; Rev. 22:18-19; John 5:39; Rev. 21:1-8, 22:8-9; Matt. 18:3; John 3:3, 14:6).

New Age Teaching (continued)

10. Spirit beings, or entities, are able to provide spiritual insight and guidance. They are helpers who can show man how to become fully conscious and realize self (become divine).

11. The Holy Bible is insufficient as a guide for man. Other "bibles" from other religions, ancient religious texts and writings, and fresh new revelations either from people living today or spirit entities are equally as valuable and reliable.

12. Man is part of and one with the creation; the creation is "God," thus man is also "God." He is co-creator of the universe. Through an evolutionary process, man is "awakening" and returning to godhood.

This chart is from the book *New Age Cults and Religions*, by Texe Marrs. Permission is hereby granted the reader to reproduce this chart (pages 46, 47, and 48) in any quantity as long as the author and source are given credit.
© 1990 Living Truth Publishers, 8103 Shiloh Court, Austin, Texas 78745

never change it and if a Christian knows the Truth he will always be pleasing his Lord when he uses that Truth against a lie of Satan."

Even the most extreme of New Age cults and religions is to be confronted successfully with the overpowering might of Scripture. Recently a woman phoned and told me that she needed to research satanism. "Is there a book you would recommend on the subject," she inquired. "Yes," I responded immediately, "the Bible."

The fact is, we can never understand the depths of depravity involved in Satan worship unless we first come to grips with what God says about the nature of satanic powers—and the ultimate fate and doom of those powers. The Bible records the wisdom of God and demonstrates His strength in relationship to the Adversary. It records the Truth and guidance we need for everyday living. In its manifold pages is the evidence and ammunition we need to confront the cult recruiter face-to-face. It provides the strength we must have to lovingly but with authority challenge the cultist with the absolute, unvarnished, life-changing Truth.

Yes, I thank God that He called on me to write this book unmasking the New Age cults and religions; yet, mine and any book is only a pale substitute for God's Word. If we are truly to understand what is the New Age and recognize the dangers inherent in its cults and religious sects, we must turn to what God says in His Bible.

Unholy Bibles of the New Age

Peter advised us that God's Word is like a light that shines in the dark place, for Scripture comes from God (2 Peter 1:19-

21). Meanwhile, John, in Revelation 22:18-19, warned men against adding to or subtracting from the Bible:

> If any man shall add unto these things, God shall add unto him the plagues that are written in this book: And if any man shall take away the words of the book of this prophesy, God shall take away his part out of the Book of Life.

Peter also cautioned: "There shall be false teachers among you, who privily shall bring in damnable heresies, even denying the Lord that bought them, and bring upon themselves swift destruction" (2 Peter 2:1).

Regardless of these admonitions, the New Age cults and religions have published and are using a great number of false bibles and scriptures. New Age teachers have always used the standard texts of the Eastern religions such as the Hindu *Baghavad-Gita* and the *Tibetan Book of the Dead*, as well as the writings of Jewish mysticism called the *Kabbala* and the gnostic scriptures often called the *Apocrypha*. However, many of the newer bibles supposedly come from the spirit world, being dictated to human contacts through automatic writing. Other New Age bibles come from the vivid imaginations of various New Age leaders. Whatever their source, all of these false bibles are designed to take man's attention away from the true Word of God and direct it instead to untruths, half-truths, and distortions.

Throughout this book, as we look at individual cult groups and religions, we will examine the various false bibles and scriptures being promoted by each. It is important to realize that these bibles have not been hastily thrown together. Clearly, demonic powers using arcane knowledge and sophisticated occultic philosophies have been involved in the production of these books. For example, one New Age bible, *Oahspe*, is 1,088 pages in length and filled with mysterious symbols and strange diagrams. *Oahspe* bills itself as "a New Bible in the Words of Jehovih" (Jehovih is Oahspe's "true" name for Jehovah). *Oahspe* is today distributed by the New Age religious group known as *Kosmon*. The book was first printed in 1882. So we see that the false bibles of the New Age are not revolutionary new phenomena--some of them have long and infamous histories.

In Part II of this book I will discuss more of the origins and claims of the *Oahspe* bible. I will also examine *The Keys of Enoch*, a beautifully illustrated book of some 600 pages supposedly given to a New Age leader by two spirits who identified themselves as "Enoch" and "Metatron." We will unravel the gross and outrageous claim of the Christ Foundation concerning its unique set of scriptures, *A Spiritual Sex Manual*, and we will delve into the odd background and current popularity of the *Urantia Book*, a 2,097 page set of scriptures which presents a rather bizarre account of the lives of Jesus and Lucifer.

Intended to Confuse

Many New Age bibles are no doubt intended by the Adversary to confuse, deceive, and keep people away from the one true Bible. They are also useful in introducing a mass audience to the concepts and beliefs of the New Age religion. For example, a group called *New Age Light* in New Zealand publishes a false bible entitlcd *The New Age Testament of Light*. Supposedly dictated to a man named Arthur Garside by a spirit who boasted of being "the Universal I AM." The other-worldly author of *The New Testament of Light* proclaims:

> I Am indeed the Light Force, Intelligence, and Divine Light of the Universe, and there is no other one thing outside of or beside me ... I Am the universe itself and all that is in it ... Jesus, the Master/Teacher served Me by performing My Will to perfection ... Jesus of Nazareth was the greatest of all the Masters to manifest on Earth.

Clearly, these are not the words of God at all since they suggest that Jesus was only a "Master" and that God is the entire universe, indistinct from His creation.

One New Age bible that is quite interesting because of its name and supposed authorship is *The New American Bible*, subtitled *Ecology of Mind*. Attractively bound with a glossy green cover and gold embossing, its authorship is shown on the front cover of the book to be: "By God and Michael Mathiesen." In this 442 page volume, Mathiesen insists that while sitting at his computer one day, God came and took over the computer screen and proceeded to give him messages. These messages became the text of *The New American Bible*. Again we see the undeniable traces of New Age influence when the "God" of Mr. Mathiesen describes himself in this book as "Universal Mind" and insists that man will be punished severely unless by the year 2000 he organizes himself into a World Government.

Perhaps one of the most widely distributed bibles in the New Age is *The Aquarian Gospel of Jesus the Christ*, whose author identifies himself simply as "Levi," but was born as Levi H. Dowling in 1844 in Bellville, Ohio. In *The Aquarian Gospel*, Levi writes that a great being called "Visel, the Goddess of Wisdom," came to him and said "Oh Levi, son of man, behold, for you are called to be the message bearer of the coming age--the age of spirit blessedness."

The Aquarian Gospel of Jesus the Christ embraces a number of New Age doctrines including reincarnation. It purports to be the true story of Jesus but its account is radically different than the one in the Holy Bible. The Jesus of *The Aquarian Gospel* tells his disciples that God is everywhere and that all people in fact worship him, regardless of their different religions. The universal God, says this false Jesus, is simply "Wisdom." This new Jesus travels to India to teach and learn from the gurus, and also journeys to Persia, Assyria, Ur in the Chaldees, and finally to Egypt.

In Egypt Jesus goes into the temple at Heliopolis and is received as a pupil. Eventually, he is initiated into the Egyptian Mysteries after successfully completing his seventh initiation. It is through this process of initiation that Jesus earns his title, "The Christ."

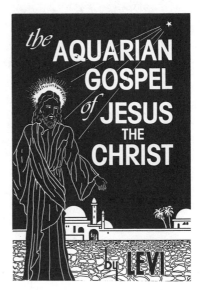

The Aquarian Gospel of Jesus the Christ is only one of numerous false bibles in the New Age.

And More New Age Bibles . . .

Listed below are only a few of the many bibles, near-bibles and scriptures being promoted by New Age cults and religions:

> *Essence of Life: The Book of Answers*
> *Dianetics*
> *The Seth Material*
> *The Unknown Life of Jesus Christ*
> *The Lost Teachings of Jesus*
> *The Spiritual Teachings For Children* (series)
> *The Book of Mormon*
> *The Starseed Transmissions*
> *God Calling*
> *The Jesus Letters*
> *Happy Birthday Planet Earth*
> *New Age Teachings for an Awakening Humanity*
> *The Urantia Book*

Oahspe
A Course in Miracles
The Book of Knowledge: The Keys of Enoch
A Spiritual Sex Manual
The Portable World Bible
The Rays and the Initiations
The Secret Doctrine
Isis Unveiled
The Dawn Horse Testament
The Satanic Bible

What is a Cult?

Say the word "cult" and a number of images are conjured up in people's minds. Usually pictures come to mind of destitute and hapless individuals with blank eyes and mindless stares. We envision the cult follower as flexible as rubber to the will of a guru; he or she is seen as a person living in a make-believe world. A member of a cult is often thought to be a weak sponge of a person who will carry out any deed, no matter how dastardly or unethical, up to and including murder, if called upon by the guru or prophet who promises him some form of eternal bliss.

Actually, while in extreme cases this may be an accurate description of cults and their members, the term "cult" has a broader and more encompassing meaning. In *Webster's New Collegiate Dictionary*, the word cult is defined as "a system of religious beliefs and rituals; also: its body of adherents."

A cult is a group whose membership is intensely devoted to a particular goal or leader and whose unusual lifestyle or peculiar attitudes and behaviors separate its members from society as a whole. If a small cult develops and grows in authority and numbers over time, it may mature into a sect or an actual religion, complete with such trappings as a cadre of trained priests or pastors, formalized ritual worship, sacraments, holy days, and so on.

It is true that many New Age cults and religions are shrouded in secrecy. The inner teachings of the group are kept from the majority and initiates must proceed through a number of steps or degrees of initiations in order to become illumined, wise, or divine. But not all New Age groups are cloaked in secrecy. Many are open to the public, and though initially they may present themselves as possessing a body of occultic, or hidden beliefs, their membership is readily provided a set of written scriptures, books, tapes, or other tangible resources which they can use to immerse themselves more deeply into the activities of the group.

So what exactly is a New Age "cult or religion?" Recently, Dr. William BeVier of the Religion Analysis Service, in an issue of *The Discerner*, provided a very succinct but accurate definition of a cult. He wrote: "I define a cult as a group or movement, which claims some affinity with Christianity, that holds a non-biblical view of either the person of Christ or the work of Christ, or both." Dr. BeVier's unfettered, direct definition is a good one.

We can also add a few more distinctions. Throughout this book, my major emphasis will be to unmask New Age cults, religions, and organizations which, while they may not appear to be a present danger to the life and health of individuals, nevertheless are unchristian or anti-Christian in one respect or another. Therefore, like Dr. BeVier, I do not necessarily define a cult or a religion the same way that a non-Christian would. In the framework of this book, *"A cult is a body or organized group of activists or believers who have involved themselves in a spiritual or social movement in opposition to the clear and direct Word of God."*

Essentials of the Faith as a Measuring Stick

The Bible gives us a small number of *essentials of the faith*. Organized spiritual groups which depart from these essentials can properly be classified as cultic. Now, I do not refer to the *nonessentials* of the faith, and of course there are some within Christianity--including some in major denominations and churches--who have in the past over-emphasized the nonessentials. However, this book concerns itself only with defending and explaining the *essentials* of the faith. Therefore, throughout the book, my goal is to shine a spotlight on groups which are detrimental to the Great Commission of Christ and whose outlook, worldview, teachings, or acts constitute either a direct or an indirect assault on traditional, true biblical Christianity. The cults and religions described herein stand in opposition to Christianity even though some most vehemently deny it.

The essentials of the faith which enable us to separate the New Age group from the Christian include an absolute belief that *there is in fact a personal and loving God who is the Creator of all things.* Another essential is that *Jesus Christ is wholly God and came in the flesh as God.* This essential of the faith includes the well-established doctrine in Scripture that Jesus is and was the only Christ and Messiah, that He was a man of flesh and yet undeniably truly God.

Another essential of the faith which separates biblical Christianity from the New Age sects and groups is the clear understanding from the Bible that *man is not an evolving god*, that he is and will always remain subservient to the great God of the universe. Moreover, another essential of the Christian faith given little credence in New Age circles is the Christian's undeniable practice of praying to and *calling on Jesus Christ alone as the mediator between man and God.* The true Christian does not speak with the spirits or even with the departed saints in heaven. But instead, he knows that he has a mediator and intercessor in heavenly places who hears his petitions and his prayers and knows the desires of his heart. That intercessor is Christ.

The essential Christian belief that *the Bible is the inspired, infallible, inerrant, and literal Word of God*, given to man through God and undefiled by nature of its divine authorship is another important feature of true Christianity which separates its practice from those of the New Age cults and religions. Most New Age groups profess that the Bible is either inadequate, flawed, distorted, or otherwise limited, or they claim that it is one of only a number of Holy Scriptures and inspired texts. This view is diametrically opposed to that of the true Christian.

Thus, in this book, the groups which we discuss have the marks of a cult not necessarily because their leader is a cruel dictator, or because the group is guilty of crimes as defined in secular legal definitions, or even because a group may be overtly satanic or occultic. There are a number of types of New Age cults and religions. Some groups are more destructive than others. What distinguishes a cult from a Christian denomination, sect, or religious group is simply its variance from the essentials of the Christian faith.

The apostle Paul in Galatians 1:6-9 states that if anyone, even an angel from heaven, proclaims any other gospel than the one proclaimed in the Holy Bible and set forth clearly by the Apostles, that person is *accursed*. Moreover, in II Corinthians 11:4 we find that there is *another gospel* and *another Jesus*. Then, in Romans 16:17-18 we see that even if a person claims to be Christian yet teaches false doctrines contrary to that stated in the whole gospel of Christ, that person is not of God but is simply following the lust of the flesh and the will of the evil one.

True Christianity Defined

True Christianity is defined as a belief in the *Gospel*, a Gospel that Paul set forth in I Corinthians 15:1-4. This Gospel declares the majesty of Jesus Christ and speaks of His sacrifice for our sins. It relates the glorious news of His resurrection and subsequent appearances on earth and assures us of His Lordship and His faithfulness to all those who place their faith in the finished, completed work of Christ. The basis of Christian salvation is a profound belief and faith in Jesus Christ as Lord and Savior. The result of salvation is new life, inner peace and an intense desire to serve God.

New Age cults and religions are at variance with Christianity primarily because of their unscriptural teachings about the finished work of Christ and the person of Christ as compared with Scripture. Regardless of the other traits, characteristics, or marks of the specific cult or religion--and even though some of their works may be good--by these fruits we may know them. As Peter stated in Acts 4:12, only in Jesus Christ alone can man find hope: "Neither is there salvation in any other (name); for there is no other name under heaven given among men whereby we must be saved."

How do we discern whether a particular group is a cult or religion in opposition to Christianity? There is only one rule for this kind of accurate discernment. Each of us must, as did the Bereans, go directly to the Scriptures, studying God's Word to show ourselves approved workmen who need not be ashamed, able to rightly divide the Word of Truth (II Timothy 2:15). Without the Scriptures as our measuring stick, we are lost, hopeless, and without a compass, for as we read in Proverbs 14:12: "There is a way that seemeth right unto a man, but the end thereof are the ways of death."

Types of New Age Cults and Religions

There are basically nine types of New Age cults and religions. These nine types are listed below along with a brief description.

1. *Eastern Mystical.* Cults and sects in this category fall along the traditional lines of such major Eastern religions as Hinduism, Buddhism, and Confucianism. Such groups emphasize the oriental and Eastern religious concepts. While Islam, the Moslem faith, cannot properly be categorized as New Age because of its exclusive belief in a personal God, there is a type of mystical Moslem sect called the Sufis which fits into the Eastern Mystical religious category.

Members of Eastern Mystical cults and groups focus on such techniques as meditation, chanting, and the use of rosaries and mandalas. Invariably they advocate either holism (all is God) or polytheism, a belief in multiple gods, with the accompanying belief that all of these gods are integral parts of the whole fabric of reality.

2. *Mystery Teachings.* This type of cult group loves to cloak and shroud its esoteric body of beliefs within the framework of some ancient mystery teaching. Some call it the Perennial Philosophy, the Ancient Wisdom, or Divine Wisdom. Whatever terminology is used, cult leaders focus the group's attention on the gods, goddesses, and mythological fables and stories of ancient Greece, Babylon, Rome, Egypt, and the Orient. There is also an emphasis on the concept of *archetypes*--the envisioning and molding of gods and goddesses through man's own creative, imaginative faculties.

A further emphasis is placed on astrological signs, with mythological deities usually connected with the signs of the zodiac. The New Age groups involved in Mystery Teachings commonly instruct new recruits that they must remain *chelas*, or students, until they are progressively initiated into deeper levels of Gnosis, or knowledge of the mysteries. The promise of the unfolding of the mysteries is a seductive lure used to draw in curious seekers.

3. *Deceptive "Christian".* A number of groups come cleverly cloaked as "Christian." Such cults may be either "liberal" or "conservative" in outlook. Those that are of a "conservative" nature are not truly conservative at all, they are simply stereotyped as such by the media. Thus, such groups only *appear* to be conservative. They often are led by strong, dictatorial-type leaders adept at keeping members obedient and submissive. The Bible is often twisted in one way or another and minor passages are over-emphasized and fashioned into major doctrines in order to keep members in bondage. Eventually, since power corrupts and absolute

power corrupts absolutely, the leader of a warped Christian cult or religious sect may go too far and seriously endanger and harm the physical and mental health of cult members.

A classic example of extremism in this regard was the mass suicide and murder of hundreds of people who traveled to Guyana, South America with cult leader Jim Jones of the People's Temple. New Age groups often attempt to smear traditional Christianity by claiming that such men as Jim Jones and even Adolf Hitler were "Christians." The truth is far different. Jim Jones most definitely could be classified as a New Ager since he taught a warped view of the person and deity of Jesus Christ and twisted scripture to suit his own unethical acts and desires. In regards to Adolf Hitler, even a cursory look at history reveals to us that Hitler, raised as a Catholic, began to take up the occultic magical black arts and finally joined the Thule Society, a patently occultic cult group whose teachings can be traced back to 19th century Theosophy.

The "liberal" Deceptive Christian group or church is equally as dangerous spiritually as the conservative cult. Perhaps more so, for the liberal leader or pastor puts on a front, a veneer of Christianity, while at the same time often denying every essential of the faith. Oftentimes, the leader will vigorously embrace New Age doctrines and practices while refraining from the term "New Age" itself. Usually, such leaders keep their flocks captive through flattery, or they may encourage political and social activism in neglect of the scriptures in order to keep their flock motivated toward reforming the world system. The members of such groups are often shocked for their church or organization to be labeled "New Age;" but, again, by their fruits ye shall know them.

4. *Occultic.* Occultic groups range from those who advocate and practice the black magic arts to those who profess the value of occultic astrology and esoteric occultism, finally to the more bizarre and aberrant groups involved in devil worship and Satanism. Most New Age cults and

groups are occultic in nature. But a number, such as the Lucis Trust and the Church of Satan, are overtly so. Those groups which proclaim as their purpose the "illumination" of humanity and lead their disciples and followers into a study of ancient occultic philosophies, as well as those which practice ceremonial rituals of a black or Satanic nature, most definitely can be categorized as occultic.

Some groups who practice magic attempt to deny the dark nature of these practices, contending that theirs is "white magic" and that only "black magic" is evil. In reality, there is little or no distinction between black and white magic, as such practitioners as Anton LeVey, founder of the Church of Satan, and Dr. Michael Aquino of the satanic Temple of Set, have frequently attested. Certainly the Bible makes no distinction.

5. *Earth and Nature.* These cultic groups and religious sects and factions honor and revere Mother Earth and all types of nature. Included in this category are the various witchcraft, goddess, and pagan groups. The earth religion is quite ancient and has its roots in primitive Babylon and Egypt. A number of Native American Indian religious groups practice earth and nature rituals. The essential doctrine taught by these groups is the reality of pantheism, that man is simply part of nature and that nature is itself divine. Commonly, such groups worship an energy force which is believed to permeate the universe. However, witches also quite often personify their deities, being known to call on the horned god Pan, for example, who was known to the Greeks as the god of the forest. Many witches also believe in Diana, the huntress, likewise a nature deity.

Goddess worshippers harken to the pagan goddesses of olden times; they believe that the goddesses connect modern-day worshippers to the earth and provide a means of empowerment for the believer. Also in this category we can place the various pagan groups including those who worship the Norse gods and other mythological figures.

6. *Human Potential.* These groups and organizations often disguise the New Age content of their programs and messages. For example, the Pacific Institute, founded by Lou Tice, once offered a seminar course to businesses, corporations, and governmental agencies which was called "New Age Thinking." But in the mid-80s, as it became increasingly clear that the New Age involved religious and spiritual dimensions and doctrinal elements hostile to traditional Christianity and even bizarre in relation to the commonly shared beliefs of Americans, the Pacific Institute dropped the term "New Age" from its course description. The course was repackaged as a "Creative Thinking" seminar.

Human potential groups are epitomized by the slogan "Be all that you can be." They offer self-improvement, increased creativity, success in the marketplace, etc. Generally, they emphasize positive thinking and positive affirmation techniques and attitudes. Self-love is a cardinal teaching of such groups, and pop-psychology is their greatest tool.

Occasionally, human potential groups give away their ulterior motives by presenting their materials and teachings in a *spiritual* framework; for example, a human potential group leader may tell members of a business seminar that they are "destined for divinity" or that their human potential is so unlimited that by human endeavor, raw will power, or by practicing the techniques offered by the group, the individual can develop latent god-like powers and even command miracles and supernatural happenings to occur. In other words, many human potential groups, even those which start off related more to psychology and self-improvement than to religion, eventually concentrate the mental energies of their audiences into a spiritual or religious channel.

7. *Prosperity and Health.* This type of group appears to be non-doctrinal and devoid of occultic and mystical aspects; yet, such aspects are often veiled or hidden beneath the glitter and glamor of the cult group's teachings and the

flamboyance of its leader. Like the human pote
cult leaders of the Prosperity and Health variet
positive thinking and narcissism. They promise
the use of mind dynamics and by changing one's inner
attitudes and thoughts, the individual can enjoy unparalleled prosperity and be guaranteed of excellent health and
long life. Healing miracles are often emphasized; <u>Happiness
and riches are seen as easily attainable and this is the lure
which draws in new recruits</u>. Sometimes, elaborate systems
of thought-control are offered. For example, what the New
Age calls "self-talk" has been repackaged and made to
appear more pseudoscientific by calling it "neurolinguistic
programming."

Among the groups that fall in the <u>Prosperity and Health</u>
category are Unity Church, Unitarianism, Christian Science,
Church of Religious Science (Science of Mind), and New
Thought.

8. *Astral/Galactic.* The astral/galactic cult, religion, or
organization is often seen by the general public as far out,
zany, and bizarre. UFO societies are often a type of Astral/
Galactic cult. Their tales of mysterious abductions and
strange, curious green men and other creatures from, say,
Venus or the earth's immediate planetary system, and their
adventurous accounts of galactic and interplanetary en-
counters, extraterrestrial influences, and strange sightings
of flying saucers and other advanced or wierd UFO craft are
sometimes reported in the media in sensationalist language.

But many people involved in these groups are well-
educated, rational, intelligent, and thoughtful. They are not
the kooks they are often made out to be by the media.
Moreover, careful study and examination of UFO groups
reveals that there is a spiritual and religious doctrine that
many of their leaders are intent on spreading to all of us. It is
this spiritual and religious element that we will discuss later
in *Texe Marrs Book of New Age Cults and Religions* when we
get to the section on UFO Societies and Cults.

Another group of New Age cults and organizations that

fit into the Astral/Galactic type are those promising their followers and adherents experiences beyond-the-senses through *astral* or *soul travel*. Commonly called "out-of-body" experiences (OBE), it is the contention of such groups as Anthroposophy and Eckankar that man can learn techniques that will enable him to leave the limitations of the body and soar into the astral world--into heavenly dimensions and etheric realms of visionary worlds and utopias. Such out-of-body experiences are said to enable men and women to escape the bonds of earth and to communicate with the great, all-wise, all-knowing spirit entities who populate the other-worldly dimensions.

For example, L. Ron Hubbard, founder of Scientology, once claimed that through soul or astral travel he was taken on a fantastic trip to "heaven." There he gazed upon magnificent edifices and was able to observe breathtaking architectural wonders. The streets glistened and everything seemed to be spiffily immaculate. However, Hubbard claimed that on a subsequent trip to heaven, he found that the powers that controlled that realm had been painfully remiss in their responsibilities. Now there were potholes on the streets, things were generally unkempt, and the buildings were in a sad state of disrepair.

9. *Political/Economic*. This type of New Age group or organization usually focuses on one or a handful of specific political, economic or social goals; for example, achieving world peace, cleaning up the environment, One World Government, One World Religion, ending world hunger, radical feminism, global democracy, rights and benefits for gays (homosexuals and lesbians), animal rights, vegetarianism, etc. Some groups also exist to further such financial aims as the establishment of a one world mercantile, or commercial, system free of trade barriers between nations.

These groups often attempt to hide or otherwise conceal their spiritual and religious underpinning. Yet, when a trained analyst of cults studies carefully the publications, speeches, and public activities of these groups, the *hidden* spiritual and religious nature of their agenda often surfaces.

For example, groups supporting radical feminism will very often promote goals similar to those of the Earth and Nature cults. Goddess worship and the end of patriarchal religion (fundamentalist Christianity, Judaism, and Islam being the prime examples) are ever-pressing agenda items for radical feminist groups. For another example, the New Age organization known as the Hunger Project, whose ostensible goal is to stamp out world hunger, has spent virtually none of its millions of dollars of income to feed the hungry around the world. Instead it is the contention of the Hunger Project that its money can best be used to promote the development of a "global consciousness." The claim is that once this global consciousness is achieved, then people everywhere will share naturally and the hunger problem will be instantly dissolved.

The Eclectic Nature of the Cults

Few of the New Age cults, religions, and organizations fall strictly into one of the above categories. Most often, a group combines a number of methods, techniques, and teachings in an eclectic fashion. One example is the commonplace practice of *necromancy*, communication with the dead, with entities who are called "spirit guides" by the New Age. Groups who contact and follow the guidance of spirit guides include the Eastern Mystical, Mystery Teachings, Occultic, Astral/Galactic, and on occasion, the Deceptive Christian cults. Generally, however, from an examination of their espoused purposes, activities, and spiritual or social teachings, each of the cults and religious groups and organizations covered in this book can be classified into one or another of the nine types.

In this book information is provided primarily on the first eight types. Regrettably, I did not have sufficient space to include detailed information on the Political/Economic groups and organizations, though I intend to do a future book exclusively exposing the work of these nefarious groups, many of which are employing literally hundreds of millions of dollars in an attempt to convert the world into a hodgepodge of New Age institutions, practices, and systems. Among the Political/Economic groups and social organizations which are not covered but certainly merit classification as New Age are the following: the Green Party; Sovereign Military Order of Malta; ACLU; Rockefeller Foundation; Carnegie Endowment; Bread For the World; Hunger Project; UNESCO; Aspen Institute; Better World Society; Club of Rome; Esalen Institute; Earth Celebrations 2000; The Council on Foreign Relations; the National Organization for Women (NOW); Planned Parenthood; and the Trilateral Commission.

In addition, such political and economic philosophies as *fascism* and *communism* could well be included in the New Age political/economic category because of their fervent belief in secular humanism or, in the case of the fascists, this ideology's poisonous spiritual and physical race doctrines. Communism, like the New Age religious sects, exalts the human being, and the communist ideology is extremely amenable to the notion of a Cosmic Intelligence devoid of individualistic personality. Meanwhile, the fascist tenet of the "Superman" with god-like qualities beyond good and evil--as proposed, for example, by German writer Frederich Nietzche--can be closely linked with the racial doctrines espoused by such New Age groups as the Lucis Trust, World Goodwill, the Tara Center, and others.

It is important to realize that the goal of the New Age leadership is to establish influence in all areas of society--in education, entertainment, economics and finance, politics, law, medicine, and of course, in the religious field. This is why there are so many, varied types of New Age cults and organizations. The ultimate objective is to create a One World Religion, a One World Economy, and a One World Government. The way to acheive this is to permeate society and create a pervasive network of interlinking, though ostensibly independent organizations and groups.

Tactics and Techniques of Cults

Unhealthy and destructive cults share many of the following traits and characteristics:

(1) They are headed by a charmingly hypnotic or dynamically charismatic leader.

(2) They use manipulation, fraud, and deception to recruit and hold members.

(3) They isolate and separate members from friends, family, or the constancy of outside contact to create a loss of reality and keep a person out of touch with the real world and with other, external sources of information.

(4) They induce a form of hypnosis in disciples, a state of altered consciousness or high suggestibility, through use of such techniques and exercises as vain repetitions or chanting, meditation, and visualization on mandalas or other occultic symbols.

(5) They demand that new recruits share intimacies and reveal hidden sins or secrets in their lives. Once confessed and in the open, the individual may be held in check by threats of having these secrets revealed; in addition, members frequently develop a sense of group consciousness and closeness because of their shared intimacies.

(6) Rejection of traditional values. New members are encouraged to change their lifestyle, their career goals, their education, their preferred reading selections, and their ethical and religious belief systems. The cult insists on the imposition of new values or an entire new paradigm or worldview. True biblical Christianity absolutely must be abandoned by the cult member.

(7) Sleep and food deprivation. Vegetarianism produces an altered state of consciousness and may make a person vulnerable to demonic contacts and out-of-body experiences. Lack of sleep disorients an individual, slowing or diminishing rational thought processes. This may render a person

open and susceptible to cult influences and allow the new value system to be imposed on the individual by the cult leadership. Over a long period of time food and sleep deprivation can have devastating effects on the individual. Occasionally a new dietary regime which includes untried and experimental herbs and natural substances has been known to create toxic poisons in the body and literally kill people.

(8) A feeling of chosenness or special calling is induced. The individual is made to feel special and superior. He is told that he is a "new being," an initiate on the road to total happiness and bliss. Also, it may be revealed to the new initiate that he or she is one of the elect chosen to accept the new values and abandon the old. The person is made to feel a part of the "in crowd," spiritually advanced, fully conscious, and cosmically superior to the ignorant, uncouth masses, especially the "jaded old fundamentalist Christians with their legalism and outmoded, old-fashioned morality and belief system."

(9) Proselytizing is encouraged, even required, of the new recruit as well as veteran members. The New Age cults and religions are very evangelistic; most are determined to go out into the highways and byways and recruit new members for their spiritual and other causes.

(10) Total loyalty and obedience is demanded of members. Most cults have a particular guru or spiritual leader, whether dead or living, for whom members must continually express their love, affection, and highest veneration. He is constantly held out as superior and god-like, and pictured to be a supreme, holy and enlightened teacher.

(11) Peer and group pressure and love-bonding tactics are used. The individual is often showered with love and attention when she or he first joins the group. This tactic is designed to drive away doubts and reinforce the human yearning to belong and conform. It is a common practice among New Age cults for members to hug, touch, and flatter each other. New members usually receive a showering of attention. Also, the use of what appears to be amusing, child-like games, greetings, prayer chains, and similar tactics are

often used to enhance the charm of the collective group and induce a spirit of cooperation, family togetherness, and, for militaristic groups, a common *esprit d'corps.*

(12) Self-esteem attacks are employed. If love-bonding does not work or produce the desired psychological result in the new recruit or member, the opposite tact may be used; that is, the person's self-esteem may literally be attacked. He or she may become the subject of a vicious verbal assault. Cult leaders and other veteran members may accuse the individual of all kinds of heinous acts and thoughts, real or imagined. Regardless of the person's pleadings and cries of repentance, he or she is cruelly badgered and made to feel lowly and a worm. Once the individual's self-esteem is sufficiently destroyed and a feeling of worthlessness is induced, then, suddenly, the group changes its tactics and commences to love-bond, once again showering the individual with kind words, hugging, and touching. Bouts of alternating crying and hilarious laughing and sobbing may ensue. It may take alternate periods of love-bonding and esteem-attacking to wear down and mold the individual into a malleable and flexible tool easily manipulated by the cult.

Mind Control is the Goal

It is plain from reviewing the above list of tactics and techniques that mind control is a paramount goal of the cult. The person's mind must be attacked so that he or she comes under the effective control of either the cult leader or the cult group. The collective is usually encouraged; this is why the New Age continually stresses that personal salvation is passé, that individual transformation has passed away along with other outmoded traditions of biblical Christianity. Instead, in the radiant New Age, a *group consciousness* is encouraged. Group salvation is in vogue; the community is everything and the individual is simply a part of the community as a whole. His desires and wishes must be molded to conform to the needs of the "Community." The good of all must be considered, members are told. The lie is that the individual will be most happy once he or she learns to tailor or subordinate the personality to fit the needs of the collective group.

In the late 60s and early 70s, a number of cult groups were able to successfully separate young people from their family and friends, thereby creating an artificial environment in which cult tactics and techniques could more effectively be used to manipulate new recruits. Today, the cults and religious sects have become more sophisticated and more insidiously devious in their techniques and strategy. Study the list provided here of tactics and techniques of the cults described and you will find that *most can be employed without the need to physically separate the individual for an extended period.*

Nowadays, most New Age cults and religions are able to exert group pressure, accomplish their love-bonding or self-esteem attacks, induce states of hypnosis, cause the individual to reject old values and take on a new worldview, and voluntarily agree to sleep and food deprivation, without complete physical isolation.

Regular group meetings, visits at home by experienced group members, the constant practice by the person of such techniques as meditation, visualization, and chanting; and the requirement to read a voluminous amount of cult literature at home, all mean that the cults no longer need to sequester the individual away from the real world. The desired objectives are now most often achieved without brutal group pressure and harassment and without undue physical and mental coercion.

Fraud, Deception, and Brainwashing

When one uses the term brainwashing, an image of a prisoner of war being tortured in a secluded, grimy cell by enemy interrogation experts comes to mind. But as Stephen Hassan relates in his thought-provoking book, *Combatting*

Cult Mind Control, "Today, many techniques of mind control exist that are far more sophisticated than the brainwashing techniques used in World War II and the Korean War." Hassan explains that "Some involve covert forms of hypnosis, while others are implemented through the highly rigid, controlled social environment of the destructive cult." Above all, he stresses, "It should be recognized that mind control is a very subtle process."

Hassan himself relates how a process of mind control was employed on him by the Moonies (the Reverend Sun Myung Moon's Unification Church) to the extent that he became practically a walking zombie. In a deluded mental and spiritual condition, Steve Hassan, an educated, articulate, and bright young man, fell under almost the complete control of his cult captors. He became a puppet without a string being attached. The process took only three days. Here is how Steve Hassan describes the results of the brainwashing that he experienced from this New Age cult:

> By the end of those three days, the Steve Hassan who had walked into the first workshop was gone, replaced by a new "Steve Hassan." I was elated at the thought that I was "chosen" by God and that my life's path was now on the only "true track." I experienced a wide range of other feelings, too: I was shocked and honored that I had been singled out for leadership, scared at how much responsibility rested on my shoulders, and emotionally high on the thought that God was actively working to bring about the Garden of Eden. No more war, no more poverty, no more ecological destruction. Just love, truth, beauty, and goodness. Still, a muffled voice deep within was telling me to watch out... *1 Kings 19:12*

The Lure of Cults

It is a misconception that the cults are only after our young people. True, cult recruiters and true believers do indeed scout college campuses and even the high schools searching for new souls. But today the New Age cults and religions find a much more attractive market for their wares among middle-aged and elderly people than they do among the youth population. This New Age penchant to grasp on to a more mature audience is causing untold suffering and casualties among older adults who should know better but who often fall under the sway of the cults during a particularly vulnerable moment in their lives.

As I visit New Age bookstores around this nation and drop in on New Age groups and gatherings, I notice that it is the mature adult who, surprisingly, seems to be most receptive to the New Age philosophy. In my ministry, too, I have been startled at the number of phone calls from young, hurting men and women, especially teenagers but also people in their 20s, who call and plead with us to help them rescue and extricate a parent entrapped in a New Age cult or religious group. You would be totally shocked to discover how many thousands of mothers in the 30-40s age bracket are abandoning husbands, children, and homes to strike out on some kind of a spiritual journey looking for their own Wizard of Oz. We have also had hurting husbands call and, in tears, relate the most heartbreaking accounts imaginable of wives leaving them for a guru, or insisting that an extramarital sexual affair is "okay" because other members of their New Age cult told them that the extramarital partner is a "soul twin," a romantic liaison from a past life.

Wives, too, phone and write, their voices sometimes cracking with emotion as they explain how their husbands have become entangled in a New Age cult and how it has wrecked and harmed their marriages.

In *Woman's Day* magazine, writer Claire Safran recently wrote an insightful article entitled, "Today's Cults Want

You" in which she stated: "If you are mid-life or older, feeling a little vulnerable and have some money, you are a candidate for a cult. And if you don't think you'd ever fall for such nonsense, read the stories of three very normal women who did."

The three women profiled in the *Woman's Day* article are not at all the kind of people that you or I might imagine a potential New Age cult member to be. They were neither "spacey" nor youthful. One was a woman who could properly be called a "Super Mom." Yet, somehow, one day she found herself amidst ritual candles while a Buddha-like cult leader in a gray business suit flattered her by claiming to be the channel for messages especially designed to meet her needs from "Lao-Tsu," the ancient Chinese philosopher and founder of Taoism. In another life 2500 years ago, the voice of "Lao-Tsu" told her, this woman was his favorite sister, the one who had helped him write his mysterious poetry.

Soon, this lady, whom her family and friends had assumed to be a normal, respectable, suburban wife, declared to her family that she needed "some space." She promptly packed her bags and was off to follow her guru to a distant state. Just a few months later, disillusioned, she phoned her husband and begged him to take her back. Today, she simply cannot believe her stupidity and lack of judgment.

The stories of the other women profiled by writer Clair Safran are similar. "Cults have gone mainstream," Safran observed, "and their new targets are middle aged and older women." The article added, "Today, the cults realize that parents may have more assets--homes, cars, bank accounts--than their children."

This is indeed true, for in my own experience dealing with the New Age cults, I have found that some of the people lured into these cults are willing to pump tens of thousands of dollars into cult coffers. Some are even enticed to sell their home, their cars, their jewelry and clothes, and all of their belongings and donate it to the guru or spiritual leader who promises them self-fulfillment, a share of the "divine essence," or initiation into the higher mysteries.

In a special report entitled the "The New Victims of Cults" in the *Ladies Home Journal*, writer Diane Salvatore warned: "If you are worrying that your teenage children could be lured into joining a cult, your fear may be misplaced. Today, the most vulnerable member of the family may be your aging mother--or yourself." Salvatore gave graphic examples of elderly people who have been bilked of all their assets by New Age cults. Alarmingly, Salvatore reports that:

> Cults today are expanding their membership through a new pool of recruits: the elderly, the middle aged, and church going Christians. And, while in the past cults attracted equal numbers of males and females, today more women than men are being drawn in.

Who is Vulnerable to a Cult?

Men and women who are drawn into the New Age are not ignorant nor stupid. Often, some of the brightest people imaginable can be persuaded to believe in the most incredulous and outrageous practices and doctrines. Studies on the cults have found that these groups especially prey on people during periods of extreme vulnerability. A man or a woman going through a particularly stressful time in their lives is a prime target; for example, the death of a loved one, losing one's job, moving, going away to college, an extended illness, confinement in prison, being away from home due to military service, divorce, or the emotional state which some amusingly call "the middle age crazies"--any one of these stressful periods may render a person susceptible to the influence of New Age cults and religions.

Cult recruiters especially like to pick on women in their 30s, 40s, and 50s returning to college or those whose children have grown up and recently left home, creating what is often called "the childless nest syndrome." Men and women experiencing marital distress are also often victimized by the New Age recruiters. For example, a couple experiencing marital problems may unwittingly go to a psychotherapist or a psychiatrist steeped in New Age doctrine. By the second or third counseling session, they find that they are involved in extended group therapy in which the leader has influenced them to become enmeshed in the reading of New Age and unchristian "self-help" books and literature. The therapist may also use subtle messages to attack the couple's traditional views and values so he can gradually replace them with newer values more amenable to the New Age.

In addition to the lonely and insecure and those suffering temporary emotional stress, the New Age also preys on the *naive*. Unfortunately, most of our schools today teach such unwholesome curricula "innovations" as values clarification, secular humanism, situational ethics, and relativism--philosophies made to order for New Age cults and religions. Led to believe that anything is possible for those who think positive and have the right mental attitude, and brought up to reject traditional Christian values and morality, most young people today are ideal targets for the New Age. Many lack absolutes and are tossed like a shipwreck on the seas whenever a glib-talking or physically attractive person of the opposite sex confronts them with smooth and deceptive new ideas. Unsure of their own convictions, they are extremely susceptible to what is presented.

The cults capitalize on what are often very real and unmet spiritual needs and unfilled longings. The cultists do not usually waste time on a person who demonstrates a solid knowledge of the Bible or conveys a firm faith in Jesus Christ as Lord and Savior. However, for those whose "faith" is second-hand and inherited from parents, the situation is quite different. Most people today are not grounded in Bible doctrines, even though they may have been raised in Christian churches. Such persons find the New Age cults and religions attractive precisely because they offer *feelings, experiences*, and the possibility of meeting deep human needs while suggesting that these desired objectives can be obtained through quick fixes. The New Age promotes the mystical rather than the rational; it suggests there is a way to "know" and "become." The lure is that a person can become wise, happy, fulfilled, and successful through some type of magical formula or series of new and exciting, or mysteriously ancient initiations.

The New Age has attracted the majority of its participants from aging Baby Boomers. These are the children of the 60s who still have not found the answers they have been looking for. They believe that by searching and sorting out through the multitude of cults, sects, religions, and teachings of the New Age, someday they will be rewarded when they find that one teaching or one leader who can finally give them the key to instant enlightenment and/or illumination. These individuals have rejected Jesus Christ and the authority of the Bible but they realize that material happiness is insufficient to meet the deep inner needs of the human heart. So they seek and seek among the many New Age offerings, but their appetites are never satisfied.

Reaching Out to New Age Believers

Ronald Enroth, a professor at Westmont College in Santa Barbara, California, and author of the excellent book *The Lure of the Cults and New Religions*, explained in *Moody Monthly* magazine a few years ago some of the reasons why the New Age has made such deep inroads in our society and attracted so many. Enroth points out that, "It is important to remember that most people are attracted to cults for non-theological reasons." He goes on to explain:

> Few Mormons joined the Mormon church because they were drawn initially to the *Book of Mormon*. Not

many Moonies became members of the Unification Church out of early fascination with Sun Myung Moon's *Divine Principle*. Theological considerations are nearly always secondary.

The appeal of the cults is quite simple. Cults lure people that are successful because they are meeting basic human needs: the need to belong, to have fellowship, to have a sense of identity and purpose, to be affirmed as a person, to have answers for life's enduring problems.

Ronald Enroth gives us a means to reach the cultist with Christ and help the person discover the Truth. As Christians we should not view those in the New Age only as gullible, deceived adherents of false doctrines which need to be refuted. It certainly is true that we must be defenders of the faith, but we must remember that those trapped in the New Age are people just like us. We, too, once were in need of the Truth and were separated from God. New Agers are our next door neighbors, our loved ones, or the friend at work-- men and women created by God whom we should be concerned about and reach out to with a pure desire to assist the person to discover true joy and happiness.

We know that this can be attained only through Jesus Christ; what we must understand and ever keep in mind is that these people are victims of propaganda. They are people who often firmly believe that they have found the truth; they may well consider the message of historic Christianity inferior to the new doctrines or special revelations they have obtained through some "inspired" channel of truth. Still, if we can better understand the individual's human and social needs, possibly we can reach that person.

The significant thing to remember is that few New Agers start off initially on an unholy quest to wreck and destroy the Christian faith. Many in the New Age are idealistic, even altruistic and humanitarian in their worldview and perspective. Moreover, when first approached by cult members and invited to participate, many are in the throes of loneliness and insecurity. They succumb because they are temporarily vulnerable. Surely, we can sympathize with such men and women though we can not help them if we compromise our own principles and faith in the process.

Not too long ago I read a remark made by a woman named Jeanne Mills. Her words touched me deeply and caused me to reflect on the plight of those involved in the New Age. Mills stated:

> When you meet the friendliest people you have ever known, who introduce you to the most loving group of people you have ever encountered, and you find the leader to be the most inspired, caring, compassionate, and understanding person you have ever met, and then you learn that the cause of the group is something you never dared hoped to be accomplished, and all of this sounds too good to be true, it probably is too good to be true! Don't give up your education, your hopes and ambitions, to follow a rainbow.

What makes these words so very poignant is that Jeanne Mills is a former member of The People's Temple. Jeanne was not in Jonestown, Guyana, on November 18, 1978 and was not one of the 911 adults and children who were brutalized and eventually murdered at the instigation of Jim Jones, their New Age "Christian" leader. Subsequent to these murders, Jeanne was interviewed by a number of television and newspaper reporters and was able to explain the reasons why so many had agreed to become part of The People's Temple cult. Angered by her public renunciation of the cult, a year after the Jonestown incident Jeanne Mills was assassinated by surviving but disgruntled and vicious members of the cult who still believed in their dead cult leader.

It is so important that we thoughtfully and prayerfully reflect on the most effective way to witness to New Agers.

Though many are brainwashed and unable to discern reality, it is vital that we who are of Christ recognize the incredible extent to which those in the New Age are victimized by fraud and deception. In a perceptive poem, which he called "This is It," poet Carl Sandburg gave us this keen insight into the mind control techniques of the cult:

> Repeat and repeat till they say what you are saying.
> Repeat and repeat till they are helpless before your
>   repetitions.
> Say it over and over until their brains can hold only what
>   you are saying.
> Speak it soft, yell it and yell it, change to a whisper,
>   always in repeats.
> Come back to it day on day, hour after hour.
> Till they say what you tell them to say.
> To wash A, B, C out of a brain and replace it with
>   X, Y, Z.

Sandburg's poem should touch a chord in the minds of many in the New Age. It is, in fact, the goal of almost every New Age cult, religion, sect, or organization to convince the individual that he or she is suffering a *delusion* and that only through the initiation process or the enlightenment available through the New Age group can a person be freed from the *illusion* in which the whole world--as well as that individual--is trapped. For example, *A Course in Miracles* stresses that the student is to judge his or her surroundings and all of reality as mere illusion--what the Hindus call *maya*. Instructors of *A Course in Miracles* suggest that the student refuse to accept the reality that confronts them and instead relinquish all their beliefs about reality itself. Lesson 132 of the course encourages the individual to make this affirmation: "I loose the world from all I thought it was."

It is therefore an astonishing thing for a New Ager, after being a member of a New Age cult or religion and being brainwashed for a number of years, to come out of such a group and realize the extent to which he, or she, voluntarily, through the prodding of his captors, gave up the real world. L. Ron Hubbard, founder of Scientology, once called his religion the "total road to happiness." Instead, the frightening truth is that Scientology and all the other New Age cults and religions are pathways to imprisonment and confinement.

Though they promise a bright new life and a radiant new aeon, the New Age cult groups deliver only a murky, dim world of partial truths and mega-lies. Promising to help people become sane, they then proceed to assist the individual to enter an insane asylum of his or her own doing-- an impoverished place of mental and spiritual confinement where the mind and the senses cease to logically process information and distinguish facts from fantasies.

The Danger of Cults

The greatest danger of a cult is that the individual will lose the opportunity to come to know Christ Jesus as Lord and Savior. There is not one--no, not one--New Age cult or religion which truly exalts Jesus Christ as Lord of all. Thus, a person who becomes involved in the New Age is not able to recognize the truth of Philippians 2:9-11:

> Wherefore God also hath highly exalted him, and given him a name which is above every name: That at the name of Jesus every knee should bow, of things in heaven, and things in earth, and things under the earth; And that every tongue should confess that Jesus Christ is Lord, to the glory of God the Father.

Because they reject the indisputable biblical teaching that all of us are "dead in trespasses and sins" (Ephesians 2:1), those in the New Age cannot find salvation unless they turn to the Truth of the Scripture. They must realize who Jesus is, and call on Him in true repentance. While many in the New Age join a particular cult or religion to meet personal or social needs, the fact is that at least tentatively, these men, women, and youth do *believe* in what they are being taught in the New Age. As long as they maintain spiritual fellowship with those who worship the "God of Forces" (see Daniel 11:36-39), they will be unable to recognize the true Light. As Paul was inspired to write in Ephesians 5:1, 11: "Be ye therefore followers of God, as dear children ... And have no fellowship with the unfruitful works of darkness, but rather reprove them."

Many in the New Age operate under the assumption that they can go to their Christian church on Sunday and during the week attend a New Age study group or fellowship. *Eph 5:11* Nothing could be further from the truth. We are told to have no fellowship with the unfruitful works of darkness. We are not to yoke ourself with unbelievers through spiritual fellowship. To imagine that we can maintain one leg in each of these two opposing camps is a serious error and places a person's soul in grave jeopardy.

Many are also in real *physical* danger through involvement in the New Age cults. Pete Slover, reporter for the Knight-Ridder Tribune News Service, last year reported on a tragic situation. A New Age teacher in Dallas had convinced a very educated man--indeed a professor of business at one of America's top learning institutions--and his wife that they were gods and goddesses in previous lifetimes. He was told that he was Jupiter, she Venus. Now the couple is dead. They eventually committed suicide. Subsequently, it was determined that a total of nine others had attempted suicide after heeding the false claim of their "spiritual guide" and becoming involved in spirit communications.

Almost every day my ministry receives letters from anxious people whose loved ones are caught up in the New Age trap. They say that after the joining a New Age group or becoming fascinated with New Age occult literature, the loved one's lifestyle changed dramatically. Often, they report, the individual eventually lost his or her job, and sometimes suffered debilitating health problems because of an unsafe dietary regimen prescribed. Mental depression and suicidal manias are also commonplace among those in the New Age.

It is ironic that men and women who join New Age groups for what initially appears to be for the best of reasons--personal development, to save the whales, end world hunger, clean up the environment, ensure world peace, or help children--soon find that none of these goals can be obtained through what the New Age has to offer. Instead, distressed, worn-out, and having sunk into a valley of despair, the person finds that years of his or her life has been wasted. But it is at that moment, and most often at that moment only, that the person begins to realize that there *is* an answer to his misery. *That answer is found through Jesus Christ alone.*

PART 2

NEW AGE CULTS AND RELIGIONS

A COURSE IN MIRACLES

It is called *A Course in Miracles*. It comes advertised as a new "bible" dictated by none other than "Jesus." It has taken the United States by storm and is now reaching out its silkily deceptive and slippery tentacles to every country on the globe. Already some 500,000 copies of this new bible have been sold and as many as four million people have studied the *Course*. Gene Keefer, in *Critique* magazine in 1989, reflected on the amazing popularity of *A Course in Miracles* when he wrote, "To say that *A Course in Miracles* is catching on is to make one of the great understatements of the decade, maybe the century. Less than 25 years ago, it was only a vortex of energy, whirling around . . . Today, it seems to almost be everywhere."

Keefer went on to say that "faithful Christians who first come to know about *A Course in Miracles* must feel uncomfortable with the thought that the Jesus-in-spirit is not at all like the man of flesh and blood they came to know from reading the Bible." He adds that the new Jesus presented in *A Course in Miracles* gives many "an uneasy feeling." Indeed, the *Course* presents another Jesus--a radically different Christ--and encourages readers to reject the old Jesus. Evidently, hundreds of thousands of people with a New Age bent of mind like what they see in the new Jesus.

A number of New Age organizations have sprung up to promote *A Course in Miracles*, and there are a number of big names involved. One is Tara Singh, a teacher from India who claims to have lived in the Himalayas, Central America, and Europe before coming to the United States in 1947. Singh had a close relationship with such luminaries as Theosophist leader Krishnamurti, India's Prime Minister Nehru, and British occultist author Aldous Huxley. In 1976 Singh came into contact with *A Course in Miracles*. Since then, he has published a number of books, videos, and other products praising the work. One is entitled *Raising the Child for the New Age;* another is *How to Raise a Child of God.*

Perhaps the biggest promoter of *A Course in Miracles* is a group called The Foundation for Inner Peace, headed by Judith Skutch-Whitson, its president. Skutch-Whitson is also affiliated with the New Age's Institute of Noetic Sciences, an organization headed by former astronaut Edgar Mitchell among others, and she is a member of the Board of Directors of the American Society for Cyclical Research. Skutch-Whitson's Foundation for Inner Peace publishes and distributes *A Course in Miracles* around the world. She also is frequently interviewed by television, radio, and New Age magazines on behalf of the *Course.*

There are many others involved in *A Course in Miracles*. For example, pop-psychologist Gerald Jampolsky. Jampolsky has written a bestselling book, *Love is Letting Go of Fear,* and is a personal friend of the Crystal Cathedral's Robert Schuller. Indeed, Jampolsky has appeared on Schuller's "Hour of Power" television program. Jampolsky is a frequent guest of Unity churches and other New Age groups. He stalks the nation selling his books and enthusiastically touting the message of the *Course.*

Yet another big name in the New Age who is a believer in the *Course* is Kenneth Wapnick, who has taken this new bible and interpreted it for the masses in a number of bestselling books. Wapnick claims to be a Catholic Christian. But in an interview with the *SCP Journal* in 1987, Wapnick frankly admitted that:

> The *Course* is not compatible with Biblical Christianity. There are three basic reasons. One is the *Course's* idea that God did not create the world. The second is the *Course's* teaching that Jesus was not the only Son of God. The third involves the *Course's* assertion that Jesus did not suffer and die for our sins. ?!

It appears that in this one statement alone, Wapnick has shown us the reason why *A Course in Miracles* has decidedly hellish origins. *A Course in Miracles* claims to be a legitimate revelation of the true Jesus Christ, but the truth is, this is one of the most heretical courses and the most diabolically seducing that I have ever personally come across. AMEN!

The Origins of the Course

How did *A Course of Miracles* come into the world? Its origins are undisputed. In the mid-1960s, a Jewish, atheist psychologist named Helen Schucman, a professor from a university in the state of New York, claimed that a spirit entity began to send her visions and speak to her mind. Asked who this spirit was, Schucman revealingly exclaimed "*It* said *it* was Jesus." The Voice (as she called it) told Schucman to "take notes," that she was to give a profound teaching to the world.

For almost ten years Helen Schucman dutifully took down the notes of the Voice inside her brain. The results were published in 1975, and by 1980 over 60,000 sets of books had been distributed--without the benefits of media advertising and mainly on the basis of recommendations by enthusiastic students of the course.

Although a do-it-yourself New Age course, *A Course in Miracles* is also now being taught in many New Age churches throughout America as well as Europe. Its influence is especially deeply felt in Unitarian churches and such New Age-oriented denominations as the Church of Religious Science, Unity, and others. However, the course has also caught on with such liberal Christian denominations as the Methodists, Episcopals, Disciples of Christ, and some Lutheran groups. It is also increasingly popular within the Catholic Church. In fact, it is now common as I travel around America for faithful Catholics to come up to me and say that they left their local church after a priest or a nun began teaching *A Course in Miracles*, causing great distress and sadness and the eventual breaking away of the individual from the Catholic Church.

The *Course* comes in three volumes which sell for about $30. Volume I, the principal text, has 622 pages. Volume II, a workbook for students, is 478 pages in length. There is also a *Manual for Teachers* (88 pages). This is really a set of teachings promoting the basic premises of Hinduism and Buddhism, but it is deceptively presented in Western terminology and does not easily give itself away as a doctrinal Hindu/Eastern Mystical text. Indeed, it comes across as a very holy and loving text which promises peace and contentment for its students. Those who are unfamiliar with the Holy Bible and have rejected traditional Christian doctrines are almost sitting ducks for *A Course in Miracles* because of the seductive nature in which it presents its teachings.

The Teachings of A Course in Miracles

It is important that we take a look at those teachings. First, the *Course* claims that we are in charge of and are part of our own atonement. It insists that Jesus' crucifixion was not for the sins of the world and that we individually are responsible for our own salvation. Obviously, this is at direct variance from the Bible which tells us that all have sinned and fallen short of the Glory of God, but that through His grace and through the redemption that comes by Jesus Christ, we are saved through faith in Him (Romans 3:23-25).

The *Course* also claims that God does not condemn us for our evil or even hold us personally to blame for our bad deeds. It also rejects the Biblical account of Adam and Eve being driven out of the garden. Judgment is depicted not as something that God undertakes, but something we ourselves must determine. However, the Bible says that Jesus has been appointed as Judge of both the living and the dead (Acts 10:42, and see II Corinthians 5:10).

Like all New Age teachings, the *Course* proclaims that *everyone* has God's Word written on their hearts and that salvation is universal. *All* will be saved. But the Bible says that the natural man does not receive the things of the Spirit of God for they are foolishness to him and he cannot understand them. Only he who is born again through the free gift given by God (John 3:3 and I Corinthians 2:14) have God's Word inside as a testimony, a witness, and a guide.

The Course also teaches another cardinal New Age doctrine--that there are "Teachers" in the spirit world whom we can call on for assistance and help. This is simply *necromancy*, or communication with familiar spirits (demons), a practice which is expressly prohibited in the Bible (see Deuteronomy 18).

The Course vs. The Bible

Here are a number of other discrepancies in *A Course in Miracles* as compared to the truth of the Bible:

1. The *Course* teaches that the world we see is simply an illusion, that material matter does not exist. God did not create it. When we turn to scripture we see, however, that the heavens declare the glory of God and are the work of his hand (Psalm 19:1; John 1:1-3; Colossians 1:16; Hebrews 1:2-3).

2. Jesus is Christ but *not* the only Christ--we are *all* Christs, author Helen Schucman was told by her spirit guide who called itself "Jesus." Yet, the Bible shows clearly that Jesus is the *only* Christ. For example, John the Baptist freely confessed that he was not the Christ and that a greater one than he was to come (John 1:20). Jesus Himself in Matthew 24:4-5 warned that in the last days many would come in His name claiming to be the Christ and would deceive many.

3. The *Course* maintains that the Word (or thought) could not have been made flesh and that this is a false belief. However, the Bible testifies that the Word (Jesus) was in the beginning, that the Word was God, and was with God (John 1). Moreover, every spirit that acknowledges that Jesus Christ has come in the flesh is from God, the Bible teaches, and every spirit that does not acknowledge that Jesus Christ came in the flesh as God is the spirit of the Antichrist (I John 4:1-3; John 1:1-18).

4. According to the *Course*, Jesus was not punished on the cross because of our sins or because we are bad. This, it says, is a distortion. Obviously this is in direct contradiction with John 3:16 and with a score of other biblical passages.

5. The *Course* tells its readers that their works and their holiness will result in their individual salvation. For example, it states "My salvation comes from me. It cannot come from anywhere else." Clearly, this is heresy for we see in God's Word that salvation is found in no one else but Jesus Christ, for there is no other name under heaven by which we must be saved (see Acts 4:10-12 and John 3,14).

6. We are all part of God, says the *Course.* "You are part of Him who is all power and glory, and are therefore unlimited as He is." Furthermore, the *Course* teaches that "God's name is holy, but no holier than yours. To call upon His name is but to call upon your own." These teachings can be found nowhere in the Bible; just the reverse is true. To worship ourselves as God and to exalt ourselves in this manner is simply to defame and blaspheme God. God alone, the Bible teaches, is holy. (See Romans 1:25; Ezekiel 28:2; Psalms 143:2; Jeremiah 17:9; Revelation 15:3,4; and Ephesians 2:1-13, 4:18).

7. According to *A Course in Miracles*, all our sins are washed away by realizing that they were merely "mistakes." Sins are but dreams, said the false Jesus who came to Helen Schucman, and no one will be punished for their sins, for no one is a sinner. How deceptive is this teaching, for if we are not sinners then Jesus died on the cross in vain, and He was either a fool or a lunatic. However, the Bible testifies to the Truth--that if we claim to be without sin we deceive ourselves and the truth is not in us. But if we confess our sin, He is faithful and just and will forgive us our sin and cleanse us from our unrighteousness (see I John 1:8-10; Romans 3:23; 6:23; and Ephesians 4:18).

8. Naturally, since it is a New Age bible, the *Course* teaches that there is no death, that man is an eternal creature who will live on and on. This is simply a reiteration of the Hindu and New Age belief in reincarnation and karma. Easily we see that this is a lie, for Hebrews 9:27 says that man will live one life on this earth and afterward will face the judgment of God.

A Counterfeit Bible

A Course in Miracles is most definitely a counterfeit bible. This is a false bible that even comes with a new type of Lord's Prayer. Helen Schucman has stated that when she received the new Lord's Prayer from the Voice that claimed it was Jesus, she literally burst into tears. "The beauty of the language," she remarked, "the profundity of the thoughts--in a sense the equivalence of the Lord's Prayer for the *Course*--seemed to be so clear." This new Lord's Prayer is certainly different from the original. Below is just a part of it.

> Forgive us our illusions, Father, and help us to accept our true relationship with You in which there are no illusions and where none can ever enter. Our holiness is Yours. What can there be in us that needs forgiveness when Yours is perfect? The sleep of forgetfulness is only our willingness to accept Your forgiveness and Your Love. Let us not wonder at temptations, for the temptation of the Son of God is not Your will. And let us receive only what You have given and accept this into the mind You love. Amen.

Forget All That You Have Learned

The discrepancies between what *A Course in Miracles* teaches and the truth of the Bible is casually dismissed by the followers of this new religion. The *Course* itself encourages its readers to forget all that they have ever learned and to willingly accept its new conceptions of spirituality:

> Let us be still an instant and forget all things we have ever learned, all thoughts we have and every preconception we hold of what things mean and what their purpose is. Let us remember not our own ideas of what the world is for. We do not know. Let every image held by everyone be loosened from our minds

behind-person also
Thought for the...
(2)

and swept away. Be innocent of judgment, unaware of any thoughts of evil or of good that ever crossed your mind of anyone ...

Moreover, to make it even more palatable to the doubter, the proponents of the *Course* say that you can pick and choose whatever parts of the *Course* suit your own life-style and worldview. For example, John Macri, who started an Indianapolis group to study the *Course*, told an interviewer, "It doesn't go against any religion. There is nothing anti-religious about it. You can accept whatever parts you want to. If you have problems with parts, that is okay."

According to Macri, it is acceptable simply to believe in this one principle from the *Course*: "God is in everything I see because God is in my mind."

Is it "Christian"?

It is difficult to understand how some who call themselves "Christian" can embrace this clearly heretical new bible. We can only assume that either they are greatly deceived as Christians or that these disciples of the *Course* are simply deceiving themselves in their insistence that they *are* Christians. Today, the very term "Christian" has come into disrepute because of the machinations and deceptions of those who seek to mislead and confuse us. Certainly those who would promote and teach *A Course in Miracles* are not born-again believers as Jesus taught in John 3:3. The fact that this new bible is 1,188 pages long is ample evidence that spirit entities and intellectuals such as Dr. Helen Schucman who have rejected the One True God are dogged, determined, and will persevere to bring their views into this world under the guise of "Christianity."

The Course and Christian Science

Ultimately, *A Course in Miracles* is simply a more refined and sophisticated type of *Christian Science*. Judith Skutch-Whitson, president of the Foundation for Inner Peace, the group which publishes *A Course in Miracles*, has said that, "Sickness is incorrect thinking and can be healed by correct thinking. It is a mistake that must be corrected at its source. Healing is of the mind, since only the mind can make mistakes." Clearly, this is the same philosophy taught by Mary Baker Eddy's Christian Science and by Ernest Holmes in his *Science of Mind.*

Another similarity between the *Course* and other New Age teachings is the emphasis by the *Course* on *experience* rather than salvation by grace as a free gift from God. As Skutch-Whitson has remarked, "The *Course* states that a universal theology is impossible, but that a universal *experience* is imperative."

It is also apparent that this new bible is a dramatic attempt to water down and homogenize traditional Christianity. Skutch-Wilson herself gives an indication of this when she states:

> Christianity is the dominant religion in the Western world and history but some of its beliefs are not very Christian. The *Course* tries to help us understand spiritual teachings without the distortions...

> Some Biblical scholars, in fact, have told us that the material seems to be very close to what the early Christians probably believed...And when people are ready, they can feel the essence of a teaching rather than be distracted by the words.

What we see here, then, is a New Age bible that misuses Christian terms such as Father, Son, and Holy Spirit, turning the meaning of these words upside-down to present another gospel and another Jesus.

THE ACADEMY FOR FUTURE SCIENCE (THE KEYS OF ENOCH)

In January, 1973, J. J. Hurtag was lifted from the earth by a "Light being," who called himself the master Enoch, and swept away into the stormy constellations of the sky, soon to find himself standing before the almighty Divine Father. This is the testimony of the man  who is the founder of *The Academy for Future Science*. J. J. Hurtag, an engineer, is also the author of a false New Age bible, *The Book of Knowledge: The Keys of Enoch*, about 600 pages, color illustrated, which includes some of the most sophisticated and most confusing gobbledygook known to man.

The title page of *The Book of Knowledge: The Keys of Enoch* claims it to be "a teaching given on seven levels to be read and visualized in preparation for the Brotherhood of Light, to be delivered for the quickening of the People of Light." According to Hurtag, this complicated "bible" contains "the biocomputer keys to our consciousness time zone revealed to me by master control messengers: Metatron and Ophanim Enoch."

He goes on to say that this is an ancient scroll in the language of light. *The Keys of Enoch* is claimed to be a blueprint of the many levels of spiritual consciousness as taught by "two higher teachers of universal intelligence called Enoch and Metatron." Enoch identified himself to Hurtag as the same Enoch mentioned in the Holy Bible.

According to The Academy for Future Science, *The Keys of Enoch* is a tool for "the building of communities of light to prepare the human race for the externalization or appearance of the Masters from other worlds of light." The Academy teaches that humanity is moving into a new spiritual cycle when all will collectively become "the Christ." In this new era of higher human evolution, mankind will be connected with the Master Plan and will become united with other great worlds populated throughout the galaxy.

The Academy for Future Science is closely connected with certain UFO societies and groups. J. J. Hurtag, for example, is well-known among UFO authorities and is considered an expert on the subject. It is his claim that in 1973 a spirit-being named Enoch enveloped him with a great wall of light, and both he and Enoch sped upwards into the heavens. There they met up with another being of great majesty called Metatron, the Creator of Light in the universe.

Finally, Hurtag says, he was taken directly into the throne room, near the pyramid of the living light, before a great Throne. There he saw the "Ancient of Days" face-to-face. According to Hurtag, the Ancient of Days has glowing white hair and a face of overwhelming love and joy. Seeing the great one, Hurtag proclaimed "Thou art worthy O Lord YHWH to receive glory and honor and power, for Thou has created all things and for Thy pleasure the aeons were created."

While in the heavenly realms, Hurtag was supposedly told by his guides, Enoch and Metatron, that man is not to eat the food of "the false powers of the earth, nor encourage my seed to marry with the fallen spiritual races of the earth, nor join in false worship with those who serve the fallen mind energies of the earth."

It is apparent that Hurtag's book, *The Keys of Enoch*, is in reality a massively clever conglomeration of occultic doctrines which he has picked up over the years through intense study. For example, when Hurtag mentions the externalization of the Hierarchy, this is simply a throwback to the teachings of Alice Bailey of the Lucis Trust, who published a prominent New Age occultic book, *The Externalization of the Hierarchy*, in the 1940s. Hurtag also borrows freely and unabashedly from the Bible. For example, he says that while he was before the Throne he saw a burning scroll rolled as a cylinder and out of this burning scroll a light was projected into his "Third Eye." Such phraseology reminds us of the biblical accounts of Ezekiel and other prophets, though Hurtag's imaginative account is greatly embellished with New Age and occultic symbology and terminology.

Hurtag says that he composed a scroll on parchment from the divine scroll of light that was coded into the "Third Eye" region on his forehead. This scroll is said to be the 64 keys of Enoch as explained in *The Book of Knowledge: The Keys of Enoch.* They are a prophetic message showing how the seven seals of the book of Revelation of the Bible will come to be broken, or unsealed, and how the last days will transpire. The version of prophetic events soon to come that we find in Hurtag's scrolls certainly is at great variance from what a Christian reads in Bible prophecy.

The Brotherhood of Light

In common with other New Age groups, Hurtag's New Age bible maintains that there is a group called the *Brotherhood of Light*, spirit beings from the heavenly realm, who are available to share their wisdom with the *Brotherhood of Man.* The beings who compose the Brotherhood of Light are said to work directly for the Eternal One, YHWH. Although Jesus Christ is an indistinct part of the teachings of Hurtag and The Academy for Future Science, His role is greatly deemphasized. He most certainly is not credited by this cult group as the creator of the universe as depicted truthfully in the Holy Bible.

Hurtag's teachings are that, through a process of visualization and consciousness imaging, an individual will achieve a higher understanding. The masters who are the Brotherhood of Light will transmit into the mind of the person *through the Third Eye region of his forehead and into his brain* direct knowledge, or gnosis. Thus, the person will be able to understand the holy doctrines of YHWH.

Through continued contact with the Brotherhood of Light, eventually, The Academy of Future Science proclaims, an individual can become a Christed individual, a higher evolved entity. Those chosen as higher evolved beings receive the promise of "New Life" in the myriad other universes. They are transformed into beings of pure light and thereafter live an existence of pure bliss.

Satan can come as an angel of light.

Meanwhile, here on earth the dark forces (no doubt including biblical Christians) will be overcome. "Advanced powers" will soon oversee and direct dramatic changes upon our planet, "intervening to control man's wanderlust for a cosmic holocaust."

In other words, Hurtag maintains that the Brotherhood of Light will, in the last days, come forth to save the planet earth from extinction through nuclear catastrophe.

The Third Eye of Agni

New Agers and Hindus alike call the site where the invisible Third Eye is located the *Agni Point*, or *Agni Center*. In Hindu mythology, the Lord Agni was the fire god, represented by lightning. The New Age occultic teaching is that the Agni Center is the Third Eye in which cosmic fire and light enter to bring a form of higher consciousness and inner transformation to initiates. We should recall that Jesus Christ described Lucifer in this manner: "I beheld Satan as lightning fall from heaven" (Luke 10:18).

In some occultic teachings, the initiate is taught that a cosmic string of fire, or lightning, comes down from the spiritual realm and enters the initiate's forehead exactly where a mark is placed between the eyes. This is the *Third Eye* region. It is thought to be the chakra (Hindu) or energy point in the body which, when developed, enables the individual to develop god-like abilities, powers, and knowledge.

strength

Programmed by 6-6-6

In *The Keys of Enoch*, we find similar occultic construction. However, not only do we discover in *The Keys of Enoch* the Hindu occultic doctrine of the Third Eye, but Hurtag's *The Keys of Enoch* suggests to us that man is initiated in his Third Eye by *light messages from the Brotherhood of Light*.

Those light messages are said to come in a numerical electrical sequence. Astonishingly, we are further told that this numerical electronic sequence is the number *666*! It is through the number 666 that the heavenly beings supposedly communicate with men, sending and receiving spiritual information. This is done, says *The Keys of Enoch*, through use of "specific light and sound harmonics ... by means of a pyramidal focus created ... over the Third Eye."

By using this heavenly sequence of 666, it is explained, the individual's thoughts are elevated as if they were a "seed crystal." Blessed by the 666 force, the individual thereafter

The Urantia Book teaches that man's mind is programmed by electronic light sequences sent to the Third Eye in the forehead by beings from another dimension.

communicates directly with the "councils of light in the heavens," which is yet another synonym given in *The Keys of Enoch* for the Brotherhood of Light.

The New Age bible that is *The Keys of Enoch* reveals to us also that every man has a Third Eye and it is through the individual's Third Eye that the Father in heaven oversees creation with His own "Eye of Horus." When we realize that the Eye of Horus is the all-seeing eye of Horus, the son of Osiris, the Egyptian Father God, we understand clearly the connection of these teachings with the ancient philosophy of occultism.

In effect, The Academy for Future Science and its false bible, *The Keys of Enoch*, instruct initiates to communicate with demonic powers through a light-link. Here is the procedure of how this is supposed to be done:

> The Eye of Horus is the eye of the lords, serving the Living Father of Creation which is placed upon the Third Eye region of the elect. Therefore, this alignment of the divine eyes permits you to acquire wisdom and to work within the complete network of the divine hierarchy.

Contrast with Christianity

The "divine hierarchy" which members of The Academy for Future Science connect with is certainly not the divine hierarchy of Jesus, the true God of the Bible. Those who become involved with this New Age religious group and are held spellbound by the pseudo-scientific language of its 618 page "bible" will be taken on a journey far from the truth. Contrasts with the real Bible are many. For example, *The Keys of Enoch* teaches that the Antichrist is *not* a man, though Revelation 13 clearly shows him to be a man. The Antichrist, suggests Hurtag, is the collective spirit of all of those who stick to the "contaminated," man-made doctrines of Biblical Christianity.

Hurtag says that his New Age scriptures are superior to the Bible but that even more highly advanced revelations are forthcoming. He insists that in the coming era the Bible will be augmented and supplemented with certain "sacred scriptures" revealed to man by interplanetary messengers. This receiving of new sacred scriptures will occur when the New Age race is ready to move upward to a higher evolutionary plane. Then the lower beings who refuse the New Age doctrines must return to the primeval earth and begin the reincarnation process all over again, as the Kingdom of God--a New Age Utopia--is built here on earth.

Thus, The Academy for Future Science teaches a doctrine of the "elect:" "The elect are the people of The Plan."

*A*DELPHI

Adelphi leader Richard Kieninger claims that strange members of an invisible spirit world who make up the elite group called the *Brotherhood* have initiated him into a higher knowledge and spiritual state. Kieninger claims that Adelphi was established to carry out "the Great Plan of these disembodied spirits of the Brotherhood."

Adelphi, in Garland, Texas, a suburb of Dallas, has gone through some trying times recently. It seems that another organization which Kieninger established, the Stelle Group, dismissed Kieninger from its leadership claiming that he had bilked the organization out of a significant sum of money and that he was also guilty of sexual misconduct.

Specifically, it was charged that Kieninger had failed to come through on his grandiose scheme for a utopia on earth. It is Kieninger's plan to buy an island, which he claims exists in the Pacific Ocean, and rename it "Philadelphia."

Philadelphia, according to Kieninger, is slated by the Brotherhood to be a heavenly city on earth. The directors of the Stelle Group, however, contend that such an island does not exist at all, that actually it was merely a figment of Richard Kieninger's fertile and untrustworthy imagination, designed to delude members and relieve them of spare cash.

None the worse off, Kieninger in 1988-89 decided to emphasize Adelphi, which, after extended litigation and legal maneuverings, appears now to be totally a separate entity under the direction of Kieninger and associates.

The Great Plan of the Brotherhood

According to its own publications, which include the *Adelphi Quarterly* newsletter, it is Adelphi's purpose to help disciples realign themselves with "The Great Plan of the Brotherhood." To that end, Adelphi conducts public seminars to teach participants what the Brotherhood wants humanity to do in achieving spiritual goals.

Adelphi teaches that the cosmic universe consists of seven planes of existence made up of matter and energy. These range from the physical plane to the plane of pure spirit and love, which is the seventh and ultimate plane. Another teaching is the spiritual evolution of man. According to the Brotherhood, man proceeds throughout twelve levels of development before he fully realizes his true purpose and divinity.

The central and most desirable goal of those who believe in Adelphi is to be initiated into the Brotherhood. If Richard Kieninger's example is an indication (see section on The Stelle Group), initiation occurs at a mystical ceremony in which, evidently, the individual literally receives a mark somewhere on the body in a form of bloodletting.

Yet another key feature of Adelphi's teachings is the Theosophist doctrine of the ancient continents of Atlantis and Lemuria. In fact, Adelphi seems to claim to be the *New Lemuria*, an embryo of a great society soon to take hold and bloom on planet earth in which men will be able to exercise fully their psychic powers and become god-like. As part of this teaching on Lemurian and Atlantis history, initiates are also instructed on the spiritual role and meaning of the Egyptian religions, and the building of the Great Pyramid.

Belief in the Ten Lemurian Laws

Like practically every other New Age group, Adelphi also is a believer in the *Law of Karma*, which Adelphi instructors call the "Natural Law of Cause and Effect." Finally, Adelphi teaches that the coming great society of "Philadelphia" will incorporate what is called the *Ten Lemurian Laws*, which are held to be akin to the Bill of Rights in the U.S. Constitution. According to founder Richard Kieninger, everyone on earth is insane to a certain degree because of the sickness of society and its failure to recognize the true spiritual laws of the universe. Thus, Kieninger has stated, "In reaching Initiation, you are essentially going sane." As a person works the Ten Lemurian Laws and achieves increasingly higher levels of initiation, Adelphi teaches that the person progressively achieves sanity and eventually may become an ascended master, one of the elite of the Brotherhood.

ALETHEIA

Aletheia sells itself as a "dynamic health training center." Its founder is a man named Jack Schwartz who operates the *Aletheia Center* and the *Aletheia Institute of Massage* in Ashland, Oregon. The center provides a wide range of New *holistic(holism)* the view that an organic or integrated whole has an independent reality, which cannot be understood simply thru understanding its parts ② of, concerned with, dealing with wholes or integrated systems rather than with their parts.

Age and holistic health learning experiences and studies. For example, in its most recent course schedule we find such short courses as *Understanding the Human Energy Centers (Chakras and Glands); Introduction to Biofeedback; Kinesiology; Mythology for Self-Discovery; Breathing For Self-Regulation and Expansion of Consciousness; <u>Advanced Human Energy Systems (Auras)</u>; Transcending Into Knowingness; Exploring The Paraconscious; Energy and Motion With Light, Color, and Sound;* and *Health Imagery and Breathing.*

Schwartz promotes the "Aletheia experience" as a potential way to achieve not only individual peace of mind but *world* peace and love. Through Aletheia even the survival of the human race on the planet might be assured. How does the Aletheia program claim to achieve such astounding goals? In its publications we are told that man can achieve peace of mind, universal love, self-understanding, financial prosperity, health, and enduring relationships through a "transmutation of the mind" and by linking up with "the unlimited power of universal intelligence." Thus again we find revealed the impersonal force which the New Age calls "God."

It is apparent from their logo, which is an adaptation of the oriental yin/yang, that Aletheia is simply another Eastern mystical holistic health system. In fact, Aletheia offers multiple ways to achieve the oriental transformation so familiar to New Age believers. Chief among them is the belief in the hazy form of God which Aletheia calls "Universal Intelligence." Tap into this Universal Intelligence and you will find the greatest source of wisdom and wealth in the universe, touts Aletheia: "Successful people tune in this infinite intelligence and receive the answers and wisdom they need to achieve their success."

The teachings of Aletheia are eclectic, representing a virtual hodgepodge of New Age faddism, spiritual experiences, holistic health speculation, and psuedo-scientific trappings. Recently, even the Catholic Church's teachings on Mary received the attention of founder Jack Schwartz and

eclectic - selecting from various systems, doctrines, sources.

his wife, Lois. On May 25-June 7, 1990 they personally conducted a tour to Medjugorje, Yugoslavia, the site where many claim that Mary, the Mother of Jesus, appeared to children.

They called this tour "a spiritual adventure to Medjugorje, Assisi, and the Omeramergau Passion Play." The European tour no doubt included Assisi, Italy as well as Medjugorje, Yogoslavia, because it was at Assisi that St. Francis, patron of nature in the Catholic Church, first formulated his now popular religious teachings advocating the worship of nature. In their brochure, Jack and Lois Schwartz advertise Assisi as "An enchantment of nature."

ANANDA

What are we to make of an organization that goes by the Hindu name of Ananda--billing itself as the *Ananda World Brotherhood Village*--yet sends out promotional material with pictures of Christianity's Jesus Christ? The simple conclusion is that Ananda is a group promoting the synthesis of all the world's religions. While emphasizing Hinduism, the organization unabashedly promotes Pope John Paul II, the worldwide head of the Catholic Church, and declares that all religions basically are the same regardless of their outward form, dogmas, or rituals. Sri Kriyananda, the head of Ananda, has stated, "Direct experience of truth, like the experiments of science, is the true essence of all religions." According to Kriyananda, "The quest for inner experience will become the religion of the New Age."

To promote its own vision of the New Age, Ananda's disciples are busy in their headquarters at Nevada City, California, building two new impressive shrines, or temples, which they believe will contribute to world peace and the unity of all religions and spiritualities. These are the brain-child of leader Sri Kriyananda, an American whose real name before he converted to Hinduism was J. Donald Walters. Swami, or Sri, Kriyananda is the founder and spiritual director of Ananda.

Kriyananda claims to have received in meditation a vision that he was to build a "Golden Lotus Shrine of All Religions." At the time, as Donald Walters, he was serving the Hindu guru Paramhansa Yogananda in India. Walters promptly wrote to Nehru, the prime minister of the government of India, and requested permission to build this Golden Lotus Shrine of All Religions near New Delhi, India. Nehru quickly approved the project; however, Walters could not get it off the ground because of a lack of funding and, by his own admission, a lack of spiritual maturity on his part. Today, Kriyananda (or Walters) proclaims that the time is right and that his retreat facility at Ananda is "the expanding light needed to transform mankind and bring all of humanity into a relationship with the Divine Essence."

Ground has also been broken for a second temple to be called the "Chapel of Divine Inspiration." Ananda explains that the Chapel of Divine Inspiration will enable the organization to conduct special conferences with the leaders of all the world's religions and thereby establish universally recognized teachings. The stated goal is "Towards oneness in God for all mankind."

The Oneness of all Religions

In a letter to seekers who request information about the Ananda community, Kriyananda explains the purpose of Ananda. First, he announces that spirituality in its purest form was brought to the world by Krishna and Buddha as well as by Jesus and Moses. In fact, he writes, all world teachers serve the *same* God. Thus spouting the New Age doctrine of "oneness," Kriyananda goes on to remark:

There is an urgent need today to demonstrate the essential *oneness* of all religions. For, clearly, all of them are devoted to principles that are *universal*. Every one of them has a goal of uplifting human consciousness, and of expanding human sympathies. All of them teach us to love our fellow man, to honor truth, and to be humble. Most (though not all) religions teach that one should love God and obey His commandments ....There is widespread unanimity.

At their essence, Ananda teaches, all religions are the same; therefore, the group has decided to immortalize in architecture this universalist teaching. The Golden Lotus Shrine of All Religions, according to Kriyananda, affirms Ananda's dedication to these universal spiritual values.

How to Realize "Self"

Ananda's nebulous concept of religious world unity does not in and of itself draw many followers. Therefore, Ananda and its founder Kriyananda also promise the individual manifold rewards if he or she actively participates in Ananda projects. Ananda says that the goal of every human being is "self-realization" and that, through Ananda, individuals can fellowship with others while realizing this self-realization. The term "self-realization," in the New Age view, means achieving *divinity of self*. Thus, Ananda promises to teach individuals how to become deities in their own right.

At their facilities in California, Ananda offers a number of programs. One is called *Lessons in Yoga: 14 Steps to Higher Awareness.* This program is not only offered in residence, but is available through the use of written study guides and tapes designed for home study as well. The individual learns such things as "Yoga and meditation, pathways to god, steps of self-realization, how to control your subconscious mind, how to become a dynamo of energy, how and why to develop your magnetism, what is a guru, esoterica of a spiritual path, and secret teachings of the Bible." It is apparent that a number of these topics are extremely enticing to individuals who lack self-esteem and spiritual depth and are interested in self-development.

Also at the Ananda facilities, participants can take advantage of "the superconscious attunement ceremony-- an evening of heart expanding, chanting, meditation, and healing prayers." At this ceremony, an Ananda publication points out, the individuals will be served "leisurely, family style, vegetarian dinners." Like all Hindu retreat centers, Ananda abhors meat.

The spiritual tradition of Ananda comes from the life and teachings of the Hindu guru Paramhansa Yogananda, author of *Autobiography of a Yogi*. Its literature claims that miracles seem to happen spontaneously at the Ananda community and that those who practice Raji Yogi, a form of spiritual as well as physical Yoga, will awaken their human consciousness and attune it to the divine.

The Ananda group also operates a press, Crystal Clarity Publishers. Among their books in print is *How to Be a Channel,* by noted West Coast psychic Barbara Courtney; and *The Reappearance of Christ.* In the latter book, author Kriyananda says that the central message of Jesus Christ was simply that mankind must love God, the "Divine Essence." This, he insists, is "what the early Christians practiced and what modern Christians have generally forgotten."

In summary, Ananda offers us "another Jesus" and "another gospel" (see II Corinthians 11:4 and Galatians 1), derived, in fact, not from the Bible but from the Hindu scriptures (the *Bhagavad Gita*).

Anthroposophical - religious or mystical system or movement similar to theosophy

ANTHROPOSOPHY AND THE WALDORF SCHOOLS (RUDOLF STEINER)

It has been called by its supporters "Christian occultism," seemingly an oxymoron and a contradiction in terms. Its founder, Rudolf Steiner, called it *Anthroposophy* and named the group whose membership believes in "Steinerism" the *Anthroposophical Society*. Rudolf Steiner was the author of over 100 books and lectures. A Western occultist, he studied and borrowed freely from dozens of other occultic systems, especially Theosophy, to create this strange new system which he dubbed Anthroposophy. Therefore, Anthroposophy's religious system has a little bit of everything in it. This is sort of a smorgasbord of occultism. Indeed, its proponents call it the "rainbow teachings," symbolizing the multifaceted nature of Anthroposophy.

Today, Anthroposophy has deep roots in American and German society, as well as in other countries around the world. There are major branches of Anthroposophy located in Los Angeles, New York City, and Chicago, and in most other cities in the U.S.A. The society also has over 500 Waldorf Schools, which teach Steiner's principles and aim as their central goal the development of the spiritual consciousness of young school-age children.

Rudolf Steiner's Influences and Ideas

Rudolf Steiner himself was born in 1861 in Austria. Holder of a doctorate degree, he was fascinated by the ideas of such mystical thinkers as Johann Wolfgang von Goethe, the German writer who single-mindedly pushed the occultist, pantheist ideas of his day. It was both Goethe's and Steiner's

110 ☐ Anthroposophy and the Waldorf Schools

assertion that the universe contains and expresses a creative *force*. This force, which some call "God," is both positive and negative, dark and light, good and bad; however, though it appears to be a duality, it is in fact a *unity*. Moreover, the force is *in* everything and *is* everything. Steiner eventually concluded that men could become more fully an expression of this creative force by uniting with the spirit world.

In 1902, Rudolf Steiner became a member of Helena Blavatsky's Theosophical Society. Eventually, he became Secretary of Theosophy for all of Germany. He enthusiastically embraced such Hindu beliefs as reincarnation, the law of karma, and the existence of spirit entities. He also began to claim that Jesus was Lord, but not in the sense that Christians know Jesus; rather, Steiner's claim is that Jesus is simply the "Lord of Karma," as well as only one of many "Christ" figures.

In 1913, Steiner's many interests caused him to decide to form his own group, the Anthroposophical Society, so that his teachings could extend even past those of Theosophy into new, previously uncharted forms of occultism. A decade later, he made Dornach, Switzerland, a town near Basel, his world center and was able to obtain funds for the building of a unique architectural structure which he called the *Goetheanum*, after his hero, Goethe. Today, the Goetheanum, rebuilt after a fire destroyed the original facility, serves as the world headquarters of Anthroposophy and also houses its School for Spiritual Science.

Evolution and Steiner

Steiner's central thesis is that both physical and spiritual evolution are a fact. For him, evolution is presided over by certain spiritual beings who mold and form man and guide him as he progresses in consciousness to become super-human. Steiner's Anthroposophy is a great promoter of occultic meditation techniques--clearing the mind, visualization, inviting in spirit entities, soul or astral travel, and so forth. Through meditation, Steiner said, man could discover his true origin and destiny and travel the path of knowledge to attain true wisdom of the universe and man's place in it.

Steiner rejected the biblical account in Genesis of the fall. His own version was that the fall was simply man's losing his consciousness of the spiritual worlds of which he was once a part. It is the goal of Anthroposophy to bring man to a knowledge of the spiritual world and return him to the state of heavenly bliss he enjoyed before the fall. Naturally, to accomplish this, Steiner taught, man must live through successive lives, finally becoming perfect and fully conscious.

According to Steiner, the earth is also undergoing an ongoing process of evolution and reincarnation development. His teachings on geography and geology are very similar to those of Maria Montessori, the Italian educator whose work is being carried on in thousands of Montessori schools in America today. According to Steiner, the planet has undergone four embodiments--as saturn (warmth), the sun (air), the moon (water), and the earth (mineral). The earth is now supposed to be in its fourth reincarnation. Each of these cycles is guarded over by spiritual beings.

Interestingly enough, Steiner's teaching is that some of these spiritual beings are in conflict with other spiritual beings, and that this is causing a number of problems and complications. It is because of this conflict in the spirit world, he said, that man fell and lost his perfect nature. In effect, Steiner is merely alluding to the reality of demonic beings in rebellion against God, though he vehemently denies the scriptural account of Lucifer's rebellion and ouster.

The conflict which Steiner referred to is said to be a war between spirits who lived on the sun, whom he called the Sun Beings, and those who lived on the moon, the Moon Beings. Moon Beings are said to be Luciferian spirits who adversely effect man's behavior whereas the Sun Beings are positive creatures who will eventually triumph over their adversaries and bring man to his destined state of perfection.

The teachings of Anthroposophy are therefore in line with those of the *Illuminati* in general, as well as the many pagan religions which teach the existence of a sun god, or deity, and his subordinate spiritual beings (which Christians know as demons), sometimes described as Beings of Light, Light Bearers, or Lords of the (Sun) Rays.

Anthroposophy and Christ

Possibly the most dangerous feature of Anthroposophy is its claim that it is the *true* Christianity and that biblical Christianity is a fake. Some Anthroposophy groups even refer to themselves as *Christian occult societies*. It has been reported also that one of C.S. Lewis' closest friends, Owen Barfield, a fervent Anthroposophist, has been actively speaking to many Christian groups, causing much confusion. C.S. Lewis himself, though he was at odds with Barfield on a number of issues, contributed in his own way to occultism and Anthroposophy with his promotion of pagan mythologies and magical superbeings and other fantasy creatures in his novels.

Rudolf Steiner claimed that Christ was not a person but could be experienced inwardly in a mystical manner. According to him, Christianity was a form of mysticism, and truth could be found not only in the Bible but also in certain other texts, including the Hindu scriptures known as the *Baghavad Gita*. To Anthroposophy the gospels are *esoterically* understood and are for the *initiated* only. Meanwhile, Jesus Christ is claimed to be a supreme example of *human* perfection which men should emulate. However, the unique nature of Christ as God Almighty, as proclaimed in Colossians 2:9, John 1, and in many other places in the Bible, is totally rejected by Anthroposophists.

The Coming of the Sun God and the Two Jesuses

Instead of the second coming of Christ, Anthroposophy teaches the coming of the great sun spirit, also known as the

Sun Being or as the Hidden One. This is said to be "Christ" in another form--the *Christ Essence*, which was previously incarnated as a man in the form of Jesus Christ but will now return in yet another form.

Although the first chapter of the Gospel of John clearly reveals that Jesus Christ came in the flesh *as God*, Anthroposophy teaches that Jesus was simply an ordinary mortal until the age of 30. It is taught that Jesus received the Christ Essence at his baptism by John the Baptist. Then Anthroposophy's teachings become even more muddy and murky. According to Steiner's writings, there are, in fact, really *two Jesuses*. One was the Jesus of Matthew and Luke, the other a reincarnation of the Persian deity Zoroaster. One of these Jesuses was said to be a human being whose body was prepared by the Spiritual Beings, including none other than the Buddha.

This teaching of the two Jesuses is most complicated. According to Steiner, one Jesus was a highly evolved intellectual person, whereas the other one, the one described in the Bible, was an empty ego which had never been incarnated before as a person. Then, at the age of 12, the two Jesuses were merged as one spirit. Steiner explained that this is why Jesus' parents, Mary and Joseph, were so astonished at the wisdom and maturity their son displayed when he carried on a learned conversation with the scholars in the temple at Jerusalem.

Finally, Anthroposophy's writings propose that at the age of 30, the Zoroaster "Jesus" departed from Jesus of Nazareth. This occurred at the moment the Christ Essence came and settled within the Jesus of Nazareth. The ultimate weirdity of this teaching is Anthroposophy's insistence that Jesus never really existed in the flesh but was some sort of "phantom." This is akin to teachings of the Gnostics. In fact, much of Anthroposophy's teachings are gnostic in origin.

Anthroposophy also has an occult explanation for the sightings of Jesus after His resurrection. Mary Magdalene, his disciples, and all the others who saw Jesus actually merely saw Him *clairvoyantly*, with the use of their *Third Eye*. The claim is that any of us can see Christ today and we can become one with the Christ Essence simply through the practice of *meditation*. It is by meditation, Anthroposophy teaches, that we empower ourselves and gain entrance into the spiritual world beyond our present material limitations.

The Waldorf Schools

Anthroposophy began its growing system of Waldorf Schools after receiving a huge grant of money from the owner of the Waldorf-Astoria cigarette factory in Stuttgart, Germany. This same individual was responsible for the luxurious Waldorf-Astoria Hotel in New York City. Waldorf education could well be the most visual application of Anthroposophy. Waldorf Schools are becoming increasingly popular in Germany, Holland, and the United States, and they have also been founded in Australia, New Zealand, Great Britain, and in other countries.

The Waldorf system of education attempts to keep children away from the disrupting influences of modern society and particularly what Anthroposophy feels are unspiritual influences. (For example, relationships with those who believe in fundamentalist Christianity). One of the subjects taught in the Waldorf Schools is Steiner's *eurythmy*, his spiritual dance. Eurythmy is based on the Hindu concept that both God and man are involved in a form of cosmic dance and that energy is ever in motion. It is thus seen as necessary to teach children the inner dynamics of music and language so that, through motion and with the music of the spheres (spiritual music, or sound), the child's path to spiritual consciousness can be shaped and hastened.

In eurythmic dancing, children and adults use sweeping and stately movements of the arms. The trunk sways in a gradual motion; the field is ascetic. Grown women who practice this dance do so with their dresses on, which hides the shape of their bodies; their hair is typically parted in the middle and is often gathered in a bun at the back.

Most Anthroposophists have at one time or another taken up eurythmy. There has even been a rock music group called the *Eurythmics*, the leader of which was reputed to be a witch.

Children in the Waldorf system are taught a special form of Steiner speech therapy. Painting and colors are also quite important and the use of the rainbow as a symbol is greatly encouraged. You may occasionally see on automobiles some of the bumper stickers promoting and advertising Waldorf Schools which almost universally include some representation of the rainbow.

In the early years, such Steiner doctrinal staples as reincarnation and karma are not emphasized by the Waldorf Schools so as not to scare off parents uncertain about the value of New Age concepts. Instead, great care is taken to convince parents that the teaching methods of the Waldorf Schools are imaginative and promote creativity in children. In later years principles such as karma and rein-carnation are taught in a mild form. However, in some schools there might well be blunt instruction in these topics.

The curriculum in most Waldorf Schools does emphasize the importance of such topics as the Norse myths; the ancient pagan gods; the history of India, Babylon, Sumeria, Persia, and Egypt; and harmony and music in ancient Greece. There is also an emphasis on nature as well as on fairy tales, fables, and legends. The Old Testament is even taught, the children often being led to believe that the sagas and stories of the Old Testament are basically yet more examples of fairy tales, nature stories, fables, and legends.

Steiner's Serpent

Anthroposophy has a number of symbols in addition to the rainbow. One is the *serpent*. The teaching is that the Goetheanum serpent is one that has its tail within its mouth, being formed as a circle. This is said to be an indication of the individual being part of the macrocosmic spirit, the all.

Another popular symbol among some is the *dome*. Anthroposophy's Goetheanum headquarters is shaped in the form of a dome. The dome has its origins as an occult symbol in the worship of the ancient goddess, a concept which Steiner no doubt found appealing. Steiner was an accomplished theosophist and occultist. Then he became a teacher of Rosicrucianism. Thus, he undoubtedly knew that the dome represented the breast of the goddess, that it is a sign of fertility. He knew, too, that in occultism the dome symbolizes the man who has achieved perfection and has become both masculine and feminine, integrating the two poles, though the feminine strain reigns dominant.

The Church of Anthroposophy

Though most members of Anthroposophy meet in individual study groups, conducted in one of many centers, or at the major center in Dornach, Switzerland, there is also a formal religion which is called the *Christian Community*. According to Geoffry Ahern, who conducted an insightful study of Anthroposophy and subsequently authored the book *Sun at Midnight*, there may be as many as 350 priests in the Christian Community of Anthroposophy. West Germany has most, but there are also Anthroposophical priests in the United States, Great Britain, and Holland.

These priests teach their followers of the transforming power of love, which they characterize as the "Christ Impulse." The church has extensive rituals of an esoteric nature. The priests' chasubles have figures of eight to represent the infinity (to occultists, the figure eight symbolizes the eternal victory of their master, Lucifer). The colors of the priests' garments relate to Steiner's spiritual science and especially to his revelations about the human aura. There are a number of sacraments in the church including baptism, confirmation, marriage, counseling, anointing, and ordination. These sacraments were given to Steiner by his spirit guides.

Nature Teachings: Gnomes, the Earth Force, and More

In the future, Anthroposophy will no doubt experience growth. This seems to be an ideal form of New Age religion, and its extension into education through the Waldorf Schools will also likely prove a continuing success. As the environmental movement grows stronger, earth worship increases in popularity, and the goddess religion advances because of its connection with Gaia, the Greek earth goddess, and other pagan goddesses of nature, interest in Anthroposophy will also grow in tandem. This is because of Anthroposophy's emphasis on nature and the spirits of the earth.

Anthroposophy claims that such nature beings as gnomes, salamanders, sylphs, and others are real and that man's astral body is simply a part of the great "earth force." A number of Anthroposophists practice a form of agriculture and farming which they call *bio-dynamics*. They believe this to be in tune with ecological awareness. Bio-dynamics is a type of organic farming. Steiner's modern-day disciples also apply certain bio-dynamic rituals and physical preparations to their fields and crops. For example, they may use powdered quartz or cow manure as well as dandelion, nettle velarion, oak bark, and other natural substances to prepare the soil.

They also believe that gnomes, hidden below the earth's surface, help plant roots to grow, and so they attempt to communicate with these gnomes to request their assistance. Moreover, it is believed that the astral aura of cows nourishes the gnomes. Just as for the Hindus, the cows are greatly venerated by Anthroposophists, for it is felt that cows provide the important spiritual functions of bringing cosmic forces down to earth. Birds are also greatly respected because it is taught that they carry earthly substance out into the cosmos.

All in all, it can be seen that Anthroposophy provides an eclectic and thoroughly absurd system of occultism; yet, absurdity seems to be no barrier among those who are bent on rejecting both scientific facts and the supernatural truth of God's Holy Word, the Bible.

THE ARCANE SCHOOL

In 1923 Theosophist Alice Bailey began the *Arcane School*. The purpose of the Arcane School is to promote the teachings of the spirit entities Dwjhal Khul, also known as "the Tibetan," and "Master Koothumi." The Lucis Trust, World Goodwill, and Triangles, three related organizations founded by Bailey, were also begun at the instigation of spirit guides. The inspiration for the Arcane School originally came from the spirit known as Master Koothumi (or Kuthumi) and from the teachings of Helena Blavatsky's Theosophy. Indeed, in her book *The Unfinished Autobiography*, Alice Bailey remarked that the Arcane School had first been the vision of Helena Blavatsky in the 19th century, and Bailey felt that it was her task to carry out the vision of Blavatsky.

Like Dwjhal Khul (see "Lucis Trust") Koothumi is yet another of the shadowy Masters of Wisdom, members of a spiritual "Hierarchy" who supposedly exist in some kind of mythical land known as *Shambala*. These concepts are familiar to the occultists who are fans and admirers of the works of Theosophist Helena Blavatsky and especially her writings known as *The Secret Doctrine*. In effect, if we are to believe Alice Bailey and her husband Foster Bailey, co-founders of the Arcane School, and Mary Bailey, the more recent head of this school, their entire life's work is based on the prodding of demonic spirits.

The Arcane School conducts classes and lessons "in occult philosophy and cosmic law" for "the disciples of the Great One... during that critical period of our present world history when we are transcending out of the piscean era into the aquarian age." This comes from information provided by Foster Bailey in his article entitled *The Arcane School--Its Esoteric Origins and Purposes.* The teaching efforts of the Arcane School are necessary, said Foster Bailey, "to hasten the reappearance of the (New Age) Christ." Its formal goal is as follows: "Training for New Age discipleship is provided by the Arcane School. The principles of the Ageless Wisdom are presented through esoteric meditation, study, and service as a way of life."

If we are to believe the literature published by the Lucis Trust, the graduates of the Arcane School are privileged to become the elite of the New Age. Such initiates will become part of The New Group of World Servers, an unnamed and unidentified but powerful group of men and women in all walks of life who are said to be masters of occultism destined to lead the world into a New Age kingdom.

Headquartered in New York, but also with centers in Europe, the stated goal of the Arcane School is to train men and women so that they may take their next step upon the path of evolution. Alice Bailey taught that the Arcane School would enable students to recognize the fact of the Spiritual Hierarchy of the planet. (Christians of course, would recognize this spiritual hierarchy as the demonic entities under the control of Satan.) Another primary teaching of the Arcane School is that the souls of men are one, again a cardinal New Age belief.

While the Arcane School claims to be non-sectarian and non-political, in fact, the school certainly does have a religious and political basis. Each student is a believer in occultism, although there is significant leeway and freedom as to the exact occult philosophies that may be held by the individual. However, no formal pledges or vows to obey are extracted from any student during the training. They are expected to voluntarily carry out the requirements, and most do since few enter such training without an occult foundation having already been laid in their individual lives.

The Plan and The Christ

The Arcane School also teaches students to understand what the New Age calls "The Plan for humanity." They are led to understand that their loyalty and devotion to The Plan will promote their evolutionary progress. They are also made to understand the immediacy of the return of the New Age "Christ" who, in the worldview of the Arcane School, is not only the Christ of Christianity but also the Messiah for the Jews, Buddhists, Hindus, and Moslems.

In other words, the Arcane School teaches *universality* and harshly rejects any religious teaching of exclusiveness. For example, to teach that Jesus Christ is Lord of all would be a heresy not tolerated by the Arcane School and its teachers. Alice Bailey once stated:

> In the Arcane School, we make a definite effort to counter the great heresy of separateness . . . and thus lay the foundation for that new world in which there will emerge a civilization based upon the belief that the souls of men are One.

In plain language, this means that Christianity is not unique and, moreover, any suggestion that it is unique or exclusive is a "great heresy" for students of the Arcane School.

Man is Divine

Another major teaching of the Arcane School is that within each human being is a point of light, a "spark of the one Flame." Men, then, are themselves deities. Interestingly, Alice Bailey often attempted to invoke scripture to prove that man is his own god, pointing out for example that Paul spoke of "Christ in you, the hope of glory." To Bailey, this meant that there is a divine essence in each person, that man collectively is "God" as well as "Christ."

Yet, ultimately, as a student delves into the deeply esoteric teachings of the Arcane School he or she will discover that in the occultism of Alice Bailey there is a master above all other masters--a great world teacher whom Alice Bailey mysteriously called "Sanat Kumara, the Great One." Is *Sanat* merely a scrambling of the letters of the word *Satan*? It is my well-founded contention that Satan is indeed the lord of the Arcane School.

ASSOCIATION FOR RESEARCH AND ENLIGHTENMENT (A.R.E.)

He was called the "sleeping prophet." He gave over 16,000 readings to his followers. He is definitely one of the fathers of the New Age and has especially been influential in the area of New Age holistic medicine. Indeed, one of his biographers, Jeff Stern, called him the  "Father of Holistic Healing." His name was Edgar Cayce.

Born in 1877 on a farm near Hopkinsville, Kentucky, Cayce never had a formal education, dropping out of school in the sixth grade. At first, he took an interest in Christianity, even as a young boy reading the Bible and enjoying going to church regularly. It is claimed that he made it a habit to read the Bible through at least once a year, and for his entire life he taught Sunday School at a local Presbyterian church. Yet, though he claimed to be a Christian, Edgar Cayce was one of the most occultic leaders the New Age has ever known.

Today, the *Association for Research and Enlightenment (A.R.E.)*, led by the late Cayce's son, Hugh Lynn Cayce, has untold thousands of members. As many as 15 million persons worldwide have been influenced through his many writings. Recently I received a flyer from Books of Light, a New Age book club, which offered 18 different books about the work of Edgar Cayce by a variety of New Age authors. Some 600 medical doctors, chiropractors, psychologists, and other professional health workers are associated with the A.R.E. Most are listed in the A.R.E. annual directory.

According to A.R.E. statistics, small groups of people from all walks of life meet once a week in over 1,700 homes to study the Edgar Cayce readings. Their children are schooled in A.R.E. Search For God programs. Across the nation, hundreds of seminars and lectures are held in almost every major city on a variety of A.R.E. topics, from astrology and Egyptian religion, to reincarnation and karma. Tens of thousands of seekers and researchers continually access the thousands of Edgar Cayce readings that are now contained in the A.R.E. library at Virginia Beach, Virginia. There they use an index for over 10,000 subjects.

A.R.E. also has a bookstore and publishes a periodic catalog of some 65 pages. Many of Cayce's writings have been put into book form, particularly his prophecies gained from the spirit world on coming earth changes. His son, Hugh Lynn Cayce, has also authored a book, *Earth Changes Update*.

Cayce and Occultism

Edgar Cayce developed occultic tendencies quite early in life. He admitted later that as a child he had certain "play folk," real spirit people, who would appear to him and talk with him. At the age of 13, an angelic being, Cayce claimed, appeared to him and asked him what request he would make of her. Young Edgar replied that he would like to help others. At that point the apparition dissolved.

Evidently, occultism ran in Cayce's family. His father had a hypnotic control over snakes; his grandfather was a dowser and water witcher. At his home, magical stunts such as making tables move, causing brooms to dance, and the use of telepathic powers was commonplace.

One time, famed evangelist Dwight L. Moody passed through town. When Edgar shared with him the fact that he was receiving visions and hearing voices from a supernatural world, the great evangelist suggested to him that evil spirits could be responsible. But according to Cayce's biography *There Is A River*, Moody also mentioned to Edgar that he might be a prophet, a legitimate prophet of God.

Cayce's role as a professional New Age healer began when, as a young, budding salesman, Edgar developed laryngitis so acute that he could barely speak. Medical doctors could not cure him and he turned to "Dr." Al Lane, a holistic healer who used magnetic devices and herbs to effect healings. Lane was a mail-order naturopath who also practiced hypnosis. He taught Edgar Cayce how to use self-hypnosis, and while Cayce was in his own hypnotic spell, an unconscious voice in his own mind diagnosed his throat problem and was able to suggest to Edgar what needed to be done. In fact, the healing took place immediately while Cayce was still under the hypnotic spell. Awakening, he found he was able to speak normally. This convinced the young man that mind powers and trance-like states were very significant to healing processes.

Cayce the Occultic Healer

Following this self-healing episode, Cayce then began a vocation of self-hypnotic trances during which he physically evaluated the health complaints of patients who had come to him having heard of his growing reputation. For these people he gave "health readings." All that Cayce supposedly needed was to be given their name and address. Then, he claimed, he could tune in telepathically to that individual's mind and body, clearly seeing the hidden medical problem or malfunctioning. Cayce then would dredge up some kind of supernatural knowledge from a spiritual realm and make the diagnosis as well as suggested treatment.

Cayce's treatment suggestions made licensed medical doctors blink and despair because of their bizarre nature. It is because of these unorthodox treatments that Cayce today is the hero of alternative health quacks and New Age "healers" of all types. Cayce was especially big on raw, natural foods, including milk and honey; he advocated massage and manipulation, yoga exercises, tar soap, various salves, bile salts, home remedies of all kinds, patent medicines, olive oil, mutton tallow, mineral oil, brandy fumes, artichokes, numerous kinds of ointments, and even gems, crystals, and other healing stones. Regardless of the irregular nature of such treatments, Cayce was not shy about diagnosing and attempting to treat serious ailments that ranged from breast cancer tumors, to arthritis, detached retina, epilepsy, goiter, gonorrhea, gall stones, insomnia, and even mental retardation.

Finally, in 1936 Cayce's widespread fame as a nontraditional healer got him in trouble when he was arrested in Detroit for practicing medicine without a license. Cayce professed astonishment. How could the good he was trying to accomplish be so misunderstood? he asked.

After this arrest, Edgar Cayce was more careful about his medical practice (or should we call it *malpractice*?). He began to turn his attention to another area--that of prophetic dreams. Eventually he was to make hundreds of prophetic predictions, many of which came true (his supporters claim 90 percent) and many of which turned out to be false prophecies. Here for example, is only one of many of Cayce's predictions:

1958-1998 A.D. The earth will be broken up in the western portion of America. The greater portion of Japan must go into the sea. The upper portion of Europe will be changed as in the twinkling of an eye. Land will appear off the East Coast of America. There will be upheavals in the Arctic and in the Antarctic, and eruptions of volcanos in the torrid areas, and there will be a shifting then of the poles--so that where it has been frigid or semi-tropical, it will become the more tropical, and moss and fern will grow. And these will begin in those periods of 1958-1998.

Cayce predicted that eventually the sea would cover all of the western part of the United States and that the state of Nebraska will sometime in the next century be a coastal state on the Pacific Ocean.

Cayce and Past Lives

Cayce also began to give life readings to individuals, contending that these would help the individual to learn about his incarnations in previous lives and thus aid him to better understand his current life. For example, here are excerpts from a life reading Cayce gave to a 14 year old boy on August 29, 1927:

Before this, the entity lived in France when the people of that country were near to the rebellion, during the period of Louis XIII. The entity was then among those who would escort the protectors of that monarch; he was especially the one chosen to dress and change apparel for that ruler--though not in the capacity of the valet. Rather the entity was the one who set the style for the people. His name then was Neil . . .

Before that we find that the entity was in the land now
known as Persia .... Then the entity as a physician in
the court gained throughout the services rendered,
even when persecutions came through invading
forces. The name was Abiel ....

Before that we find the entity was in the Egyptian land
during the period when there was a division of the
kingdom. The entity was among those people who
were of the native folk, yet the one who brought much
comfort to many people in providing for the
application of truth ... The name then is Isois ....

Before that the entity was in the Atlantean land when
the floods came and when destruction ruled in that
land ... The name was the Amiaieoulieb.

Cayce and The Bible

The occultic nature of Cayce's readings and predictions
were heightened after he met and became enamored of a
man named Arthur Lammers, a wealthy printer from Ohio
who had sought Cayce out after hearing of his fame.
Lammers was extremely interested in metaphysical and
psychic phenomena. He wanted to learn more about the
mystery religions of Egypt and Greece, about yoga, Madame
Blavatsky and Theosophy, and the spirit world. In fact,
Lammers was a devoted Theosophist. Cayce agreed to give
Lammers a life reading during which he determined that this
man had lived many past lives. Cayce himself then began to
study reincarnation. Finally, he came to the conclusion that
the Bible was flawed, that third century scholars had deleted
all references to reincarnation from the Bible, and that
current Bible versions were therefore of limited value.

Cayce's spirit guides also taught him the following
unholy and unbiblical doctrines: that the Bible is neither

accurate nor authoritative; that Jesus was only one manifestation of Christ and that, in fact, Jesus had 30 other
incarnations by the time he was born to Mary; that Jesus was
not God with a capital "G"; that all of us were with God in
the beginning and are now working our way back to a divine
state through karma by repaying our debt in each lifetime. It
will, however, take many lifetimes to make up the debt and
return to union with God; God is not a judge and there is no
hell; there is no need to be born again in the traditional sense
of Christianity, but that all are Christians if we do good.

Obviously it does not take much of a Bible student to see
the tremendous damage that is done by believing in such
heretical doctrines, none of which has a shred of basis in the
Bible. Thus, those who study Edgar Cayce's works are drawn
deeply into a most severe type of occultism and are taught to
almost totally reject true Christianity.

One person who was deeply influenced by Cayce, by her
own admission, was actress Shirley MacLaine, author of the
bestselling *Out On A Limb* and many other New Age books.
Shirley MacLaine gives Cayce credit for her successful
"search for self." Returning the favor, A.R.E. has been very
complimentary of MacLaine's books, selling them through
its catalogs and letting others know "that lots of people"
have joined A.R.E. due to the influence of the New Age
actress. Notably, Shirley MacLaine says that Edgar Cayce,
the sleeping prophet, is responsible for her decision to take
up the banner of reincarnation and karma and bring it to
widespread public knowledge.

Hidden Dangers

There are many hidden dangers in Cayce's writings. For
example, because of his avid belief in reincarnation, Cayce
has intimated that incest is merely due to the fact that the
child and the parent could have been lovers or possibly were
married in previous lives. He has also suggested that

homosexuality could be natural in that it is simply a conscious mind pattern from past lives when an individual, say a female, may have been a man.

The greatest dangers of Edgar Cayce's teachings are spiritual. Because he wrapped his occultic message in a coat of Christianity, some may mistakenly believe that the A.R.E. doctrines are biblical. Cayce also taught that his psychic gifts were from God. Again, this could draw people away from the truth. The fact is that Cayce was an occultist, plain and simple. His teachings that Jesus was only a reincarnation of Adam, Joshua, and Zend (the father of the Persian deity Zoroaster); that salvation is accomplished through good karma by our own works, not solely by God; and that God is Mother and Father, male and female, solidly place his works in the category of unchristian.

One can accurately say that Edgar Cayce and the A.R.E. are pioneers of the New Age, not only in America but throughout the world. Edgar Cayce died January 3, 1945 in Virginia Beach, Virginia, where A.R.E.'s headquarters is today located. Regrettably, his works live on. Because of Cayce, many people today suffer under the impression that Jesus was simply just another brother mystic or saint who was initiated in temples in Tibet and Egypt; they labor under the mistake that Jesus is not Lord of all; and there can be little doubt that many have to their sorrow failed to seek professional medical attention because they relied on the quackery and the unprofessional advice of Cayce and his readings.

ASTARA

If one is seeking the quintessential New Age religion, that person will find that *Astara* certainly fills the bill. Astara is named after the Greek goddess Astraea, which means "a place of light." Astara claims to be a mystery school for today. Its literature prom-

ises to teach the seeker "the wisdom teachings which arose among the splendors of ancient Egypt when the Mystery Schools flourished under the guidance of an illumined Priest-King."

In the Astara guide *Finding Your Place in The Golden Age,* the reader is told that the group's textbook, *Astara's Book of Life,* and its lessons which lead the follower through the seven degrees of Astara, will present:

> ... the mysteries of the golden age in Greece ... the esoteric teachings of India, Tibet, and other Eastern lands...and the inner meanings of Christianity, as well as ... the arcane thought of Judaism, Islam, Buddhism, and many another of those great spiritual movements which have touched the inner consciousness of the enlightened men through the ages and enabled them to see that truth is one, though men give it many names.

Astara has many thousands of members worldwide. They usually initially get in touch with Astara after coming across one of its impressive ads in New Age publications, including astrological guides and magazines. For many seekers, Astara seems to be the *ultimate religious system.* After all, "It guides the disciple," so it claims, "toward the inner mysteries of life, death, and the ultimate initiation: immortality." These supernatural mysteries cannot normally all be found in any one religion, explains Astara literature, but Astara claims to put it all together. Astara's teachings encompass the philosophies and religious doctrines found in Yoga, Christianity, Rosicrucianism, Theosophy, Hinduism, Buddhism, and on and on.

The Founders of Astara: Robert and Earlyne Chaney

At age 30, Earlyne met and married Robert Chaney, himself a spiritualist who was in contact with an entity who called himself "Ram." The Chaneys then moved to California where they formed the Astara Foundation in 1951. By following Astara, insists Earlyne Chaney, one will become a "Light Bearer" in this century. Since Light Bearer is one of the names of Lucifer, the devil, perhaps we should take Mrs. Chaney at her word, although no doubt she would deny that she had the devil in mind.

Egyptian Religion and Spirit Beings

The primary text used by Astara is the Chaneys' publication, *Astara's Book of Life*. The cover of this book enlightens us significantly. What we see pictured is the ankh cross hanging from a chain. On the cross is a seven point star. The ankh cross consists of the ancient Tau cross superimposed by an oval or egg, thus signifying death, fertility, and rebirth. The ankh is an ancient symbol used by the pharaohs of Egypt. Egyptian art often shows the ankh in the possession of the goddess of Egypt and other deities. To the Egyptians the ankh symbolized cyclical life spans, or reincarnation.

In addition to reincarnation, through the correspondence courses offered by Astara one also supposedly learns how to develop inner psychic faculties, heal illnesses, expand consciousness, and realize one's own godhood. Also, there is a teaching of the "universal spiritual brotherhood of all men."

At the very root of Astara's teaching is *spiritism*, or demonic communications. Earlyne Chaney has testified that as a child she began communicating with the spirit entity named Kut-Hu-Mi through a system of clairvoyance. Incidentally, Kut-Hu-Mi (also spelled Kuthumi or Koothoomi) is the name often cited by a number of other New Age leaders as their own spirit guide. For Chaney, Kut-Hu-Mi taught the development of psychic powers, including the secretive yoga system called *Lhama Yoga*, which Astara promises to teach its devotees.

Astara instructs its followers in a number of other occult, mystical doctrines and practices as well. Some are even related to Freemasonry. For example, there is the Astarian sign, word, and hand grip. There is also the technique of meditation and the use of psychic phenomena. Each month, followers receive the publication, *The Voice of Astara*. In it they discover numerous testimonies from people who have benefitted from miraculous cures and opened their minds to marvelous new discoveries. They also learn of the Circle of the Secret Seven, a group of spirit guides who will intercede on behalf of Astarians in times of need. Among the techniques taught by Astara are the use of biorythms, breath techniques (which utilize the Hindu concept of *prana*, or the breathing in of energy), astral projection or soul travel, and the concept of vibratory forces. They are also taught to bring themselves into a trance state so as to communicate with familiar spirits.

A significant teaching is of the "Divine Hierarchy of Great Beings" who are said to come from the Universal Brotherhood. These spirit beings are servants who will reveal all the great mysteries of life to the learner. Of course, these mysteries can be fathomed only through Astara, it is suggested. Throughout your life you will be comforted, Astara confides, by the presence of the "Astarian Masters" who will oversee your life, and lead and guide you onward to victory. Victory is defined as god-realization.

For Truth-Seekers Only

People who are fascinated and drawn to Astara by their slick magazine ads and write for more information usually receive an intriguing letter that goes something like this:

> *Dear Seeker of Truth:* Imagine being invited to become an initiate of the Ancient Mystery School at Heliopolis, the city of the sun in long ago Egypt where many illumined minds were taught the hidden secrets of the universe and the arcane spiritual truths of the ages.
>
> Or being asked to become a disciple after Liang Lhama, in the Kashmir Valley, where adepts studied the mysteries as taught by the Tibetan Lhamas, or to join the famed school of a master teacher where a two years silence is imposed on every neophyte, or to sit at the feet of the great master teacher Plato, who influenced the Christian religion perhaps more than any other man who preceded the Christ.
>
> In this dawn of a new aquarian age, the Mysteries Schools are being reborn all over the world, but more especially America which is destined to be the protected cradle of the New Age teachings.

The letter goes on to explain that in the heart of busy Southern California some 35 years ago was reborn a Mystery School that teaches the initiation process and the wisdom teachings. That school, of course, is Astara. As one letter from Astara to inquirers states, "We have placed in your hand the key to the great door. Only you can use it." Continuing, the letter concludes, "I pray that the blessings of the Illumined One be with you as you make your decision whether or not to become an Astarian and walk the inner way with this worldwide group of enlightened seekers."

Obviously, Astara promises much, and is no doubt intellectually entrancing to curious seekers who want to enter its "Greater Hall of Wisdom."

On Campus at Astara

For those who wish to become more deeply involved in Astara than merely through correspondence, there is the Astara campus on a ten acre site in Upton, California. There, many Astarians from around the world gather twice each year for a special series of seminars and ceremonies. Dr. Robert Chaney, co-founder, conducts special Sunday services in the chapel. Nearby, in the garden there is a small shrine, or statue, of Mother Mary, again showing the masterful eclectic blending accomplished by Astara.

A God as You Understand Him Religion

I began this section suggesting that Astara seems to be almost the quintessential, or perfect, New Age religion. In its literature, Astara often includes the following statement explaining the basics of Astara and what Astarians believe in. Since the New Age is basically a "God as you understand him" religion, and is moreover a *pro-choice* spiritual movement, this statement of Astara, more than any other, characterizes the spiritual nature of the New Age as a whole. It is recreated below from the brochure *If You Are A Seeker . . . :*

An Astarian

In an Astarian there's no dogmatic trace--
    He sees the light of God in every face;
In Mosque, Cathedral and in Synagogue,
    Wherever man may lift his cry to God.

He joins the Wise Men, following a star,
    And finds a Christ, a Cross, an Avatar.
In Buddha's shrine, he feels a stir within,
    He bends the knee when chants the Muezzin.

He seeks to understand what Moses taught,
    And Honors what the Hindu sages brought.
The Mysteries of the pyramids inspire,
    He honors Zoroaster and his fire,

Respects what wise Confucius had to say,
    Will seek the wisdom found the Tao way.
Wherever hearts and hands are raised in prayer,
    In every shrine, a living God is there.

And whatsoe'er the Godward path may be
    The Astarian will give it dignity.
True brotherhood seeks only to ascend,
    All paths that lead to God must
        somewhere blend.

AUROVILLE COMMUNITY

In the south of India lies a community. Its name: *Auroville*. Peopled by approximately 600 men, women and children, Auroville has had an extremely important impact on the New Age world. Many thousands have flown in and out of the community since its conception and have gone back to their own localities somewhere in Europe, America, and elsewhere to continue the teachings and "insights" learned at Auroville.

    Rising from the arid, plains-like wasteland of the area

around Pondicherry, 160 kilometers south of Madras, India, is a large spherical temple. This is the building residents of the Auroville community officially call their *Matrimandir.* This temple, which the people of Auroville also refer to as the House of The New Creation, was the vision of "The Mother," who with her mate, Sri Aurobindo, a Hindu guru, founded this ashram in India known as Auroville.

The towering dome of Matrimandir stands some 30 meters high. Under construction for some years, the edifice is now in its completion stages. In the Sanskrit language, Matrimandir means "dwelling place of the Mother." This monument, then, stands as a recognition that these people and thousands of others who know and propagate the New Age message of Auroville worship the mother goddess, whom the Hindus call Kali, the goddess of both creation and destruction. In their literature the "sages" of Auroville state that the Matrimandir monument "is an inspiring symbol of our own transformation and that of the earth."

Sri Aurobindo is not as well-known as some other Hindu gurus who have periodically succeeded in fascinating and captivating the New Agers of North America and Europe; yet, his philosophies and those of his female companion, The Mother, made a significant impact for a number of years prior to the founding of Auroville. Finally, in 1968, Auroville--"the City of Dawn"--was inaugurated. Sri Aurobindo told his followers that he envisaged a divine light for Auroville's followers based on the new principle of the "Supermind"--the next great step in evolution, a step beyond the levels of matter, life, mind and the spirit that human beings have attained so far.

The Mother, who continues Sri Aurobindo's work after he passed on some years ago, has commented, "We are for a new creation, entirely new . . . a true adventure of which the goal is sure victory." According to The Mother, the Matrimandir monument is the "soul of Auroville." One can certainly see why this might be so. Here is how the booklet entitled *Matrimandir Auroville* describes the monument:

A large golden sphere which seems to be breaking out of the earth symbolizes the birth of a new consciousness that is seeking to manifest. The Matrimandir stands in relation to Auroville as the soul stands to the human being . . . . The spacious Inner Chamber in the upper hemisphere will be the main focus-- completely white, with white marble walls and white carpeting, and in the center a pure white crystal globe, suffused by a steady ray of sunlight falling on it through an opening at the apex of the sphere.

The symbolic language of the Matrimandir is simple: silence . . . purity . . . a ray of light . . . a transparent globe. And the most important thing is this: *the play of the sun on the center.* Because that becomes the symbol--the symbol of future realizations.

Since the pagans worshipped the great Sun God and since all occultists teach illumination by the spiritual "sun," the emphasis on the sun and its rays in the above description is a dead giveaway that Matrimandir is undoubtedly a profound occultic monument.

A fire ceremony at the Auroville Community. The dome is the Matrimandir structure now being erected.

The Work at Auroville

Sri Aurobindo taught what the Hindus call the *Karma Yoga*, which in its simplest definition means that a person must work to earn his or her divinity. Thus, Karma Yoga is the yoga of work. It can be understood then why the community of Auroville was built almost entirely with crude implements and tools wielded by the calloused hands of hundreds of volunteers from Western countries. These were and are enthused disciples who trekked to this desolate site in South India thinking that they were doing both the Mother and the Divine Intelligence a service. In so doing, it was also their conviction that they were earning for themselves a share of deity.

Auroville carries on a number of activities. For one thing, its residents run a small computer manufacturing unit. Also, there is the production and publishing of video tapes, books, and newsletters touting the Matrimandir monument and the works of Sri Aurobindo and The Mother. Auroville also works very closely with New Age environmental organizations, such as Earth Stewards. In its literature and other materials is the message that "a new evolutionary force is pressing upon the earth. A new urgency, pushing human consciousness to exceed its limits . . . forcing it to find a new light of understanding."

The Mother of Auroville

The Mother, as she is called, is today worshipped even more than Sri Aurobindo it seems. Born in Paris on February 21, 1878, she herself wrote of her spiritual development: "Between 11 and 13 a series of psychic and spiritual experiences revealed to me not only the existence of God but the possibility of uniting with Him, of realizing him integrally in a life divine."

In her mid-20s The Mother traveled to Algeria where she became an avid student of occultism. Then, at the age of

36 she sailed to Pondicherry, India to meet Sri Aurobindo and become his disciple.

Eventually she became almost a soul twin to him, and under her guidance the Sri Aurobindo Ashram grew into a community of some 1200 souls. A number of works have been published in the name of The Mother. Auroville residents are quick to credit her as being a wonderful, highly evolved Master almost without peer.

The Mother and Numerology

It seems that The Mother has a special fascination for *occult numerology*. For example, in the 1988 yearbook of Auroville International, The Mother waxed eloquent about the vital date of *June 6, 1966*. She noted that this was the sixth month, the sixth day, of the sixty-sixth year--or four sixes. "Four sixes--this represents the complete square of the creation ... Four sixes ... this is very rare ... this occurs only once in a century ... 6/6/66 is very important," she wrote. The Mother also revealed that:

> "On 6/6/66 someone was born here--here; I mean someone who lives here in the Ashram ... In this atmosphere and especially on this date for conscious development. It is a date chosen by him. Yes, he has chosen it. We shall see what he will do. We must follow his development. It is good: he has many possibilities. It is interesting--how these dates which have an occult significance influence physical domains also. We shall see in this child."

Anyone who knows Bible prophecy can understand the darkness of what The Mother of Auroville is suggesting. The beast of Revelation 13 is the man with the number 666. In proclaiming that in her community of Auroville a man was born on the sixth day, the sixth month, of the year sixty-six, that he himself "chose" this date before he was incarnated, and that this has "occult significance," is extremely re-vealing.

The Mother and the Enneagram

The Mother and her followers are also into *occult symbols.* One of the most popular being promoted by this group is the *Enneagram,* an ancient Hindu occultic symbol which consists of a unique pattern of a circle enclosing a nine-pointed triangular configuration with a dot and a smaller circle in the middle. The Enneagram currently is an item of keen fascination in the New Age. Sri Aurobindo connected the Enneagram not only to the Mother Goddess of the Hindus but also to the goddesses of Greece and Rome.

Also tying the Enneagram in with occult astrology, Aurobindo maintained that the secrets of the Enneagram are so important that he who unravels its secrets "will enjoy riches and wealth and be sexually fertile."

Regrettably, the Enneagram is also in vogue and gaining popularity amongst a number of Christian groups, with both

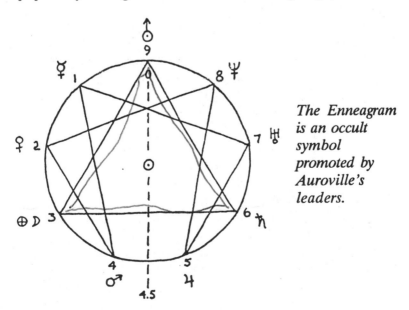

The Enneagram is an occult symbol promoted by Auroville's leaders.

Protestant and Catholic, whose leaders evidently are ever on the lookout for something new to give their audiences. It is especially popular in Catholic circles, with both priests and nuns promoting the use of the Enneagram to determine basic personality types, compulsions, and obsessions. One Catholic priest has even attempted to relate each of the nine points of the Enneagram with nine personality traits of Jesus! But it is not only used in the Catholic Church. Though its ancient occultic origins are undebatable, I have also received reports that the teaching of the Enneagram is being popularized at Southern Baptist retreats and in Methodist, Episcopal, and Charismatic circles.

BAHA'I

"One God, one religion, one mankind, one planet." This is the goal and the essential doctrine of the *Baha'i*, a major New Age religious group which boasts of over five million members worldwide, some 100,000 of whom reside in the United States of America. The Baha'i faith is proud to call itself *a* religion; but its aim is to become *the* world religion. Its founder, Baha'u'llah (1817-1892), is regarded by the Baha'i as the most recent in a long line of Messengers of God that stretches back beyond recorded time, including Abraham, Moses, Buddha, Zoroaster, Jesus, and Muhammad.

The Baha'i religion was begun in Persia (now Iran) by a young man known as The *Bab* (which means in Persian, "the Gate"). The Bab announced the imminent appearance of the Messenger of God awaited by all the peoples of the world. He further declared that his purpose was to prepare mankind for the glorious advent of this coming, renewed "Christ."

However, the dominant Muslim clergy did not take too kindly to the message of The Bab. Swift and cruel persecution followed his announcement. He was arrested, beaten, imprisoned; finally, on July 9, 1850, The Bab was executed in the public square of the city of Tibri. Some 20,000 of his followers likewise perished in a series of massacres throughout Persia. Today, overlooking the bay in Haifa, Israel, the Baha'i have on public display a majestic building with a superb golden dome. Set among beautiful gardens, its striking architecture is no doubt a wonder and a puzzlement to the Jews who live nearby. This is the shrine where it is claimed The Bab's earthly remains are entombed. The Baha'i consider it a great holy place.

A believer in the message of The Bab was the man *Baha'u'llah* (1817-1892), who is officially credited as being the founder of the Baha'i faith. A rich young man of royal blood whose family traced its lineage all the way back to the ruling dynasties of Persia's imperial past. Baha'u'llah became engulfed in the wave of violence unleashed at the time of The Bab's execution. The Muslim overlords of Persia stripped him of his wealth and vast estate and set him packing to Baghdad where, in 1863, he announced himself as the One promised by The Bab, the great Messenger of God.

In prison, Baha'u'llah addressed a series of letters which, today, the Baha'i treat as holy writ. These papers, now distributed in book form throughout the world, proclaim the coming unification of humanity and the emergence of a World Order, World Civilization, and the uniting into One of the world's religion and faiths.

A Perfect New Age Religion?

Baha'i is almost the perfect New Age religion. Indeed, Baha'u'llah is called by his modern-day disciples the "Herald of the New Age." The current leader of the Baha'i faith, who oversees an administrative body known as the Universal

Bahá'í House of Worship,
Apia, Western Samoa. ▷

BAHÁ'Í HOUSES OF WORSHIP

Bahá'í Houses of Worship are open to all peoples. Although their architectural styles differ widely, the nine sides and central dome common to all of them symbolize at once the diversity of the human race and its essential oneness. Devotional programs are simple, consisting of prayers, meditations, and the reading of selections from the Sacred Scriptures of the Bahá'í Faith and other world religions. Music is provided by unaccompanied choirs.

As conceived by Bahá'u'lláh, the House of Worship is intended as the spiritual center for various dependent institutions dedicated to scientific, humanitarian, educational and administrative service.

Bahá'í House of Worship, Längenhain (Frankfurt) West Germany. ▽

Bahá'í House of Worship, Panama City, Panama. ▽

Bahá'í House of Worship, New Delhi, India. ▽

Bahá'í House of Worship, Sydney, Australia. ▽

Bahá'í House of Worship, Wilmette, Illinois, USA. ▽

Bahá'í House of Worship, Kampala, Uganda. ▽

*This page from the brochure **The Baha'i Faith** pictures Baha'i houses of worship around the world.*

House of Justice, has declared, "The human race, as a distinct, organic unit, has passed through evolutionary stages and the stages of infancy and childhood in the lives of its individual members, and is now in a culminating period of its turbulent adolescence approaching its long awaited coming of age."

According to a Baha'i Statement on Peace promulgated by the group's Universal House of Justice, the Baha'i faith is destined to correct "the record of the substitute faiths that the worldly wise of our age have created." The statement boasted that Baha'u'llah, the new "Messenger of God," is more perfect than all of the other Christs and Messiahs who came before him. The same statement also calls for the banning of nuclear weapons and the inauguration of a massive global disarmament. It declares that the time has come for a One World Order and the "recognition of the oneness of mankind":

> Unbridled nationalism ... must give way to a wider loyalty, to the love of humanity as a whole. Baha'u'llah's statement is: 'The earth is but one country and mankind its citizens.'

The Baha'i also call for the emancipation of women and for universal education, world peace, and common spiritual principles to be accepted by all of humanity.

But perhaps the central thesis of the Baha'i faith is its call for a World Order, a World Order which its leaders say can be founded "only on an unshakable consciousness of the oneness of mankind, a spiritual truth which all the human scientists confirm." They say also that "A recognition of the oneness of mankind is the first fundamental prerequisite for a reorganization and administration of the world as one country, the whole of humankind."

Finally, in the Statement of Peace declaration, we read: "In the Baha'i view, recognition of the oneness of mankind calls for no less that the reconstruction and the demilitarization of the whole civilized world--a world organically unified in all the essential aspects of its life, its political machinery, its spiritual aspiration, its trade and finance, its script and language, and yet infinite in the diversity in the national characteristics of its federated units."

Baha'i, therefore, states precisely the goal of the New Age: Total unity of mankind under a god other than Jesus Christ.

Evangelizing the World

Believers in the Baha'i faith go all-out to promote their religion. In their monthly newspaper, *The American Baha'i*, we see constant reminders of their furious activities. For example, we read encouraging reports of steady growth of enrollment in the Baha'i assemblies in greater Atlanta, Phoenix, Portland, San Jose, and other American cities. Also, already there are more than 400 community-based Baha'i schools in America. Meanwhile, a major fund-raising drive is being conducted to raise $300 million to complete an impressive building complex on Mount Carmel in Israel, which is to be called "The Ark." It is claimed that The Ark will be the *spiritual shelter of mankind*. It will be "the seat of God's throne on planet earth."

That the Baha'i are influential throughout the world and even in America--despite their small numbers in the U.S.A.--is indisputable. Baha'i believers are building new churches in America, and their architecture is often stunning and beautiful. In *The American Baha'i* newspaper we see a panorama of world leaders gravitating toward the Baha'i faith. For example, in a December 1989 issue is a picture of His Royal Highness, Prince Philip, Great Britain's Duke of Edinburgh, and United Nations Secretary-General Javier Perez de Cuellar. The caption reports that the Prince is introducing to the United Nations Secretary-General the "Sacred Literature Trust," a project which translates and publishes collections of the sacred texts of the various world religions. The Baha'i is one of eight major world religions affiliated with this Sacred Literature Trust.

In Atlanta, Georgia, the Baha'i have established and are nurturing a growing relationship with the Martin Luther King, Jr. Center for Non-violent Social Change and with other black groups such as the NAACP. They also work hand-in-hand with radical feminist groups such as the National Committee on Women and the National Organization for Women (NOW). Across America Baha'i spokesmen have been invited to make presentations on their favorite subjects, unity and peace, to such varied groups as the Kiwanis Clubs, the Sojourners, Lion's International, and the Rotary Clubs. Mayor Tom Bradley of Los Angeles and a score of other American political leaders have praised the efforts of the Baha'i.

It could well be that because of their unity doctrine and their vast numbers and growing influence the Baha'i religion will become a focal point for the New Age Movement in the coming years. Its teachings and goals are certainly impeccable in terms of the New Age worldview. The Baha'i teach not only of spiritual principles but are active in the political realm as well. Baha'i followers are involved in all arenas of society--in education, in establishing the quality of the sexes, in uniting various religious groups, and in the parliaments and in congresses of many nations.

The World Religion of the Future?

Historian Arnold Toynbee once predicted that Baha'i will become "the world religion of the future." Writer Leo Tolstoy described it as the "highest and purest form of religious teaching." Of course, we must realize that men like Tolstoy were not Christians. For if they were, they would realize how far off the mark from the teachings of Jesus Christ are those of Baha'u'llah and his modern-day Baha'i worshippers.

It is significant that the Baha'i have made their head-quarters--consisting of spacious and lavish buildings and facilities--on Mount Carmel in Haifa, Israel. Clearly, this group intends to become a major factor in the race for men's souls as we speed toward the 21st century.

BLUE MOUNTAIN CENTER OF MEDITATION

Amidst the beauty of nature in Petaluma, California is found the *Blue Mountain Center of Meditation*, a religious study group founded by Ecknath Easwaran, a man who came to the Blue Mountains of this part of California from southern India, the Hindu region of India that Ecknath Easwaran once called home. His followers say that Easwaran came to the United States on the Fullbright Scholarship Exchange Program following a successful career in India as a writer, lecturer, and professor of English literature. In 1961, the Blue Mountain Center of Meditation was established in Berkeley, California where, at the University of California, Easwaran taught the first accredited college course in meditation.

The teachings of Easwaran are an energetic combination of Christianity, Buddhism, Hinduism, and other transcendental concepts. An author of many books, the eclectic Easwaran does not hesitate to proclaim the spiritual genius of Saint Francis, Saint Paul, and Saint Augustine, and he has demonstrated great admiration for the Catholic Church's Mother Theresa in his book, *Love Never Faileth*. On one hand Easwaran speaks of Mahatma Gandhi as if he were a deity. Then, he is able to quickly transition into a positive-sounding sermonette about Jesus, as goggle-eyed, admiring followers rapturously sit at his feet.

According to Easwaran and his followers, in every man lies the spark of divinity; it is the birthright of every one of us. It is through studying the insights of the Buddha, the Hindu pantheon of deities, and yes, even Christ, that man can travel the path to his own union with the Godhead.

In addition to his books, which are sold nationally under the imprint of the Nilgiri Press, the Blue Mountain Meditation Center holds monthly workshops taught personally by Easwaran. There are also retreats at least twice a year; and according to their most recent *Blue Mountain Center News* newsletter, each Tuesday night Easwaran personally gives a talk on meditation at the United Church of Christ in Petaluma, California.

The retreats of the Center are conducted at the Santa Sabina Retreat Center, originally a Catholic convent. These retreats emphasize meditation but also include such subjects as the "healing of the earth" and other environmental issues. They are normally attended by small groups because Easwaran has not yet gained the wide following of other guru types who have come to America. His following is scattered and dispersed, mainly consisting of those who read his books on the subject of meditation and spiritual growth.

BOULDER GRADUATE SCHOOL

The Boulder Graduate School, in Boulder, Colorado, claims to "combine academic excellence with experiential learning in an atmosphere that integrates body, mind, and spirit." Actually, to put it bluntly, what the Boulder Graduate School does is provide its students a series of jolts from the outer perimeter of the New Age movement.

Offering Master of Arts degrees in Health and Wellness and in Psychology and Counseling, Boulder Graduate School includes in its classes instruction in almost every facet of the New Age. A recent catalog of courses listed "Native American Healing; Shamanism; Gnosticism; Goddessism; Oriental Religions: Hinduism, Buddhism, and Confucianism; Music, Sound and Healing; and Wilderness Rites of Passage." There were also courses in "Western Herbology" and "The Art and Science of Touch, or Movement."

Considering its wacky range of courses, the credentials of the staff of the Boulder Graduate School seem to be impressive; many have a PhD and some are medical doctors. Its nursing courses are evidently approved by the Colorado Nurses Association and on an informal basis by the American Nurses Associations Board on Accreditation.

The school, whose motto is "The Next Generation of Knowledge," is truly a New Age university. It offers classes at night and weekends and allows the individual to tailor his curriculum to whatever occultic path or New Age lifestyle to which he is addicted or in which he finds an interest. This institution is a prototype for all the universities and colleges of the future. In fact, as we examine the college catalogs and bulletins of such premier and vaunted learning institutions as Yale, Princeton, Southern California, the University of Texas, University of Michigan, and others, we find New Ageism creeping into many of their courses as well. But at the Boulder Graduate School, it can correctly be stated that New Age instruction is not simply *a part* of the curriculum. It is *the* curriculum.

BUDDHISM

Known as the religion of enlightenment, *Buddhism* was founded by Gautama Buddha. He was born with the name Siddhartha Gautama in what is today Nepal about 560 B.C. and died at the age of 80 in the following century. He fostered the religious teachings which came to be known as Buddhism as a violent protest against Hinduism, the religion then and now prevailing in his homeland. Especially despicable, according to the Buddha, was the Hindu doctrine of caste systems.

In the succeeding centuries, Buddhism spread to Burma, Thailand, Laos, Cambodia, Vietnam, Sri Lanka, and on into China, Korea, and Japan. In Japan a different form of Buddhism known as *Mahayana* (the Greater Vehicle) came into vogue.

There are literally thousands of different sects and schools of thought in Buddhism. Some have said that this is more a *family* of religion than a single religion. Yet, there are certain constants in the teachings of the Buddha which all Buddhists hold in common and which make it a false religion for those who are traditional Christian believers.

Recently, the Associated Press carried a story with the headline "Buddhism Takes Hold in the United States." Religion writer Ira Rifkin reported that Buddhism is sweeping across America and has now emerged as a major religion. According to Rifkin, about 150 leaders of Buddhist groups met in Los Angeles in 1987 to create a national organization designed to enhance the spread of the faith in this country. The occasion was the first convocation of the American Buddhist Congress which was held at the Qwan Um Sa Korean Buddhist Temple. It was called "an historic occasion and a great step forward in propagating and preserving the teachings of the Lord Buddha."

Rifkin also noted that some 30 Japanese Buddhist sects exist in the United States, while a statement issued by

Buddhist leaders in 1986 in Boulder, Colorado indicated that North America holds the greatest variety of Buddhist traditions of any country in the world today.

1.5 Million Buddhists in America

There may be as many as one and one-half million Buddhists in America. Large numbers live in California, Colorado, Hawaii, and other West Coast states. But sizeable pockets of Buddhists can even be found in the Northeast and Midwest. However, Southern California takes the cake as far as the spiraling growth of Buddhism is concerned. An estimated 500,000 Buddhists live in Orange County in Greater Los Angeles, according to religious statistics cited by Havan Pola Ratanasara, president of the Buddhist Sangha Council of Southern California.

Buddhism and the New Age

It appears that Buddhism is also a central feature of such New Age groups as Benjamin Creme's Tara Center and the Lucis Trust, founded by the late Alice Bailey. Both organizations greatly venerate and honor the Buddha, and Creme maintains that people everywhere should meditate and visualize the Buddha as a point of light.

Benjamin Creme is the promoter of a New Age "Christ" whom he names as the Lord Maitreya. It is interesting that Buddhism claims that after his death, the god-consciousness of Buddha was transmitted into a spirit entity known as the "Maitreya" in the spirit world. Supposedly, this Lord Maitreya is to return again to the world to become the New Age Christ and show man the way to godhood and perfection. As one expert, M. Williams, states in *Buddhism* (page 181):

> At the moment of his attaining Buddhahood, he (Gautama Buddha) had transferred the divine

essence to Maitreya, the loving and compassionate
one ... Maitreya watches over, promotes the interest
of the Buddhist faith, while awaiting the time he is to
appear on the earth as the Maitreya, or the fifth
Buddha of the present age.

The Major Teachings of Buddhism

Once we understand that Buddhism proceeded from and is
simply another form of Hinduism with minor modifications,
we then begin to realize why the teachings of the Buddhists
are so prevalent today in the New Age. Buddhism is a flexible
religion that greatly accommodates even the most bizarre
and far out teachings and doctrines. So it is a natural to be
used as a cornerstone of the eclectic and syncretic New Age
World Religion.

Listed below is a brief description of some of the major
concepts and teachings of Buddhism:

1. *The Eight-fold Path:* Those who would themselves
become little Buddhas are said to tread the eight-fold
path, which includes right understanding, right
thoughts, right speech, right action, right means of
earning a living, right effort, right mindfulness, and
right concentration. All of these are thought to lead
to singleness of mind, wisdom, and finally to *nirvana*,
a state of heavenly bliss.

2. *The Four Noble Truths:* When the Buddha became
enlightened, he supposedly perceived four truths
about the state of humanity. The first is the truth that
man suffers through sickness, old age, etc. A second
truth is that this suffering is caused by man's
inadequacies; for example, his lust and greed. Third,
man, through his will and through certain spiritual
techniques and knowledge, can break through this
suffering. Fourth, by undertaking the eight-fold path,

man may finally put an end to his suffering and achieve nirvana, or union with the divine "all that is."

3. *Karma:* Buddhism teaches that negative karma results from man's thoughts and acts. This karma is carried over to the next life as is the good karma collected. In other words, man accumulates certain types of energy forces which mold and shape his future existences on the path to nirvana.

4. *Samsara*: Samsara is simply a synonym for reincarnation, the repeated process and cycles of birthing and death. Unlike the truth of the Bible (see Hebrews 9:27) where we find that man is appointed once to die and then to face God Almighty in judgment, Buddhism, as does other New Age religions and cults, says that man is destined to be born over and over and over again. An individual must live many lifetimes. During these lifecycles he may alternatively progress through incarnations as a lowly insect, an animal, a human, or he may become an insatiable ghost or even a demon.

5. *Enlightenment:* Buddhism says that man can become *enlightened*. He can become a Buddha himself, though this may require many lifetimes. It is claimed that one of the wisest and most effective ways to achieve enlightenment, especially as taught by New Agers today, is to contact the spiritual beings that exist in the other spiritual realms so they can be way-showers and guide a person along the eight-fold path.

6. *Goddess worship:* Though not every Buddhist practices goddess worship, many do. In the far East, the most popular feminine deity is the Chinese River Goddess, Qwan Yin, often called the Goddess of Mercy. She is also popular among New Agers in the West. Qwan (or Kwan) Yin is called on by people who have everyday problems, and it is claimed that she is

able to help them understand how to be happy and joyful, how to recognize the beauty within, and finally, how to succeed in attaining the paradise state of nirvana.

The Buddhists have a collection of scriptures which are called the *Tripitaka*, which means "three baskets." It is called three baskets because it really constitutes three major divisions. The first tells one how to live, the second discusses the basic ideals and teachings of Buddha, and finally, there is the *Dharmapada* which sums up all the teachings of Buddhism in a concise and easy way to learn. Other scriptures are known as the *Sutras*. These are especially taught in the New Age.

The Art of Meditation

The philosophy called *Zen Buddhism* is widely popular in the New Age today. Emphasizing meditation, Zen Buddhists chant using a *mantra*, a word or phrase that is recited over and over again in the belief that much recitation will somehow cause the spiritual world to intervene or the physical plane (the material world) to be changed. The syllable "om" (or "aum") is most used as a mantra, but any type of word will do. A number of those who have studied Hinduism use the names of Hindu goddesses and gods as mantras.

Also in Zen Buddhism there is the *mandala*, a diagram or drawing which contains circles within larger circles and is also sometimes composed of triangles and other occultic symbols. The mandala is thought to be a spiritual diagram, or rendering of the universe--a sort of labyrinth to help people find salvation. Many mandalas are colorful. Worshippers usually visualize, centering in on and focusing on a mandala. They literally achieve a trance-like state. Such occult techniques as meditation, the chanting of mantras, and centering on a mandala produce self-hypnotism and make the individual vulnerable to demonic influences and susceptible to warped psychological feelings and intuitions.

Popularity Among New Agers

It is undeniable that Buddhism is increasingly finding support in the New Age. In fact, it is almost inseparable *from* the New Age. For example, in *People* magazine recently was an article about the booming Japanese Buddhist sect of *Nichiren Shoshu* (Soka Gokkai). According to the article, thousands of Americans now daily retire to a secluded place in their home where they have set up an alter for the Buddha, complete with candles, water bowls (which make a ringing sound), and other artifacts of a spiritual nature. Families then commence to chant as they kneel quietly and clasp their hands together in a praying mode. Rosaries may be used, as rosary beads are extremely popular among Buddhists and Hindus alike.

Though the Bible warns against vain repetition, to the devotees of Nichiren Shoshu chanting is magical; what they are doing is worshipping a scroll called the *Ghonson*, which is behind the doors of the altar. The common chant is: "nam-myoho-nenge-kiyo," which means "I bow to," or worship, "the lotus satra."

There are hundreds of thousands of Nichiren Shoshu members today; the sect is especially influential among Japanese-Americans, but increasingly it is finding favor among others looking for a new spirituality. Although most sect members reside in Los Angeles and elsewhere in Southern California, there is also a temple in Houston and other centers in Chicago and other cities.

Many prominent Americans have expressed a belief in Buddhism, particularly Zen Buddhism. Among them: California governor Jerry Brown, actors Richard Gere, Patrick Duffy and John Travolta, and singer Tina Turner. Positive articles on Zen Buddhism are constantly found in such magazines as *Life, Time, Newsweek*, and even *Reader's Digest*, not to mention the various women's magazines.

Zen Buddhism: Inroads into Christian Churches

Zen Buddhism has also found its way into many Christian churches. M. Scott Peck, bestselling author of the #1 New York Times bestseller *The Road Less Traveled*, is a promoter of Zen Buddhism. Sadly, a number of Protestant and Catholic churches frequently invite Peck to speak to their congregations. Even Southern Baptist churches have done so; yet, he does not attempt to hide his New Age orientation.

Also, my ministry continually receives reports about Zen Buddhist instruction given by nuns, priests, and laymen at Catholic retreats. Zen Buddhism has also gained support among Methodist and Episcopal pastors and priests, and it is not uncommon at all to find occult forms of Zen Buddhist meditation being taught in these churches. Christian psychiatrists and counselors, regrettably, are often among the biggest promoters of Zen Buddhist meditation though they rarely call their recommended therapy by that name.

Buddhism is most definitely unholy and unbiblical. The core teaching of Buddhism is that man must attain his own salvation through works, doing so through a series of incarnations. In contrast, Christianity teaches that man is saved by grace alone through the atonement of our Lord Jesus Christ. Moreover, in I Corinthians 2:5, Paul wisely taught: "That your faith should not stand in the wisdom of men, but in the power of God." Thus man cannot work his way to self-empowerment. We see also the clear Bible teaching that Jesus Christ is "*the* Way, *the* Truth, and *the* Life," and that no person can come to the Father but by Him.

In sum, Buddhism teaches that there is no one personal God and that man is responsible for his own salvation. There is also no Father in Heaven who has provided a way through the atonement of Christ on the cross for us to be saved.

Buddhism does not lead to enlightenment as it boasts, but is instead only one of many religions which, in fact, lead men into pervasive darkness.

THE CENTER FOR DANCES OF UNIVERSAL PEACE

The Center For Dances of Universal Peace, located in Fairfax, Virginia, and connected with the Sufi Moslems, is an organization whose goal is to promote mystical holy dancing throughout the world. According to the organization's statement of purpose, "The Center's programs seek to mine the resources of deep mystical understanding and practices that are found in all the sacred religions of the Earth." The group was founded by American mystic Samuel L. Lewis in 1964 under the inspiration of two of his spiritual teachers, the Sufi leader Hazrat Inayat Khan and American sacred dance pioneer Ruth St. Denis. Lewis passed away in 1971 and currently, Neil Douglas-Klotz is the leader.

The Sufis encourage a circular form of dancing called the *dervish*. The Center For Dances of Universal Peace believes that by teaching all peoples to practice a form of sacred dance in which they circle around and around in concentric circles, this will help lead to world peace and a oneness of all mankind. The dance is finding popularity among members of Buddhist, Hindu, and Sufi Moslem groups alike as well as various New Age and peace-oriented organizations.

The center combines its dances with mystical music, combining Zoroastrian, Christian, Catholic, Celtic, Jewish, and other traditions. As they dance, there are fables and storytelling going on in the traditions of the goddess and other Eastern teachings. The Center conducts retreats and workshops around the world and has established small groups in Germany, Japan, the United States, Holland, Canada, France, and even inside the Soviet Union.

Though The Center for Dances of Universal Peace claims that it favors no religions or ideologies, in fact, it is exclusively mystical in nature and its publications are filled with images of the mother goddess in her various incarnations, whether as Isis in Egypt, Mary for the Catholics, the sorceress of the ancient pagans, as an unnamed, beautiful blond woman with a flowing white gown holding up a flame, or even as the Statue of Liberty. It should also be noted that Neil Douglas-Klotz has published a new esoteric version of the Lord's Prayer which reinterprets the model prayer given by Jesus in the New Testament to fit the desired goals of New Age mysticism.

CHINOOK LEARNING CENTER

Fritz Hull, who with his wife, Vivienne, founded the Chinook Center in 1972, insists that his center is not involved with the "New Age." It is instead, he recently told a newspaper reporter, "A place that integrates living and understanding, teaching people to live in harmony with the earth." Nonsense. The Chinook Center, believe me, is most definitely classic New Age. Housed on scenic Whidbey Island outside of greater Seattle, Washington, Chinook occupies some 64 acres of what was once an old Finnish farm house. This is a tranquil, woodsy setting where the group produces organic crops and educates its youngsters in its own Waldorf School (see section on *Anthroposophy*).

The learning program that Chinook offers three to four

thousand New Agers from around the country each year leaves no doubt about the New Age direction of the group. For example, there is a seminar called "The Gateway Experience" in which participants are invited to "follow our bliss" and work for "the dream of the earth." Chinook has also conducted workshops on Sacred Dance and seminars on Mending the Sacred Hoops, Sexuality of the Earth, and the Cosmic Dance.

Fritz Hull, Chinook's founder, is a Presbyterian minister who each Sunday morning offers a "universal communion" during his services in downtown Clinton, Washington. Another official of Chinook is a man named Wes Veatch, a minister with the Disciples of Christ denomination. Hull and Veatch are sure that a new cycle is before us. In a newsletter (*The Chinook Letter*, Fall 1987), Hull wrote: "Ahead is a new cycle of history . . . A new 'tough love.'" He remarked that a shift is taking place on the earth. This shift involves, "The waning influence of conservative and fundamentalist religions." According to Hull, the Christian fundamentalist is putting out a lot of loud rhetoric, but biblical (fundamentalist) Christians do not "foster a compassionate society." At the same time, he insists that the new shift in society opens the way for the mystical movement "to emerge with greater power than ever before."

According to its own claims, there are over 800 Chinook Associate and Covenant members and over 5,000 on the Center's mailing list. One of the most notable members is a man named David Spangler, widely known throughout the New Age for his books. Spangler once stated that Lucifer has come to bring man to wholeness in the New Age. He is a channeler of a number of spirit beings, including an entity who calls himself "Limitless Love and Truth." Spangler and other New Agers are greatly desirous of merging Christianity with the New Age, thus their campaign to de-emphasize the term "New Age" which is obviously a thinly veiled attempt at doublespeak.

THE CHRIST FOUNDATION

Are these the actual words of Jesus?:

> I come to be one with you. This is Jesus speaking. I
> speak to you through the pages of this book and tell
> you of the wisdom of the ages. I come to tell you of
> love, and of love between man and woman. I come to
> teach you and to show you a better way, one that will
> give you the ecstasy and the fulfillment for which you
> long, one that will lead you to the outermost reaches
> of Who You are. I am Jesus, come again. Read Me.

A gross and disgusting example of the New Age attempt
to pervert true Christianity is the New Age book, *A Spiritual
Sex Manual.* Published by an obscure group in Washington
state that calls itself "The Christ Foundation," the book is a
sex manual that gives detailed instructions. Only a foul
demon spirit could have inspired the human authors and
publishers to print this despicable book.

No doubt many with a New Age worldview and others
who are skeptics of Biblical Christianity will love this book
because it comes packaged with beautiful prose and messages of "love," "peace," and "wholeness." It is an expen-
sively and spectacularly produced book, with romantically
pink paper, beautiful illustrations of roses and so forth.
Moreover--and this is the startling news--*the publisher
claims the book is personally written by Jesus himself.* "Jesus"
supposedly even signed the foreword of the book. The living
woman who is the one to whom "Jesus" transmitted this
book says in it that she is the reincarnated Mary Magdalene
who once was Jesus' lover.

In *A Spiritual Sex Manual,* "Jesus" gives a glowing and
approving account of his sexual affair with Mary Magdalene
(they supposedly slipped away from the disciples into the
nearby fields outside of Jerusalem). Then "he" goes on to

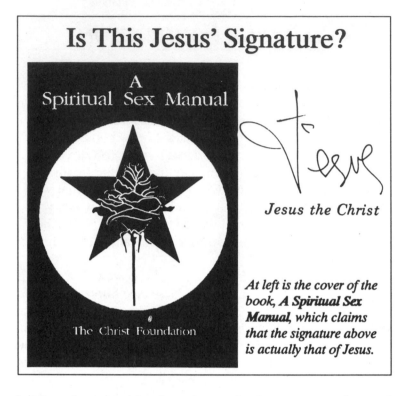

Is This Jesus' Signature?

A
Spiritual Sex Manual

The Christ Foundation

Jesus the Christ

At left is the cover of the book, A Spiritual Sex Manual, which claims that the signature above is actually that of Jesus.

detail various sex rituals and acts readers can practice and master for their physical enjoyment and spiritual growth.

This "Jesus" talks vaguely about "God's Plan for the Salvation of the World." He seems to be a wonderful teacher who simply wants men and women to enjoy sex as a loving and holy act, in *or* out of marriage. If a person has not discovered the real Jesus--the Jesus revealed in the Holy Bible--he or she could well be suckered in by this sex instructor imitation.

The Holy Bible warns us about the imitation Jesuses to come, for example, we read:

For if he that cometh preacheth another Jesus, whom we have not preached, or if ye receive another spirit . . . ye might well bear with him (2 Cor. 11:4).

But though we, or an angel from heaven, preach any other gospel unto you than that which we have preached unto you, let him be accursed (Gal. 1:8).

CHRISTIAN SCIENCE
(Church of Christ)

If you are interested in a religion whose founder wrote: "The sick through their own beliefs have induced their own conditions," who also taught that evil is an illusion, that the term "Christ" refers merely to a principle, and that God is simply Mind, then *Christian Science* is for you. Christian Science, formally named the Church of Christ, Scientist, was incorporated in 1879 by Mary Baker Eddy.

Eddy asserted that her teachings were the "final revelation of God for mankind." She also insisted that her book, *Science and Health With Key to the Scriptures*, was equal to the Bible in authority. But since Mrs. Eddy wrote that she had found hundreds of errors in the Bible, it can be assumed that she believed that her works *superior* to the Bible. Today, in the meeting halls and churches of Christian Science, her books receive equal credence with the Bible at worship services.

Mary Baker Eddy first came to learn of what she called Christian Science from a man by the name of Phineas Parkhurst Quimby. In 1860 she suffered from a spinal problem and visited Quimby seeking a cure. She had heard that Quimby was advocating something that he called "Christian Science," a healing through one's own mind power. So impressed was Mrs. Eddy (then Mrs. Patterson) that she began to research this area herself. Eventually, she published her book, *Science and Health With Key to the Scriptures,* the first edition of which was riddled with grammatical and other errors. The book's contents were apparently plagiarized heavily from the works of Quimby and other authors and especially a man named Frances Leber, a German-American philosopher who had written a manuscript entitled "The Metaphysical Religion of Hegel."

The Teachings of Christian Science

According to Mary Baker Eddy, the Bible should be interpreted in a metaphorical and spiritual sense, but certainly not literally. This is the reason for her distorted interpretations of the Bible. For example, Christian Science denies the deity of Jesus Christ. Eddy stated that the Trinity for Christian Science does not consist of God, His Son, and the Holy Spirit, but instead the Trinity is comprised of "Life, Truth, and Love." There is no personal God in the Christian Science teachings, only an impersonal, pantheistic God, a God who is Mind, Principle, Intelligence, or Mother. In Christian Science, even the divine birth of Jesus is explained away. Mrs. Eddy's concept was that Mary simply conceived a "spiritual idea" and named it Jesus. So Jesus resulted as a thought from Mary: "Jesus was the offspring of Mary's self-conscious communion with God."

Christian Science emphasizes healing. Periodically one reads in the newspapers of Christian Science parents being prosecuted because they failed to seek medical attention for a critically ill child. Eddy taught that there is no disease, sin, or death, that these are all illusions of our minds. By removing this illusion and recognizing that our thoughts can heal, there is no need for medical doctors. There is no way for us to determine how many innocent young children, as well as adults, have suffered and died because of this quack rejection of trained medical doctors.

The heretical nature of Christian Science can be seen most clearly in its doctrine of the atonement--more accurately, its rejection of the biblical doctrine of atonement of Christ Jesus. Eddy's *Science and Health With Key to the*

Scriptures says that, "The material blood of Jesus was no more efficacious to cleanse from sin when it was shed upon the 'accursed tree' than when it was flowing through his veins as he went daily about his father's business." Furthermore, Eddy asserted that Jesus did not die as a result of his crucifixion, for death is illusory.

The unholy doctrines and teachings of this heretical Christian sect can easily be seen from a sampling of quotes from the church's own pamphlet entitled *Jesus and the Christ:*

> The irresistible Christ is the power of Mind ... The power of Mind is the Messiah, and salvation depends on the demonstration of God as the Mind of man.

> So you and I as persons ... are human concepts of the real man, the Christ, concepts evolved by the so-called human mind.

> All that has ever existed is God and His Christ ... The Christ is not resurrected nor has it ever ascended.

> The Christ Science verifies the unreality of evil ...

> Divine Science takes men beyond the mortal belief of earth and stars for the recognition of the Kingdom of God within man and throughout the vastness of Mind. In the discovery of Christian Science, the world has been given the answer to what has been called the riddle of the universe.

> The Christ is and has always been the spiritual idea of divine Principle, and to claim any aspect of the Christ as a personal attribute or accomplishment is to misunderstand Christ.

> What is designated as the Antichrist is the belief of carnality or hatred.

In summary, Christian Science is a religion that over-emphasizes healing to the neglect of Jesus Christ, our Lord and Savior, and it denies His works on the cross on our behalf. Eddy describes her teaching as "scientific," but in reality it is simply the administration of placebos. Moreover, Christian Science can be extremely dangerous to one's physical as well as spiritual health.

A Fall in Numbers

Once Christian Science was the premier cult among early New Age believers. It was the focal point of what was called the New Thought Movement. But today, Christian Science is greatly diminished in numbers and reputation. Practically each year for the last two decades, cult and religious researchers have reported that the number of people who identify themselves with Christian Science has declined. Nevertheless, this was a forerunner of many other groups, including the health and prosperity gospel, often dubbed "name it and claim it," that has become so prevalent in some Christian charismatic circles today.

In fact, D. R. McConnell, a former professor at Oral Roberts University, in his book, *A Different Gospel*, clearly shows how current, well-known evangelist teachers of the health and prosperity gospel have plagiarized the works of such groups as the Christian Scientists and others, and have simply recast some of the teachings of New Thought into a newer framework of doublespeak more acceptable to conservative Christianity. Kurt Koch, the late and great German evangelist, in his revealing book, *Occult ABC*, briefly discussed the infiltration of Christian Science and New Thought teachings into the Christian church. He wrote: "The finest flower of Christian Science is Agnes Sanford's book, *The Healing Light*. This book has such a plausible Bible framework, and the ideas of Christian Science are so sublimated, that many Christians, indeed even a bishop, have been deceived by it."

Regardless of its loss in members, the Church of Christ, Scientist, with its Mother Church in Boston, Massachusetts, still exerts considerable authority over some 2500 congregations located in over 50 countries around the world.

CHURCH OF DIVINE MAN

The *Church of Divine Man* has a strong and enthusiastic following on the West Coast. Based on the principle that every man and woman is psychic and is able to develop their psychic gifts, the Church of Divine Man has a number of associated church assemblies and other organizations. For example, there is the Yin-Yang High School Seminary, the Santa Rosa Psychic Institute in Santa Rosa, California, the Berkeley Psychic Institute in Berkeley, California, and also psychic institutes in San Jose, Palo Alto, Marin, and elsewhere in California. There is also Delphi University in Richmond, California, which offers courses in a number of New Age areas, including astrology. The Church of Divine Man also oversees a group of missionary healers who visit homes and hospitals.

The California branch of the Church of Divine Man was founded by Lewis S. Bostwick. Though he holds in common with other New Agers the belief in reincarnation and karma, Bostwick emphasizes the here and now, and provides advice on how people can attain happiness, success, wealth, health, etc., through psychic communication.

Many of Bostwick's parishioners have claimed miracles. For example, recently in *The Voice Within*, the church's California newspaper, one of the group's ministers testified that she had witnessed another minister in the church heal a woman by creating the antibodies needed to heal the disease that she had been inflicted with for months. He did this, she said, by showing the person how to accomplish her own healing through her own psychic powers.

In Washington state, a former associate of Bostwick's, M.F. "Doc" Slusher, publishes the Church of Divine Man publication, *The Inner Voice*, and has founded churches. In *The Inner Voice*, Reverend Gail Coupal recently explained the basis of the church's belief system when she wrote:

> The spiritual healings we do at the Church of Divine Man are based on faith . . . It is the healees' belief in themselves that allows the healing to take place. The spiritual techniques that we teach--grounding, center- ing, creating and destroying roses, and running ener- gies--are all based on faith. People's belief that they can heal create change in their physical reality. This is the vital ingredient which allows things to happen.

> Faith, believing your spiritual self, is not something that is outside of you: Rather, it is a spiritual part of you . . . Your faith is a spiritual energy. You do not have to do anything to have your faith. Rather, you can simply allow your faith to be, to own it for yourself.

Although there are many other teachings of the Church of Divine Man, the above statement, more so than any other, explains how this group diverges from the true Christian church. According to the Church of Divine Man, faith is not believing in God, a personal God who is our Heavenly Father; instead, faith is "believing in your spiritual self . . . Not something that is outside of you." Moreover, you do not have to be born again and have Jesus Christ as the object of your faith. Rather, this New Age church teaches that you "simply allow your faith to be." In other words, man himself, his mind, is the central deity of the Church of Divine Man.

In Washington state, the Church of Divine Man has centers in Bellingham, Everett, Seattle, and Tacoma; also there are locations in Portland, Oregon, and Vancouver,

B.C., Canada. In addition, the publications of the Church of Divine Man encourage parishioners to attend psychic fairs, aura readings, church retreats, kundalini workshops, meditation retreats, clairvoyance training sessions, and similar meetings.

CHURCH OF RELIGIOUS SCIENCE (SCIENCE OF MIND)

"I hardly know the person that I was--poor little struggling person that I was," said the Reverend Peggy Bassett in a telephone interview from Washington, D.C., where she was attending an International New Thought Alliance conference. Ms. Bassett was referring to the woman that she was before she came to believe in the teachings of *Science of Mind*. Bassett reported that in 1962 she first stepped into a *Church of Religious Science* meeting and was shocked at what she saw, attributing her reaction to a conservative Southern Baptist upbringing in the small Arkansas town of Friendship--population 500--where she was raised. Today, Bassett, 65, of Huntington Beach, California, is the first woman president in the 62-year history of the Church of Religious Science. Like her predecessor, Bassett believes strongly that when man recognizes his true union with the infinite, he *automatically becomes Christ*. Currently, she is pushing the church to become more involved in peace and "social justice issues," including the environment and AIDS. She also promotes a close relationship with the Soviet Union.

The Church of Religious Science was founded under

another name in 1927 by Ernest Holmes, who borrowed from the metaphysical writings of Unity Church's Charles and Myrtle Fillmore, Phineas Parkhurst Quimby, and Mary Baker Eddy, founder of Christian Science. *Science of Mind*, a book by Holmes published in 1938, is the classic textbook of those who are in the Science of Mind religion.

Holmes wrote that one's inherent self-worth emanates from the divine part. Like Christian Science and other mind science groups, Holmes insisted that Jesus was not God, but that we are all collectively both Christ and divinity. Holmes also did not believe in a literal heaven or hell, nor did he confess that Jesus' resurrection was a literal fact. Through developing the powers of the mind, said Holmes, man's potential is unlimited and he is able to do miraculous and supernatural acts.

The Church of Religious Science has congregations across the United States. Many of them do not use that name but they are still in one way or another affiliated with the overall group. *Science of Mind* magazine is also a popular staple of New Age bookstores.

The Flamboyant Terry Cole-Whittaker

Perhaps the most famous teacher and minister of the Church of Religious Science is a flamboyant and attractive blonde woman named Terry Cole-Whittaker. Called a Doris Day look-alike, Terry made it big on television in the late-70s and early-80s; soon however, she fell victim to burnout and quit her television program which had been beamed to millions and millions of viewers in major markets. Nevertheless, she remains a popular seminar, workshop, and conference speaker and her books are consistent bestsellers.

Whittaker draws a big audience with such declarations as "You've never been judged except by your own faults." She also attracts a large audience by teaching the principles of *A Course in Miracles*, a false New Age bible, and is one of the most popular proponents of the prosperity gospel. In her church she held "Dressing to Win" seminars and told her yuppie crowds that they were entitled to "divine wealth." She also crowed, "Our ministry isn't into sin, guilt, disease, pain, or hunger."

Terry often speaks of her prayer ministry and she has stated that it is through the Holy Spirit that she receives salvation. In Terry Cole-Whittaker's 1986 book, *The Inner Path From Where You Are to Where You Want to Be*, she demonstrated that she is perfectly aligned with the cardinal teachings of the New Age when she wrote: "God is That Which Includes All Beings. God is All of It and the Everything, and God cannot be apart from It, any of It, anyway." Recently, she has begun to promote the goddess and Mother Earth religious ideas, and she now has proclaimed that the New Age has already arrived and that enlightened men and women are "walking on the earth as sons of God."

THE CHURCH UNIVERSAL AND TRIUMPHANT (ELIZABETH CLARE PROPHET)

Guru Ma, her church followers call her: "Mother of the Universe." She herself says she is "the one present messenger of God's voice on earth." Her heavenly messages come from such spirits as "Jesus," "Agent K-17," "Koothoomi," and "Count Saint Germain," the ascended Master whom she recognizes as the "Hierarch of the New Age." If she is getting messages from these spirit entities, according to many reports those messages are making her fabulously wealthy. I am referring to Elizabeth Clare Prophet, founder and head of the *Church Universal and Triumphant.*

Prophet is one of the most colorful figures in the New Age religion. Her church has tens of thousands of members-- the exact number is unknown--throughout the United States mostly but also overseas. Her worship services and cere- monies are broadcast on cable television systems around the nation, greatly expanding her audience. Mostly this is a church based on communication with spirits, among whom have been mentioned Ray-O-Light, Agent K-17 of the "Inner Secret Service," El Morya, Helios, Amazonia, Cosmos, Ra, Mu, Merlin the Magician, Astara, Hercules, Venus, Zoroaster, and many more.

Its founder is a firm believer in reincarnation, and the Church teaches that Prophet's daughter, Moira Lewis, is the reincarnation of the late president John F. Kennedy. Also, it has been claimed that a second daughter, 23-year old church spokeswoman Erin Prophet, is the reincarnation of the Hindu leader Gandhi. Moira Lewis, 21, recently left the cult. She explained that she had always been the rebel of the family and that when her mother and stepfather, Elizabeth's fourth husband, realized the extent to which she rejected the Church's teachings, she was thrown out. Since then, she has given interviews to anti-cult organizations and has exposed a number of facts about her mother's cult.

The Church Universal and Triumphant (CUT) has made the national news because of reports that its leader had claimed that the world was coming to an end, and that nuclear catastrophe was on the immediate horizon. The cult promptly began to build earthen bomb-shelters. Then came reports that the New Age cult had begun to stockpile arms and munitions in its headquarters community near Paradise Valley, Montana, a picturesque area bordering Yellowstone National Park. These rumors became known as facts when Vernon Hamilton, described by federal officials as the secur- ity chief of Prophet's Church Universal and Triumphant, was arrested in July, 1989 in Spokane, Washington, for allegedly purchasing arms under a false name.

Federal officials said that Hamilton planned to purchase more than $130,000 worth of high-powered weapons and ammunition--an arsenal designed to arm 200 people. The revelations caused frantic discussions and anxieties to be raised among residents of the nearby Montana community, who feared another Jim Jones People's Temple massacre. In an article in the *Spokane Chronicle*, former cult member Kenneth Polini turned up the heat on the controversy when he stated: "Unfortunately, this does have the potential to be another Jonestown." Polini, former security chief for the church prior to Hamilton, added, "I really hate to say that, but it does."

However, the allegations of Polini were dismissed by the church as comments coming from a "sour apple," and church leaders professed innocence and surprise over the arrest of Hamilton, claiming that they knew little or nothing about the details of the arms purchases.

Mother Mary and the Teachings of CUT

Elizabeth Clare Prophet's teachings were originally borrowed from Guy Ballard's I AM group; however, the innovative Prophet seems to have added a number of fresh new concepts, practices, and twists to her presentations and to community life. In an interview with *People* magazine (June 4, 1990), Prophet was referred to as "Mistress of the Universe." She told *People* magazine, "We have all lived thousands of times," and confided: "As a child I walked and talked with Jesus." In the church's literature, the charismatic and flamboyant Prophet has also written that she got the idea to found her group when Mother Mary appeared to her on a street one day. Subsequently, she has claimed to receive many visits from Mary, who supposedly has told Prophet that today, in the spirit world, she, Mary, is known as "Lady Nada." Answering critics who warn that she is another Jim Jones, the smooth-talking, intelligent Prophet smiled and answered, "I don't control my members in any way."

Elizabeth Clare Prophet belongs to the conservative wing of the New Age religion. An avowed anti-communist, she has had such dignitaries as army general (retired) Daniel Graham on her program to tout his idea for a High Frontiers space defense system. In the Church's magazines and publications, communist insurgencies in Central America are often denounced. During the Soviet debacle in Afghanistan, Prophet's publications carried many reports of the atrocities committed by Soviet troops in their conquest and suppression of the Afghan people.

The worship services conducted by Elizabeth Clare Prophet and broadcast nationally on television are prime examples of wierd religious theatre. As Prophet speaks in a hypnotic, monotonal voice, behind her on one side of the altar is a small statue of Buddha. On the other side of the altar is a miniature replica of the Statue of Liberty. Hanging on the left side of the wall above the altar is a picture of a bearded, long-haired Jesus who appears to be blonde-haired and blue-eyed. To the right is a picture of what the New Agers believe Count St. Germain looks like. Between these two pictures is a print of a prototypical god-man being illuminated by beings from an effervescent sun.

Prophet calls her spirit guides the Lords of the Flame. It is to these Lords that her audience chants incessantly, in a process the church calls *decreeing*. This chanting, repeating verses and stanzas repeatedly, easily puts the congregation in a hypnotic state of altered consciousness, leaving them highly susceptible to suggestions by their leader, the Mother, Elizabeth Clare Prophet. At the conclusion of this chanting, Guru Ma, as she is called, often conducts healing services, laying hands on the foreheads and brows of worshippers who come forward to be healed. Sometimes the audience sings *Amazing Grace* and other Christian or psuedochristian hymns. The whole atmosphere seems like something out of a strange, mystical, and esoteric novel, but it is all for real.

The Dangers of CUT

The dangers of the New Age become vividly clear when we review the operations of the Church Universal and Triumphant. Hundreds of families have been broken up by this cult. Many wives and husbands flee their homes, coming to Montana from all parts of the United States in order to be there personally at the scenic community ranch in the Teton Mountains near Yellowstone. It is reported that some have given Prophet and the church tens of thousands of dollars, even their entire life savings, all in a vain attempt to achieve a higher state of Cosmic Consciousness.

In 1985, Randall King, an ex-husband of Elizabeth Clare Prophet, alleged that Prophet and the church use devious tactics to get people's money. As King explained it to *People* magazine:

> You wanted to get them hooked into the organization's belief system . . . you wanted to get them decreeing, which was the programming technique. You get a little bit more control over these people by having them repeat these things (hypnotic chants) over and over.

> They would be so caught up that, well, they would give us all their money, sell their houses, hock their jewelry, sell everything. They would give us a hundred thousand dollars and then wind up on our doorsteps in their sleeping bags and be willing to sleep on the floor, if we would just show them "the way."

Prophet has denied King's allegations but does preach that she has "the way." The Ascended Masters, says Prophet, constantly talk to her, guide her ministry, and help her perform healing and other miracles. Randall King believes that Prophet, his ex-wife, *is* in touch with these spirits and that the Mystery Teachings she reveals result from extra-worldly transmissions.

Whether or not Prophet's messages come from the spirit world or from her own vivid and potent imagination, the fact is that these teachings do indeed come from hellish origin-ations. One thing that Prophet tells her followers is that the Jesus of the traditional Christian church is a lie. Prophet's group has even published books, under the imprint of her Summit University Press, that purport to be "the lost teachings of Jesus." Like Edgar Cayce and other New Age teachers, Prophet maintains that Jesus traveled to Tibet and other Asian countries and became a Master through an *initiation process*. So it is that she denies the true God of the Bible and reveals the true source of her revelations.

DALAI LAMA

At the age of five the man whom New Agers and Buddhists alike venerate as "His Holiness, the Dalai Lama," was pro-claimed Dalai Lama by the Buddhist monks who controlled his nation of Tibet in the mountainous regions to the north of China and India. The word "dalai" comes from the Mon-golian word for "ocean," signifying broad knowledge, while the word "lama" refers to a spiritual teacher. According to Tibetan Buddhism, the Dalai Lama is a literal incarnation on earth of their master, Buddha.

At the age of 16, the Dalai Lama was forced to flee Tibet over the Himalayas with some 100,000 followers when his native land of Tibet was invaded and conquered by the Red Chinese. That was in 1959; in the intervening years, the Dalai Lama has lived in India and spent a great part of his life in the United States as well, promoting Tibetan Buddhism, but more than that, working tirelessly for the establishment of a unified One World Religion.

In the United States, in New York City, the Dalai Lama's organization, Tibet House, was established in 1987. Ostensibly, its purpose is to exhibit Tibetan fine arts and promote cultural programs; but its true interests lie beyond the cultural. This is an educational and political institution under the patronage of the Dalai Lama. Its major goal is to promote Tibetan Buddhism as a major force in the United States and the world. Its dominant theme is a one world culture and a one world community.

A Nobel Peace Prize for the Dalai Lama

The Dalai Lama is one of the premier spiritual leaders of the New Age. He has been awarded the Nobel Peace Prize and been invited to Amherst College in Massachusetts where a large group of medical researchers and college professors sat rapturously as the Dalai Lama patiently taught them that Buddhist psychology and spirituality were examples of science and equally as valid as the scientific understanding of the West. In his newspaper, *Wisdom*, the Dalai Lama offers for sale such books as *Christianity Meets Buddhism*, by Catholic priest Heinrich Dumoulin, a Jesuit. Priest Dumoulin writes in this book that the differences between Christianity and Buddhism have been greatly exaggerated and misunderstood. In essence, he promotes an eclectic blending of the two.

Also, the Dalai Lama has been invited to be the principal speaker at a number of high level New Age conferences and meetings. For example, on October 2-7, 1989, in Newport Beach, California, he spoke on the subject of "Awakening the Compassionate Heart" and the "Transformation of Consciousness" for the East-West Foundation's *Harmonia Mundi Congress*. Also at the Congress were Mother Theresa, the famed Catholic missionary, and priest Thomas Keating, an apologist for the Catholic faith. Keating was billed as "one of the foremost teachers of contemplation (meditation) within the Roman Catholic Church."

The Dalai Lama, in an interview for *Quest* magazine (Autumn 1988), advocated the Buddhist holy sexual practice called the "Tantras." When he was asked why the Buddhist scriptures are scientifically inaccurate, for example, why they claim that the moon is only 100 miles above the earth, etc., the Dalai Lama showed great flexibility. "If upon investigation," he answered, "you find that there is reason and truth in Western science, it is important to accept the fact, the real situation . . . ." But at the same time the Dalai Lama accorded a courtesy to the Buddhist literalists when he added, "If there are teachers who still hold to the literal meaning, then that is their own business. There is no need to argue with them. You can see things according to your own interpretation, and they can see things as they see fit."

This flexible attitude in terms of spiritual doctrines and teachings is common in the Dalai Lama's speeches and interviews. For instance, he has admitted that he believes in spirit entities who inhabit places and sometimes communicate with human beings; but if you or I do not believe in these entities, the Dalai Lama simply smiles and says, "Fine."

"World peace," he teaches, "is achieved based only on a sense of brotherhood and sisterhood." According to the Dalai Lama, man's salvation does not even depend on a belief in God for, as he has stated, "Whether we believe in God or not does not matter, but that we live peacefully, with a sense of brotherhood and sisterhood."

The Dalai Lama's religious views are greatly admired in the New Age because of their pragmatic and all-encompassing nature. In 1982 he told an interviewer: "I generally believe that every major religion has a potential of giving any human being good advice . . . Hence, we look and study, and we find a teaching that is most suitable to our own tastes." This is simply a restatement of the core teaching of the New Age that God is simply the deity of our own choice. We pick and choose our deities much like a customer makes selections at the counter of a cafeteria. "God as you understand him" is the keynote of the New Age World Religion.

DRUIDS

When Julius Caesar conquered Britain in 60 A.D., he was astonished and shocked at the perverse and grotesque nature of the religious system practiced by the conquered peoples. He and his soldiers discovered blood-stained rows of trees; howling, black-clad priests; screaming and violent women. Later, Caesar himself wrote of seeing mass burnings of human and animal victims in huge wicker cages. He told of the human sacrifices that were common to these pagans who worshipped the sun god, Hu, and the goddess Ceridwen. The religion that Caesar found so appalling was that of the *Druids*, also called the *Druidic Order*.

The Druids held sway in Great Britain in the pre-Christian era. The mysterious circular network of stones in the ruins of Stonehenge are one of the few remains of this unholy religion, whose god, Hu, was symbolized by the serpent and his goddess by the egg. Like the worshippers of Hu and Ceridwen in ancient days, there are today Druidic sects and orders in Great Britain, in the United States, and on the continent of Europe which continue many of the ungodly traditions of their ancient predecessors.

In today's Freemasonry there are also connections with Druidism. Albert Pike, former Grand Sovereign Master of Freemasonry, once said that the "Lost Word of Masonry" is concealed in the name of the Druid god Hu (see Manly P. Hall's *The Secret Teachings of All Ages*).

The popular fantasy stories about Merlin the Magician, King Arthur and his Knights of the Round Table, the bard Taliesin, and fair maidens, in their mythical and legendary land of Camelot are, in fact, legends that emanated from the days when Great Britain was dominated by the Druidic priesthood. This is why it is quite incredible that one Christian publisher, Crossway Books, today publishes a number of novels by a man named Stephen Lawhead with such titles as *Arthur*, *Merlin*, and *Taliesin*. In these novels

Lawhead attempts somehow to connect this ancient evil with Christianity.

It is Lawhead's assertion that *Taliesin, Arthur,* and others have factual, historical origins and that it was they who helped to convert Britain to Christianity. In fact, nothing could be further from the truth. For example, in Glastonbury, England in 1987, it was reported that modern Druidic followers and their Spirit Teacher communicated with the spirit world and were told that the new era would be brought in by "the reawakening of Arthur the King." It is also been reported that Merlin the Magician's spirit (actually, a demon) has been appearing to many occultists and spirit channelers, both in England and in the United States. Therefore, although Lawhead and Crossway Books may attempt to claim that their motives are altruistic in writing and publishing such books, theirs is simply the promotion of another gospel--an accursed gospel (see Galatians 1 and 2 Corinthians 11:4).

Devil Worshippers

Many of today's Druids are closely related to the witchcraft sects in their beliefs and religious practices and rituals. They believe that good and evil are simply flip sides of the same coin; many believe in transmigration and almost all believe in reincarnation and karma, two primary New Age teachings. They also believe that it is man's destiny to achieve unity with the gods and they particularly emphasize goddess worship and the powers of the earth and nature. Theirs is a fertility cult and a worship of occult medicine, the celestial bodies, black magic, feast days, and most of all, the veneration of their deity, the sun god.

Some Druidic groups, particularly in the United States, express a belief in nature spirits such as fairies, gnomes, and undines, little creatures of the forests and rivers to whom offerings are made. Some recognize and worship the goddess by many different names, such as Caillech, the Crone, or as

Kali. A number of Druidic groups meet deep in the forest near the major cities. There among a grove of trees they conduct their strange fire rituals; yet, the following Monday morning, they put on their business suits, or their doctors' or nurses' smocks, and head for the everyday workworld.

ECKANKAR

Who is "the god-man of the age?" Who is "omnipotent, omniscient, and omnipresent, all-wise, and is in all places simultaneously?" If your answer is Jesus, then you are not a disciple of the New Age religion known as *Eckankar*. In the book *The Precepts of Eckankar*, by founder Paul Twitchell, it is claimed that Eckankar is the highest of all religions and that "the Mahanta, the living ECK Master who presides over this religious system, is a god like no others." Indeed, the living head of this cult is said to be:

* Changeless and Self-Luminous.
* The Master, the Ruler of the Whole World.
* A peer of Krishna, Buddha, Vishnu . . . "He is Zeus to the Greeks; Jupiter to the Romans; . . . Jehovah to the old Judean; . . . Jesus to the Christian; Allah to the Mohammedans."
* The secret force behind world historical events.
* The key to the whole universal scheme of life.
* God-made flesh on earth.

It can plainly be seen, then, that the ECK Master is no ordinary human person like the rest of us. He is claimed to be God of all. As Twitchell summarizes, "this sounds very strange but it is true."

It does indeed sound strange, especially in light of the fact that the founder of Eckankar, the late Paul Twitchell, once stated that his was "a one man cult, with myself as founder, president, and disciple." That was, however, before this bizarre religion caught on with thousands of New Age seekers who have now made Eckankar an international movement of at least 75,000 active members. In addition, as many as a million persons have studied the works of Twitchell or participated in Eckankar in one way or another.

Soaring into Heavenly Realms Through Astral Travel

American Paul Twitchell began Eckankar around 1965, proclaiming he had been given the mantle of ECK Master by the former ECK Master, Rabazar Tarz, a Tibetan. Twitchell said that he was the 971st ECK Master in a long line of such human gods. According to Twitchell, it was Tarz who taught him the principles of soul (or astral) travel. Through soul travel, an individual is supposedly able to soar into heavenly realms and eventually achieve union with the great God *SUGMAD* (referred to as IT), whose secret name is *Hu*.

Eckankar's literature presents Twitchell's unique formulation and mosaic of Hindu, Druid, Buddhist, Scientology, and distinctly Western-flavored New Age doctrines. One primary teaching is that the soul must reincarnate millions of times unless a disciple masters the "science of soul travel" taught by Eckankar. In that case, a disciple (called a *chela*) can become a god right now, in this very incarnation.

Eckankar's soul travel technique involves the use of visualization, chants, and meditation, music and other means to attain an altered state of consciousness, a hypnotic state, in which the person is led to believe his spirit has left his body.

Eckankar's teachings certainly are at odds with those in the Bible, as a review of John 1:1; 3:16; Colossians 1:15;

Hebrews 1:3 and 9:27 will easily prove. The quotes below taken from Paul Twitchell's *Precepts of Eckankar* will enlighten the reader to some of the more "advanced" doctrines of Eckankar:

> The state of being god enlightened ... comes by the practice of ECKANKAR, the Ancient Science of Soul Travel ... ECK is the mainstream of life out of which all other doctrines flow. It is the basic teachings of religious beliefs, philosophy, and other doctrines in the fulfillment of life ... The revelation of ECK will be a shock when it strikes the individual. It upsets one's faith and cherished beliefs.

> Eckankar ... will lead ... the traveler on the path of Truth ... to the true teacher, the Sat Guru, who will lead him out of darkness into the heavenly light of the Highest Kingdom. Thus he will gain freedom and his knowledge will be the greatest of all wisdom, not gained from studies of books but from contacts with God (SUGMAD) Itself.

> Anyone can reach the Kingdom of Heaven by the trial and error method, but it will take millions of reincarnations to do so. No amount of prayer or any religious faith will bring about freedom from the uncertainties of life, not until one has the good fortune to meet and be accepted by the (ECK) Master.

> (Through soul travel) the chela (disciple) enters the regions of pure spirit and becomes a god.

> ECK says that through its own system of spiritual exercises, it can offer individual well-being (godhood) within this lifetime.

> The exercises, or techniques concerning Soul Travel are most important to the chela (disciple) on a path of

ECK. It is found that they have been also the foundation of those prophets, saints, and founders of religions such as Buddha, Krishna, Christ, Plato, Rabazar Tarz, and many others.

Complete surrender to the ECK Master is the only path to total freedom. This means that we must trust our higher interest in the hands of the Sat Guru. By giving the Master everything that one possesses, he in turn will give the chela (disciple) all he has. One can only gain by giving everything.

Complete Surrender Required

As the quote immediately above indicates, Eckankar requires its disciples to surrender completely to the ECK Master, the human being alive today who supposedly is chosen by the spirits to be leader of Eckankar and god of this world. It is interesting that upon founder Paul Twitchell's death, his wife, Gail, arranged for a man named Darwin Gross to become the successor and the new ECK Master. However, a number of higher initiates of Eckankar were not at all pleased and they began to foment trouble and cause strife within the organization. Finally, Gross was deposed in favor of a man named Darrel Klemp, who has his headquarters in Minneapolis, Minnesota. It would seem to be stretching things a bit to require that its members surrender everything they possess to the living ECK Master when the elite of Eckankar do not seem to be quite sure of who the real living ECK Master is today.

Eckankar is simply a New Age religion that promises much, much more than it could ever deliver. Not too long ago I received a letter from a lady in New Jersey, who became intensely involved in Eckankar. She wrote: "I have been searching for 'God' for the last 18 years. I was involved with everything from Tarot Cards, the I Ching, astrology and most other teachings that you mentioned in your books, *Dark*

Secrets of the New Age and *Mystery Mark of the New Age*. My latest involvement was with a group called Eckankar. I *thought* I had found all the answers to life." She then went on to explain that Eckankar simply did not fill her need for a walk with God. Frustrated, she finally realized that, "The only place I knew of to find out about walking with God was the Bible. I had never read the Bible so I bought one and have not stopped reading it since." She continued: "Needless to say, I have since become a born-again Christian and I am very content."

THE FARM

At *The Farm*, peyote, marijuana, and sacred (hallucinogenic) mushrooms have been used as "sacraments;" leather shoes are out because to kill animals would result in "negative karma;" and the mission of Jesus on planet earth is said to have been a failure. Led by Stephen Gaskin and composed of several hundred members, The Farm is a nature community made up of a group of ex-hippies who were flower children of the 60s. Their settlement is on roughly 1,700 acres about 65 miles south of Nashville. At one time The Farm was raided by police and Gaskin, its leader, spent a year in prison for drug violations.

The Farm began as a collective but today, evidently, the members are independent and self-supporting. It also began with group marriages and group sex, but again this did not work out, and the nuclear family and monogamous system are now employed. Former members of The Farm say that Stephen Gaskin has declared himself a messenger from God. He denies such concepts as sin and guilt, and Gaskin has said of Jesus' sacrifice on the cross, that "It wasn't exactly what he (Jesus) wanted to teach." Thus, Gaskin denies the atonement.

Residents of The Farm practice Zen meditation. Reportedly they are also into tantric (ritualistic) sex, and they hold in common with the Hindus such concepts as karma, reincarnation, and the use of mantras.

FELLOWSHIP OF ISIS

On St. Patrick's Day in 1966, Lawrence Durdin-Robertson had a revelation that God is a woman. He says that this greatly surprised him because, as an ordained priest in the Church of Ireland, he had been taught that God was male. Nevertheless, Lawrence began to study books on comparative religion and soon completely gave himself over to the goddess. His sister Olivia, a spiritualist and occultist, likewise fervently embraced the goddess, and finally his wife, Pamela (now deceased), also became a supporter. Together they decided to found the *Fellowship of Isis*, placing advertisements in occult and New Age magazines. The response overwhelmed them. They say that the fellowship now has almost 10,000 members in over 65 countries--including the Soviet Union--and the numbers are growing daily.

To join the Fellowship of Isis, persons do not have to renounce their allegiance to other religions. They simply pledge themselves to the goddess. This is a feminist and nature/earth religion. Olivia has explained that "many Catholics are also joining the fellowship; they are disgusted that statues of "Our Lady" are not given the honor and respect they deserve in the Catholic Church."

To further emphasize the strength of their convictions,

Lawrence and Olivia have turned their family castle into a literal temple to Isis. Especially on occultic and witchcraft holy days, such as Beltane, the May Day festival devoted to the goddess, special services are held at the temple. A crowd of local worshippers retreat to the basement area of the castle. There the worship area is set up. According to Lawrence and Olivia, the congregation recognizes the goddess by many names. She is "Hathor the Cow," "Sekmet the Lioness," "Lakshme," "Demeter," "Shiva," and "Kali." The Goddess is also recognized as the Blessed Virgin, Manian, the pony-goddess--a divinity made flesh in the Lady Godiva legend--Joan of Arc, Queen Elizabeth II, and "every other equestrian woman."

Inside the worship area of the temple are trays of offerings and there are icons, statues, wall hangings from India, Egyptian decorations, and African masks. There are also two enormous stuffed serpents, representing the Yin/Yang, made by the sister of Brigitte Bardot, the famed French actress who was universally known as a sex goddess. The centerpiece is the High Altar of Isis. "She started as the Virgin Mary," Olivia explains, "but we were sick of 'goody-goody statues' and did her naked. Then, to please those who might be offended, we clothed the statue in the Waters of Life."

The temple ceremony to the goddess includes such rituals as the ringing of a Tibetan gong, the drawing of water from a spring sacred to the Druids, prayers and meditations, and the worship of a live woman draped entirely in black and seated on a chair next to the statue of Isis.

According to Malise Ruthden, an English writer who wrote a story about this cult in England's *Harper's & Queen* magazine (September 1990), the woman representing the goddess Isis soon entered into a trance. Then she began to speak in solemn, Delphic tones proclaiming: "She is Isis of the ten thousand names: Obey her will, and the earth will become whole again." Meanwhile, numerous priestesses and priests appeared and performed rites.

Keep in mind that this is the account of a writer who was

invited by the Fellowship to observe one ceremony. Only the membership truly knows what goes on behind closed doors when outsiders are not around.

Later in this book we will examine in greater depth the subject of the modern-day revival of the worship of the goddess. The Bible, in Revelation 13, depicts the last days worldwide religion of the Adversary as one that will bring back the practices of the Mother Goddess, Mystery Babylon. Thus, the resurgence of interest in worshipping the goddess is significant. Those who have rejected traditional, biblical Christianity seem to be open to any pagan teaching that mocks and rejects the God of the Bible.

FINDHORN FOUNDATION

In her bestselling book *Hidden Dangers of the Rainbow*, an outstanding exposé of the New Age Movement, attorney Constance Cumby wrote: "The year 1962 was another landmark year, for that was when the Scottish community of Findhorn--the Vatican City of the New Age Movement--was founded." Cumby added, "The lifework of Peter and Eilene Caddy and their friend Dorothy McLean, the role of Findhorn was to help usher in 'The Plan' on earth. Their work was performed by following meticulously the Alice Bailey writings and 'guidance' Eilene was receiving from spirit beings and what she called the voice of 'God.'"

For a time, *Findhorn Community* (formally the Findhorn Foundation) was indeed the "Vatican City" of the New Age. In 1970, a new member showed up at Findhorn, David Spangler. As Cumby reports, Spangler received a royal welcome because Eilene Caddy had received guidance from her spirits that David had the "Christ Energies." Immediately Spangler was offered the job as co-director at Findhorn. As such he was the spiritual father, or guide, for the approximately 200 souls who resided there. Spangler promptly began to receive communications from a number of spirits, including demonic beings named Maitreya and Rakoczi, and a being who identified himself as "Limitless Love and Truth." Also, there was "John," whom many in the New Age believe to have been the real apostle John. These spirit beings, Spangler reports, convinced him that Lucifer is "an agent of God's love." Indeed, Spangler began to write books dictated to him by these spirits in which he declared:

> Christ is the same force as Lucifer... Lucifer prepares man for the experience of Christhood... Lucifer works within each of us to bring us to wholeness as we move into the New Age.

In such books as *Reflections on the Christ*, published by Findhorn, Spangler suggested that a New Age Christ was coming other than Jesus. He also suggested that those who do not have the superior spiritual capacity required of the

The Findhorn Community in Scotland.

New Age might have to be sent to a special dimension where they will be kept for 1,000 years while the New Age kingdom is being built on earth.

The members of Findhorn believe strongly that their leadership is given divine guidance by the spirits. For example, there are reports that the community was ecstatic when one of Findhorn's leaders related to residents that while walking in the garden of Findhorn, a horned and hairy creature who identified himself as Pan came to him and conversed on certain important subjects. Word soon got out that gnomes and other nature spirits were actively helping to create miracles in the fields at Findhorn. It was said that the vegetables and crops were unusually bountiful and that specimens were huge and oversized because of the spiritual energies of these nature spirits.

In 1973, David Spangler left Findhorn along with some supporters to found a New Age group in America called the Lorian Foundation. Today he is associated with the Chinook Center and is also closely allied with St. John the Divine Cathedral, an Episcopal Church in New York City. Peter Caddy also left the community and handed the reigns over to successors.

Today the glory of the Findhorn Community is only a faded memory to many. But its horrible works continue in that its influence has been felt by so many of the elite in the New Age. Apparently, many in the New Age were especially influenced by David Spangler's works. In his *Reflections on the Christ*, he stated: "Lucifer comes to give us the final Luciferic initiation ... It is an invitation into the New Age."

Interestingly, Spangler denies that Lucifer is the same being as Satan. Today the same lie, that Lucifer is the god of light and is not at all like the Satan described in the Bible, is a common belief among the New Age hierarchy.

THE FORUM (EST)

How much would you pay to sit in an audience while a leader on the stage degrades and heaps abuse on you and other participants? What would it be worth for you to be one of scores of people who begin to "urinate, defecate, convulse, sob, and vomit" during the training sessions? Well, if during the 70s and 80s you attended a session of *est* (Erhard Seminars Training) this is exactly what you might have experienced. Amazingly, some 500,000 people went through the est experience. In doing so they received something that its founder, Werner Erhard, called IT; they got "IT."

Evidently, though many today still rave about getting "IT," some were not so thrilled. Erhard, formerly an encyclopedia sales representative whose real name is Jack Rosenberg, began to be the subject of a number of lawsuits filed by people who believed they were psychologically damaged by est. Consequently, Erhard has now come out with a more toned-down version of est, which he calls *The Forum*. It is offered today through his company, Transformational Technologies, Inc.

Werner Erhard's The Forum can be had for about $525. That gets you four 16-hour sessions in which you learn to transform your consciousness and, The Forum promises, "make it happen." In its new incarnation, The Forum is looking for top dollar executives and managers and is definitely going after the business marketplace. "Excellence" is what it promises its participants. In reality what those who attend The Forum get is a bunch of hashed over, hippie-like, Hinduistic, Scientology-oriented, Zen Buddhist self-help philosophy that probably leaves them little better off, if not worse, than when they came in the front door.

It was in 1971 that Werner Erhard first offered his creation known as "est" to a very willing public. It was designed to "restructure a person's worldview, to bring it into line" with New Age feelings and experiences. By the third day of the est program, each new member was expected to get "IT." Nobody ever explained what "IT" was, although more than a few Christians suggested that "IT" might be demon spirits. Regardless, the 500,000 graduates of est, and now the thousands of New Agers and others who have completed The Forum, represent a significant group who have fanned out throughout our society to lead a number of other New Age groups, organizations, cults, and churches. Thus Werner Erhard and his seminars have been a tremendously effective influence in promoting New Age goals.

Our Space Agency Pays for New Age Training

So successful is Werner Erhard that the National Aeronautics and Space Administration (NASA) actually paid The Forum over $40,000 in 1988 for the opportunity to have Erhard personally come to NASA headquarters and teach high management officials his program. Although we would not place the blame on Erhard, one wonders what exactly it was that these employees got for the taxpayers money that was expended. We now see failure after failure of the space shuttle, the space telescope, and other NASA ventures.

Erhard has also been welcomed into the Soviet Union where his seminars are finding increasing favor among those Soviet-style bureaucrats who are into the "New Thinking" of President Mikhail Gorbachev.

While his group may not technically be a "cult" and while it does not presume to have religious aspirations, it is a fact that Erhard has denied the unique deity of Christ, as do all non-Christian cult leaders. While Erhard might say that Jesus is "god," he means it in the same sense in which each of us is god of our own realities. The deity of Christ for The Forum is simply the deity of every human being, and the gospel according to Erhard is a philosophically distilled version of Eastern Mysticism and psychology packaged in a high pressure group situation. The Forum teaches that we all create our own reality, and that no one's reality is objectively right or wrong. Instead, each person is responsible only to himself or herself. The individual is taught that he or she has limitless potential. The training in The Forum, through a form of marathon shock therapy, is intended to help the person to develop this unlimited potential.

Erhard and Scripture

Many passages in the Bible make a shambles of Erhard's philosophy. In Romans 5, Paul states that we are justified by faith and that we have peace with God only through Jesus Christ. Colossians 1:22-23 encourages us to continue in the faith. The Bible clearly tells us that we are not gods, nor can man be perfect; yet Erhard says that we are perfect now and that certainly there is no God outside of us that is more perfect. "Self is all there is--I mean that is all there is."

The fact is that any person who truly believes in Christ and follows the Bible's guidelines for daily living receives a peace within that surpasses all understanding. What a contrast with the psychiatric disturbances associated with est. According to one report in the *American Journal of Psychiatry* (March 1977), the researchers noted that a number of patients "developed psychotic symptoms including grandiosity, paranoia, uncontrollable mood swings, and delusions" following their participation in Erhard's est seminars.

The Forum now operates a number of centers or "work spaces" in the United States and abroad--in Bombay, Tel Aviv, London, Melbourne, Montreal, Munich, Stockholm, Sydney, Toronto, and Vancouver. As I mentioned, the program is also now offered in the Soviet Union. In addition, a number of other organizations have been founded by est graduates or by individuals who have in one way or another been influenced by Werner Erhard. Such groups include the Center for Attitudinal Healing. Groups spun off from est and The Forum do not necessarily use the same techniques and practices.

FOUNDATION FAITH OF GOD

The *Foundation Faith of God* was established in 1980. It appears to be a type of warped group with a combination of New Age and conservative Bible, apocalyptic teachings. For example, the members seem to have a belief in the deity of Jesus and at least some conception of the Second Coming, but at the same time they embrace doctrines such as reincarnation. The clergy of this group also conduct "angel listenings." They have convinced their members that they receive messages directly from angels and are able to write down the instructions received to help the person in his or her daily life. As of a few years ago, this group had centers and ministries operating in Las Vegas, New York, New Orleans, Atlanta, Phoenix, Dallas, Houston, Denver and Toronto and Ottawa in Canada.

The Foundation Faith of God was previously called the *Foundation Faith of the Millennium* and before that was founded as the *Process Church of the Final Judgment*. Under this earlier name, members were called *Processians* because they believed in a process in which the earth is headed toward an incredibly chaotic time and blood is bound to flow. The scary thing is that there were many allegations that mass-murderer Charles Manson was connected to the Processians. In fact, mention was made of them at Manson's trial, and it is reported that two church representatives visited Manson in his jail cell.

As Processians, members wore black robes with silver crosses entwined with a red serpent. They taught that man must love his enemies, *including Satan*. Indeed, the Processians were convinced that in the last days, Christ and Satan will be reconciled. Christ will come to judge the world while Satan will execute judgment. It was therefore believed that man should worship both Christ and Satan. In some Processian churches, the Satanic Bible was displayed along with the Holy Bible and readings were made out of each.

Today, the original founder of this group, Englishman Robert DeGrimston, has long since departed and reports indicate that the group seems to have toned down or eliminated entirely its Luciferian elements. There have been some claims that this group is moving toward a more traditional form of Christianity. Still, I would certainly caution anyone that might be tempted to become involved with this group to first check out its atrocious history and carefully consider also its current practices and teachings in light of its potential involvement in New Age occultism.

FOUNDATION FOR SHAMANIC STUDIES

The term *Shamanism* is derived through primitive Russia from a Siberian native language and refers to religious specialists--we used to call them "witch doctors"--who practice spiritism. The practice of shamanic sorcery was common to Native American Indians and Eskimos as well as to the witch doctors in the tribes of Asia, Africa, and Australia. Shamans practice in the context of their belief in *animism*. They believe that spirits, gods, devils, and other entities dwell in other realms to and from which the experienced and initiated shaman can travel. The shaman is thought by his people to be a man of power, able to conjure up and control the spirits. He is thought to be able to cast evil devils out of people to cure them of illnesses. The shaman usually employs a drum and puts on quite a show which often includes extracting some kind of a mysterious substance of the sick person's body, bringing forth strange spirit voices, etc. The shaman often uses a mask or may dress himself in an animal skin or with a headdress of horns to impress his audience and, theoretically, scare off or subjugate the spirits.

The *Foundation for Shamanic Studies* is headed by Michael Harner, the author of a bestselling book on the subject of shamanism, *The Way of the Shaman: A Guide to Power and Healing.* The foundation sees its goals as healing the earth, preserving shamanic knowledge among native peoples, and promoting Soviet/American shamanism. In the latter area, Harner states that his group is working in tandem with Soviet anthropologists and scientists to utilize shamanic counseling techniques to deal with alcohol and mental illness. Another area of work for the foundation is to study death and dying and discover how that relates to what is called the shamanic spirit journey.

The Foundation for Shamanic Studies has promoted the work of Joseph Campbell who wrote *The Way of the Animal Powers.* If you watched Bill Moyer's PBS series on mythologies, you may recall his guest, Joseph Campbell, a prominent New Ager who is a supposed "expert" on the mythologies. Campbell, now deceased, was a promoter of shamanism and primitive pagan sorcery of all kinds.

Headquartered in Connecticut, the Foundation for Shamanic Studies is tied in with such groups as the Esalen Institute and others. Its courses are offered in seminars and workshops across the nation and its faculty includes some impressive names. The group also has training sessions and centers in Europe, Australia, and New Zealand.

FREE DAIST COMMUNION (DA FREE JOHN)

Want to sit at the feet of a god-man, a man who has been praised and lauded as "greater than Jesus Christ or any other hero who has ever lived?" Well, according to the followers of the "Heart-Master, Da Free John," you and I have that glorious opportunity. Some of the top people in the New Age claim that Da Free John, leader of the *Free Daist Communion*, is one of the greatest avatars, or messiahs, who has ever walked the earth. Noted New Age author Ken Wilber (*Up From Eden*), for example, has acknowledged Heart-Master Da Free John's teachings as "unsurpassed by any other spiritual Hero, of any period, of any place, of any time, of any persuasion." Presumably this includes Jesus. Wilber also refers to Heart-Master Da Free John's work, *The Dawn Horse Testament*, as "The most ecstatic, profound, most complete, most radical, and most comprehensive *single spiritual text* ever penned." This presumably includes the Bible.

Other New Age authorities agree that Heart-Master Da Free John's teachings in his *The Dawn Horse Testament* are fantastically profound. Barbara Marx Hubbard of the World Future Society has remarked, "The teachings of Da Free John, embodied in an extraordinary collection of writings, provide an exquisite manual for transformation . . . I feel at the most profound depth of my being that his work will be crucial to an evolution toward full humanist society."

Meanwhile, Herbert Long, Th. D., of the Harvard Divinity School, has called Da Free John and his book, "A gift of unparalleled importance." According to Long, "Da Free John's work very likely marks the beginning of a new tradition, a new culture, a new vision of what it means to be a human being transformed." Donald Evans, Professor of Philosophy at the University of Toronto has called Da Free John, "the most significant contemporary writer concerning

the four religions ... More profound than Paul Tillich ...
and Martin Buber."

Who is this Heart-Master Da Free John that so many
rave about? Well, actually his real name is Franklin Jones,
or at least that is what his mother and father called him when
he was born on November 3, 1939. After he became involved
in Hinduism, Franklin changed his name to Da Free John in
1979 and was at one time called Bubba Free John. Here is a
man who loves to change names. Even his organizations
seem to change names frequently. First, his group was called
the Dawn Horse Fellowship; later it was called the Free
Primitive Church of Divine Communion. Now we have the
Free Daist Communion. In addition, Da Free John is in
charge of a number of other groups, all which evidently come
under the purview of the Free Daist Communion. These
include the Free Community Order and the Laughing Man
Institute.

Surrendering to Da Free John: Pathway to Divinity

Da Free John is not shy about bragging to be "another
Moses, Krishna, Jesus, or Buddha." He has a very effective
and direct way to gain support from followers. He simply has
told them that he is "God" and they will have to worship him
as such. The claim is that those who give in to Da Free John,
"God," are "loved to the point of Ecstasy and Wisdom."
Disciples are also on the path to "God-realization." In their
literature, the Free Daist Communion tells inquirers, "The
way of the heart, or Free Daism, requires a serious intention
of every practitioner to transcend all superficial and ego-
consoling orientations to life, and God, and truth. The way
of the heart ... is a whole, radically ego-transcending Way
of life, *to be lived in exquisite devotional surrender to Hridaya-
Samartha-Sat-Guru Da Love-Ananda*." The latter name,
Hridaya, etc., is an elongated rendition of the name Da Free

John; it is a phrase composed of words of great veneration and respect for this god-man on earth.

So we see that the pathway to God, according to Da Free John, is "explicit devotional surrender" to him personally. This is supposedly done by abiding in his presence and sacrificing your own ego and consciousness to him. In this way, "all negative karma is dissolved instantaneously." Of course, then you will have to begin giving financially to Da Free John and his work.

Critics of the Heart-Master claim that he lives a very sumptuous lifestyle. Indeed, he has purchased a small island in the South Pacific, one of the Fiji Islands. There, on this tiny, tropical "paradise," Da Free John has built a retreat center called The Hermitage. Only his closest followers live there with him; others may come only for brief meditation retreats.

Da Free John offers his disciples the gift of love and laughter. Just gazing upon a pot-bellied Da Free John sitting upon a pillow clothed only in a pair of brief tights with beads around his neck, his head shaven, pictured in a lotus pose, is enough to make one roar with laughter. So, there may be something to this particular aspect of his teachings. Otherwise, all you'll find in studying what is called the "crazy wisdom" of the Heart-Master is pure, doctrinal Hinduism.

Regardless of his seemingly outrageous demand that his disciples worship him totally and unequivocally and his bold assertion that he is God on earth, Da Free John has built a significant following around the world. His books, put out by the Dawn Horse imprint, are big sellers and his organization has regional centers in Holland, Australia, New Zealand, Canada, England, Hawaii, and, in the continental United States, in Boston; Clear Lake, California; Santa Monica, California; San Raphael, California; Seattle, Washington; and Washington, D.C.

FREEMASONRY

Freemasonry claims to be Christian, but it is not. Freemasonry says that it is not a religion, but it is. Freemasonry denies being Luciferian, but it is. In essence, these are the three key things that a person needs to know when examining the status of *Freemasonry*, or more simply, the *Masonic Lodge*.

There are a number of misunderstandings about Freemasonry. The reason why is simple: Freemasonry hides its activities and its true beliefs. The late Albert Pike, a 33rd degree Mason who once was the head of all of the Masonic organizations, in his "bible" of Freemasonry, *Morals and Dogma*, explained that:

> Masonry, like all the religions, all the mysteries... *conceals its secrets* from all except the adepts and

sages or the elect, and uses false explanations and mis-
interpretations of its symbols to mislead those who
deserve only to be misled, to conceal the Truth, which
it calls Light, from them, and to draw them away from
it.

Freemasonry: Unchristian, Unholy

There are a multitude of Masonic organizations. Probably
the two best known in America are the *York Rite* and the
Scottish Rite. But whatever group, all share in common the
same basic doctrines, and these doctrines are insidiously
unchristian and unholy. To properly understand these facts,
it is necessary for us to simply quote some of the top Masonic
authorities and discover what they themselves, the Masons,
have to say about their secretive cult.

First, we read the words of Henry Clausen, 33rd degree,
until recently the Sovereign Grand Master of Freemasonry.
In his book, *Emergence of the Mystical*, Clausen confirmed
the New Age underpinnings of Freemasonry when he wrote:

Today we are at the threshold of a new era. All signs
point to this fact ... We look toward a transformation
into a New Age using, however, the insight and
wisdom of the ancient mystics ... and the mysticism
of Eastern religions."

Thus, we have the leader of all Freemasons in the United
States of America admitting to the Masonic/New Age
connection and affirming the Freemasonry belief in the
"mysticism of Eastern religions."

Next, we turn to the book *The Spirit of Masonry*, by
Foster Bailey of the Lucis Trust. Bailey is also a high-ranking
Mason. His book was recently highly touted in the "book
review" section of the *Scottish Rite Journal* (August 1990
issue, pages 24 and 58). Bailey, an occultist, explains what
the Masons believe about the holy trinity:

"The Temple and the Heavens is therefore presided over by the Triune Deity . . . the Three Persons of the Divine Trinity. This Trinity of Persons . . . are well-known in all the world religions . . . known under various names, of which the most familiar to us are Sheva, Vishnu, and Brahma . . . In Masonry, this same Triplicity is known as the Most High, the Grand Geometrician, and the Great Architect of the Universe."

These three deities are actually the same trinitarian gods as found among India's Hindus. In the Masonic theology, the Christian trinity is simply the same trinity but with different names for the three deities.

In the book *A Bridge to Light*, published by Scottish Rite Masonry, author Rex Hutchens, 32nd degree, gives a summary of the degrees of Masonry and briefly explains what goes on during the initiation process for each. On page 312 of *A Bridge to Light*, he tells us about the ritual for the 32nd degree: "We find in the ritual a recitation of the beliefs of the Hindus of India." Then, on page 316, it is revealed to the 32nd degree candidate that the "Supreme Deity" is composed of a trinity of three gods: "Brahma, Vishnu, and Sheva," which represent, "the cyclical concepts of creation, preservation, and destruction."

In other words, *A Bridge to Light*, published by Freemasonry itself, affirms the book *The Spirit of Masonry* by the Lucis Trust's Foster Bailey. Therefore we can know for a fact that *the Hindu religion and Freemasonry are, for all practical purposes, one and the same religion*. However, Freemasonry also integrates a number of other false teachings and doctrines from the ancient mystical religions into its ceremonies, its rituals, and theology.

Is Freemasonry "Christian," then? Obviously not. Indeed, Albert Mackey, a prominent Mason, in his *Encyclopedia of Freemasonry*, on page 162, states flatly: "Freemasonry is not Christianity." Moreover, on page 184 of the *Masonic Handbook* we read this astonishing statement: "Whether you swear or take God's name in vain does not matter so much. Of course, the name of the Lord Jesus Christ doesn't amount to much." What a reversal from the Gospel of John 12:48, wherein we are told: "He that rejecteth and receiveth not My Words, have one that judgeth him, the Word that I have spoken, the same shall judge him in the last days." These are the words of Jesus. In Philippians 2:9-11 we read: "...that every tongue should confess that Jesus Christ is Lord to the glory of God, the Father." Moreover, one of the Ten Commandments is that we should not take the *name* of the Lord our God in vain.

Is Freemasonry a Religion?

Masonry is in fact a religion that worships strange gods and totally rejects Jesus Christ. The name of Jesus is even prohibited in the formal ceremonies of the lodges. Albert Mackey, in the *Encyclopedia of Freemasonry*, writes: "Masonry...is indeed a religious institution." Henry Wilson Coil, in *Coil's Masonic Encyclopedia*, on page 512 writes:

> Some attempt to avoid the issue by saying that Freemasonry is not a religion, but is "religious"...It would be insensible to say that man had no intellect but was intellectual or that he had no honor but was honorable. The oft-repeated aphorism: "Freemasonry is not a religion...but is religion's handmaid," has been challenged as meaningless, which it seems to be.

Coil then goes on to ask: "Does Freemasonry continually teach and insist upon a creed, tenet, and dogma? Does it have meetings characterized by practices of rites and ceremonies...?" His answer is most emphatically, *"Yes!"*

Albert Pike, whose book, *Morals and Dogma*, is recommended to all Masons as their guide to daily living (see the Masonic magazine, *New Age*, January 1989, article by C.

Fred Kleinknecht, 33rd degree, Grand Sovereign Comman-
der of Freemasonry, confirms that Masonry is a religion--
indeed, *the* one true world religion around which all can
assemble. In this book so revered by Freemasons everywhere, Pike writes:

> Masonry, around whose altars the Christian, the
> Hebrew, the Moslem, the Brahman, the followers of
> Confucius and Zoroaster, can assemble as brethren
> and unite in prayer to the one God . . . must needs
> leave to its initiate to look for the foundations of his
> faith and hope for the written scriptures of his own
> religion.

In other words, Pike believes that it does not matter to
which religion a person ascribes. He may be a Christian, a
Hebrew, a Moslem, or even a follower of Confucius or the
Persian god, Zoroaster. Is this in accordance with
Christianity? Does it matter which God man serves?

In fact, Pike himself goes on to show in his book the
"God" whom he himself clearly prefers and recommends to
all Masons. According to Pike, "Everything good in nature
comes from *Osiris* (the Egyptian Father God)--order,
harmony, and the favorable temperature of the seasons and
celestial periods."

Manly P. Hall, a 33rd degree Mason, on page 48 of his
Lost Keys of Freemasonry, frankly admits the *real* god of
Masonry:

> When a Mason learns that the Key . . . is the proper
> application of the dynamo of living power . . . the
> seething energies of *Lucifer* are in his hands and
> before he may step onward and upward, he must
> prove his ability to properly apply this energy.

Lucifer is indeed the real god of Masonry. Other "gods"
are mere fronts and covers. Moreover, not only does the
Mason acknowledge the Hindu trinity of gods and Osiris, the

Egyptian Father God, but during the ceremonies for the ritual of the Royal Arch degree, the candidate is asked, "Brother Inspector, what are you?" And he replies, "I AM THAT I AM." This, of course, is blasphemy in that God alone is the Great "I AM." Indeed, we see in the *Old Testament* that when Moses asked the Lord to identify His name, God proclaimed: "I AM THAT I AM." In effect, the candidate for the Royal Arch degree of Freemasonry declares himself to be God.

To determine how Masonry and Christianity relate, all a person needs to do is go directly to the *Encyclopedia of Freemasonry*. This book contains almost 1,000 pages, with articles on every conceivable subject in any way related to Freemasonry. Yet, it does not contain even the slightest of traces of information on or mention of Jesus Christ, the only Son of God. What are we to say about a religious system which comes complete with textbooks, encyclopedias, secretive handshakes, oaths, and rituals, and yet excludes the name of the only true God of the universe?

Our Bible tells us that if we will not confess the Lord Jesus Christ here on earth, He will not confess us to the Father in Heaven. I have great sympathy, then, for Freemasons, for in excluding Jesus Christ from their religious rituals and teachings, they are automatically excluding themselves from the Book of Life of the Lamb slain from the foundation of the world. Can a Mason be a Christian? Yes, initially a man could possibly be both a Mason and a Christian. But a true Christian will not stay with Freemasonry because oil and water do not mix; neither can Lucifer, the god of Masonry, and Jesus co-exist in the heart of a man or a woman.

If you would like to know more about Freemasonry, write for information about the book and audiotape entitled *Hidden Secrets of Masonry,* offered by Living Truth Publishers (8103 Shiloh Court, Austin, Texas 78745).

FRIENDS OF CREATION SPIRITUALITY (MATTHEW FOX)

A major supporter and promoter of witchcraft and earth religion is the Catholic priest, Matthew Fox, whose learning institution, *Holy Names College*, in San Jose, California and his *Center for Creation-Centered Spirituality* have been able to convince hundreds of nuns and priests to join the earth movement. Fox, a priest of the Dominican Order, has even invited one of the top witches in the world, Miriam Starhawk, to sit on the faculty of Holy Names College. Fox believes that the traditional belief in Jesus is a relic of the past--of the outmoded astrological Piscean Age. Fox teaches *panentheism*, the theology that God is in all things and that all things are in God. Another affiliated group, *Friends of Creation Spirituality*, Oakland, California, emphasizes mysticism, the environment, and the "ancient wisdom."

GODDESS, WITCHCRAFT, AND PAGAN SECTS

One of the fastest growing religious movements in the world today is *Witchcraft*, also known as the *Earth Religion*, and closely related to *Paganism* and *Goddess* worship. My estimate is that there are today in the United States some two million persons practicing a variety of forms of witchcraft and earth religion. In addition, millions more involved in promoting environmentalism often unwittingly embrace witchcraft doctrines and practices. Witches do not always identify themselves as witches. Some prefer to call themselves naturists, pagans, neo-pagans, druids, wiccans, mediums, or shamans. Increasingly, witches identify themselves as believers in the goddess or as those who practice "the Craft." The feminist movement has been one of the principal factors in the rise of witchcraft and earth religion groups and sects.

The Bible has a lot to say about Witchcraft, the Goddess, and the Earth Religion. All forms of these practices are denounced in such biblical passages as Deut. 18:10-11; Leviticus 19:26, 32; and Galatians 5:20. You may recall the Old Testament saga of the Witch of Endor (I Samuel 28). When King Saul sought out the Witch of Endor so that he could communicate with the dead prophet Samuel, punishment from God for this abomination was swift and sure. The very next day, the king fell on his sword and was killed in battle.

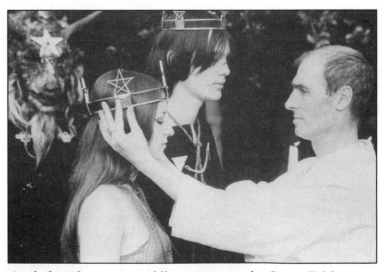

A witchcraft pagan wedding ceremony in Great Britian.

Goddess and earth worship is basically sorcery and primeval occultism. Yet these perversions are increasingly finding popular support. Witchcraft has enjoyed a great revival in Great Britain due to the works of Gerald Gardner, a male witch who died in 1964. His book, *Witchcraft Today*, caused thousands to turn to witchcraft. In America, Dr. Raymond Buckland published his *Complete Book of Witchcraft* which is used as a guide by many sects. For example, in a recent letter to an inquirer, a representative of the witchcraft group Church of the Crescent Moon commented: "Ray Buckland's *Complete Book of Witchcraft* is the best book that I have seen on basic witchcraft and I am sure that you will find everything that you need within its covers to guide you on the right path."

The signs of witchcraft and earth magic seem to be almost everywhere today. For example, computer fans have created a computer bulletin board network called *MagicNet*. Tap into MagicNet and the computer enthusiast will find an astonishing array of rituals, wiccan events, information on spells, and counter-intelligence against the Christian fundamentalists so despised by witches. And there is more evidence of witchcraft and goddess worship. In the *St. Louis-Dispatch* newspaper of May 30, 1990, was a story about "Mother Earth" appearing at a huge celebration at the Missouri Botanical Garden. Evidently a local goddess worship group dressed one of their members up in a Mother Earth outfit at a community celebration, complete with goddess gospel singers, dancers, and exhibits on global environmental problems. The international celebration was sponsored by the United Nations and funded in part by Monsanto Chemical Corporation.

Black Magic Religion

The basic Witchcraft/Earth Religion doctrine is that we are all part of the earth, that God *is* nature. Witches protest that they do not practice evil, or black magic; they say that theirs is white magic which harms no one. Indeed, the principal witchcraft motto is "Harm no one." However, this is counterbalanced by another credo which states, "Do as thou wilt."

Witches believe, as do other New Agers, in the Hinduistic concepts of reincarnation and karma. They are also prone to believe in forest, nature, and tree spirits, in fairies, gnomes and other little creatures, and in spirit beings. They especially celebrate the passing of the seasons and the coming of the new moon. Some ceremonies are held with members *skyclad*, or nude. This practice is believed to increase the release of energy forces. Occultic symbols are emphasized, especially the Satanic pentagram and the circle. Candles and incense are used in ceremonies as well as a ritualistic dagger called an *athame*. The symbolic elements of earth, fire, air, and water are embedded in rituals.

Witches do indeed cast spells and place hexes on supposed victims, just as we have seen in the movies. They also believe in healing by the laying on of hands. Some practice "astral sex" with spirit beings from beyond (incubus or succubus).

The Devil is a Christian Invention Say Witches

Almost all witchcraft, goddess, and earth/nature worshippers vehemently deny a belief in the devil. They say that Satan, or the devil, is a Christian invention. Yet many conjure up, venerate, and worship the *horned god Pan*, an ancient mythological character who is in reality the devil in another form. There have been many claims that witches sacrifice animals and even human beings to the devil. However, this practice is no doubt quite rare and uncommon, being done only by those witches and pagans into hard-core satanic ritual and magic.

Many are drawn into witchcraft and goddess worship today because they have rejected the (male) God of the Bible. Others have been conned into believing that the earth is a sacred being, a Goddess (the "Gaia Thesis") which must be protected. Many honestly feel that what they are doing is ethical and responsible. Yet, we recently received one letter from the leader of a major witchcraft group who warned that anyone contemplating becoming a witch should be very careful because "There is sexism in modern witchcraft, also there is racism in the Craft, and internal witch hunting by witches and pagans against other, real witches . . . And there is widespread abuse of power."

This is an admonition that certainly should be heeded. It should also be understood that even though those in the witchcraft and goddess sects deny that they worship Satan, nevertheless, famed British satanist Aleister Crowley was a known worshipper of Nuit, the Mother Goddess. So, there is among some witchcraft and earth religious groups a close connection with satanism and other extreme forms of occultism.

A Multitude of Groups and Covens

There are so many new witchcraft and goddess groups springing up that it is impossible in this limited space to list and describe them all, but I will mention a few. First, there is *Circle*, also known as *Circle Sanctuary*. Operating out of Mt. Horeb, Wisconsin, Circle Sanctuary publishes an annual *Circle Guide to Pagan Groups* which lists the "names, addresses, and descriptions of covens, groves, temples, churches, study circles, and other types of groups reflecting a variety of pagan/nature spirituality paths, including: Wiccan ways, Shamanism, Egyptian Magic, Scandinavian Folk Religion, Feminist Spirituality, Druidism, Neo-paganism, Native American and other native people spirituality." Circle Sanctuary was founded by one of the world's best known witches, Selena Fox, in 1974.

Another Wiccan (witchcraft) group is the *Seminary of Wicca*, also known as *Our Lady of Enchantment*. Founded by Lady Sabrina, an initiated high priestess in both Celtic wicca and Egyptian ceremonial magic, and Lord Phoenix, high priest, the Seminary is a school dedicated to teaching the ancient mystery religion of Wicca along with other occult philosophies. It offers a wide variety of regular classes and special programs, including home study courses.

The *New Wiccan Church* is a group out of California which publishes a newsletter, *The International Red Garters*. The New Wiccan Church says that its branches are "secret religious organizations dedicated to promulgating English Traditional Wicca in its various traditions, rites, forms, and orders." Among its international officers is Queen Haragno.

Pagans for Peace is a pagan/wiccan/goddess organization which has as its goal the promotion of world peace through development of the sacred energies of the earth. Yet another group promoting the earth religion is the *Children of the Green Earth*. The latter group recently received the One World Award from Baha'i for its work in planting trees. The *Rowan Tree Church* of Minneapolis, Minnesota, is a group that has also dedicated itself to the earth. Claiming to be "Neo-Alexandrian," it teaches its members how to become priests and priestesses and conducts Full Moon and Sabbat Rituals. *The Church of All Worlds*, founded at Westminister College in 1962, became well-known for publishing the journal, *The Green Egg*. It says it is "an organization of individuals who regard the earth and life on it as sacred." Like most witchcraft and goddess and nature groups, the Church of All Worlds emphasizes the evolution and divinity of man and proclaims a Golden Age soon to come when people everywhere will worship the Earth Religion.

Other groups include the *University of the Trees*, Boulder Creek, California; *Women's Alliance*, Oakland, California; the *Center for Community Resources*, Metford, Massachusetts; the *Seax-Wicca Seminary*, Charlottesville, Virginia; the *Covenant of the Goddess*, Berkeley, California; the *Georgian Church*; the *Church of the Eternal Source*; and the *Reform Druids*. In addition, there are tens of thousands of witches and goddess worshippers who practice their rituals independently of any organized group.

HARE KRISHNA
(INTERNATIONAL SOCIETY OF
KRISHNA CONSCIOUSNESS)

The New Age cult group with perhaps the worst reputation is undoubtedly *Hare Krishna*, officially the International Society of Krishna Consciousness. Actions of Hare Krishna devotees in crowded airport terminals and on street corners in attempting to con the unwitting out of their money has brought the Hare Krishnas much criticism--and justifiably so. Hare Krishna disciples have been trained to use what they call "transcendental trickery" to obtain donations through public soliciting. On one occasion, during the Christmas season, Hare Krishnas were arrested for soliciting without a permit while dressed in Santa Claus suits. As a Hindu sect, the Hare Krishnas do not celebrate Christmas and thus it was quite obvious that this was merely an attempt to deceive the public.

Recently, as colleges opened across America, Hare Krishnas scattered out on the various campuses collecting money and recruiting new converts. With their saffron robes and their shaven heads, their chanting and their crude musical instruments, they are easy to spot and avoid. Consequently, their un-American dress is now giving way to more conventional clothing; yet they remain anathema to many onlookers, being viewed as arrogant, aggressive beggars bent on deceiving the naive out of their money and perhaps their very souls.

It would be easy for us to dismiss the Hare Krishnas as a bunch of wierd, hippie-like dropouts. But the fact is that the average Hare Krishna is a fair representative of overall society. Studies have shown that some 70 percent of those in this cult formerly attended a Christian church. Disciples of Hare Krishna are no doubt deeply sincere and they genuinely believe in absolute, unswerving devotion to their Hindu guru on planet earth as well as to the Lord Krishna, the supreme Hindu deity whom they worship.

Hinduism and Hare Krishna

Hare Krishnas do not attempt to hide the fact that their religious philosophy is based on the *Bhagavad Gita*, a set of Hindu scriptures--actually a lengthy Hindu poem--written some 2000 years ago (although the Hare Krishnas and Hindus claim that its origins lie some 5000 years ago). It is significant that the *Bhagavad Gita* depicts indifference to those who are poor and suffering. It teaches unconditional surrender of one's will to a human master while neglecting the needs of the living. It is because of such scriptures as the *Bhagavad Gita* that India has toiled and labored for centuries under its despicable caste system.

Life for a Hare Krishna, whether the individual is single or a member of a family, can be very harsh and regimented. The initiates rise at 3:00 a.m. for a cold shower and begin shortly thereafter to worship the temple idols who represent various Hindu deities. These deities are even dressed and "fed." Then the devoteés are led in chants while counting their beads. Next they are off to the streets to solicit money and to preach of the love of their lord Krishna.

The life of the Krishna devoteés, then, is mostly work and praise. In the evening there is more chanting and more worship of the gods. Drugs, alcohol, coffee, and certainly meat--since Hindus abhor meat and are vegetarians--are all prohibited to the Krishna devoteé. Outside world contact is discouraged. A person is expected to depend solely on their local Hare Krishna temple for sustenance and shelter. Children are taken from parents and placed in special training schools. There they learn the principles of fundamental Hinduism.

To signify their unswerving devotion to their master, the Hare Krishna disciples are given a new Sanscrit name and a secret *mantra*, which consists of words or phrases for chanting. Women leave their hair in much a natural condition, while men shave their heads.

Beginnings and Organization

The Hare Krishna Hindu cult was begun by Swami Prabhupada, who came to America in 1966. First he drew only a small group of counter-culture hippies to his cause, but today, the Hare Krishna is a worldwide organization with 20 commissioners to administer various regional and geographical units.

Modern-day disciples of Prabhupada are formed into a world-wide confederation of ashrams, schools, temples, and communities. When Prabhupada passed away in 1977 in India, he was succeeded in America by another guru who presides over some 48 centers and foreign communities within the continental United States. Hare Krishna also has centers in Canada, Great Britain, Northern Ireland, Australia, Africa, Asia, Mexico, Brazil, Peru, Panama, Costa Rica, and literally in most countries around the world.

It is claimed by the cult that there are some three million members, one million of whom reside in the U.S.A. I have reason to believe that this is a vastly inflated figure and that the real number, in the United States at least, is no more than 100,000 at best. Interestingly, however, among apostate theologians the Hare Krishnas are today finding unexpected support. For example, at Loyola Marymount University in Los Angeles in 1990, 30 scholars, theologians, and clergy met with Mukunda Goswami, the Hare Krishna minister of public affairs. Goswami summarized the basic philosophy of the Hindu group and commented that the assistance of the theologians was needed to help fight persecution against the disciples of Hare Krishna. According to news accounts, his listeners were duly impressed.

"God is Darkness, Also"

One vehicle that the Hare Krishna movement uses to gain influence is its slick and colorful magazine *Back to Godhead*. In a recent issue (volume 23, number 5) one finds the usual Hindu philosophies of the Hare Krishnas. One article talked about the sexual affairs of the lord Krishna and a Hindu goddess. There was also a feature article on members who celebrated the Festival of the Chariots in New York City, carrying their bongo-like drums and chanting as they proceeded down busy streets in that metropolis. Here is just a sample of the philosophies spouted in *Back to Godhead* magazine:

> Religion means to abide by the laws of God. That is all. It cannot be "Hindu," "Muslim," "Christian"... Therefore, you cannot say "Christian religion," "Hindu religion," "Muslim religion." Religion is religion, God is neither Christian, nor Hindu, nor Muslim. God is God. God is one.

> God is everything. God is darkness, also. Through meditation, by concentrating one's mind upon God, the Yogis try to see Him within their heart. God is within yourself.

It is important to realize that to the Hare Krishna followers their guru is their master. He is literally the one they must worship on planet earth as a representative of the various deities and especially the supreme deity, Lord Krishna. Thus, when the founder of Hare Krishna, Swami Prabhupada, declared "I am God realized," it was believed. We see in Hare Krishna the traditional New Age view that man has the capability within himself to become fully god, fully divine, achieving union with all of the gods that exist in the universe and thereby achieving oneness. Hare Krishna devotees teach that the name of Krishna is supreme and that no other name can match it. They say that his name is higher than the God of Abraham, Isaac, Jacob, and Isaiah--higher than the name of Jesus Christ. There is no question, then, that this is a decidedly unchristian religious cult.

To learn more about the Hare Krishnas I highly recommend the outstanding book *The Roaring Lion of the East* by Marvin Yakos, published by Pentecostal Publishing House (8855 Dunn Road, Hazelwood, Missouri 63042). This is a book which reveals Yakos' stunning escape from the Hare Krishna movement. Marvin Yakos today is a devoted Christian. In his book he shows clearly how the Hare Krishna movement deceives its followers, bringing them into a most unholy worship of eastern religions and demonic influences--which are portrayed as "angels of light." As Yakos writes: "I have journeyed into this kingdom of the eastern spirit to the very edge of the deceptive pit, but then I re-entered truth with the only sources of love, truth, and salvation: Jesus Christ."

HIMALAYAN INSTITUTE

In Homesdale, Pennsylvania, nestled in the rolling hills of the Pacona Mountains in Northeastern Pennsylvania, lies a beautiful brick complex. Inside an area of some 422 acres and surrounded by spectacular views of wooded hills and valleys, this is the *Himalayan Institute*. Founded in 1971 by Swami Rama, a Hindu guru, the institute maintains that it "integrates the latest scientific knowledge with the ancient principles of yoga to manage complex problems of modern life."

Swami Rama purports to have been raised from childhood in the Himalayas by a great master of yoga. He also says that he pursued a formal education at Oxford

University in England, though he did not graduate, and then continued his studies in Germany and Holland for three years before coming to the United States. The literature of the Himalayan Institute contends that, "Swami Rama is widely respected in the East, where he held, and later renounced, the office of Shankaracharya, India's highest spiritual position."

In 1969 Swami Rama came to the United States where, reportedly, he participated with the Menninger Foundation in a study to determine, under laboratory conditions, whether conscious control of autonomic mental and physical functioning could be achieved. It is unclear whether these experiments successfully proved that Swami's mind powers are as potent as his followers claim.

The Himalayan Institute certainly possesses an impressive faculty, including a number of professors and instructors with doctorates in psychology, literature, Eastern studies, and medicine. In addition to the Himalayan Institute's headquarters in Pennsylvania, there are also regional institutes in Glenview, Chicago, and Schaumberg, Illinois; and in Indianapolis, Milwaukee, Dallas/Ft. Worth, New York City, Pittsburgh, and Buffalo. There are also institutes in Germany and India.

Swami Rama says his institute's mission is to teach people the ancient teachings and thereby "unfold human potential." In a congress held at the Himalayan Institute on June 14-17, 1990, he brought a number of people together "to explore many of the perspectives and practices of the world's great traditions of self-transformation, health, and personal evolution. These traditions include Yoga, Zen, Ayurvedic Medicine, Judaism, Christianity, Buddhism, Sikhism, Islam, and Sufism." According to Swami Rama, all of these teachings are the same in that they have one unified purpose: to teach man a knowledge of his own true nature. We see then again the man-centered, yet eclectic nature of the New Age in the teachings of the Himalayan Institute and its founder, Swami Rama.

Yoga, Diet, Meditation, and Godhood

Specifically, the Himalayan Institute concentrates on hatha yoga instruction, diet (which, of course, means vegetarian and a rejection of meat), intensive meditation, and visualization. These are all claimed to be techniques for unfolding the creative intelligence in each person. Another area that is studied by those who come to the Himalayan Institute or its centers is what is called the "science of breath," which is simply a claim that we can breath energy in and out and thus transform ourselves into divine beings.

Swami Rama himself is simply another one of the many so-called Hindu sages who have come to America during the past few decades seeking fame and fortune while desiring to spread the message of Eastern Mysticism. The main goal of Swami Rama as well as these other gurus is to synthesize the ancient teachings of the East with the modern philosophies of the West. And like his Hindu counterparts, Swami Rama seeks to swallow up Christianity by reinterpreting its message and distorting its truths, submerging true Christianity within the overall context of Hindu one worldism.

HINDUISM AND THE GURUS

An avalanche of *Hindu* gurus and swamis invaded the United States in the 1960s and 70s and our nation has never been the same since. They brought with them strange names and even stranger doctrines. First, at the turn of the century, came Swami Vivekananda. In 1893 he addressed the Parliament of Religions in Chicago and galvanized the crowd with his call for a unified world religion based on the principles of Hinduism. Then, the Beatles, with their combination of rock and mystical music, long hair, and worship of Hinduism and its gurus, ushered in this new religion for an entire generation of youth. Doctrinal, missionary Hinduism became the rage among the hippies and its influence has swept throughout the New Age community. In fact, Hinduism is the core teaching of the New Age.

Among the most popular Hindu gurus is the Maharishi Mahesh Yogi, whose teachings on Transcendental Meditation (TM) are described elsewhere in this book. Another popular Hindu teacher was Swami Muktananda, brought to this country by Werner Erhard (see The Forum/est). Muktananda emphasized the teachings of Siddha Yoga, the belief that men could become gods with supernatural powers. Yet another popular guru was the late Bhagwan Rajneesh, a vicious hater of Jesus and biblical Christianity, who was driven out of America for drug violations and a score of other criminal activities which were perpetrated at his ashram community in the state of Oregon.

Today gurus still have a significant foothold within the New Age movement. Among the most popular teachers are Sri Swami Satchidananda, Swami Prakashanand Saraswati, Swami Rama, Babaji, and Yogi Bhajan. In addition, a number of westerners have taken on the title of "Swami" or "guru," most notably Ram Dass and Da Free John. It is quite amazing that bizarre gurus from such an impoverished and spiritually ravaged nation as India could be able to convince millions of educated, affluent Americans to worship the millions of Hindu gods and practice the outrageous and absurd teachings of Hinduism. India itself is a nation where many hungry peoples roam alleyways in tattered rags and suffer great poverty. It is a country where the caste system is still honored, where beggars extend their hands and sad eyes plead for alms along the streets of every town and city.

Drinking Cow Urine and other Atrocities

Caryl Mastrisciana, author of the outstanding exposé of Hinduism, *Gods of the New Age*, shows clearly the horrors of this religion. Caryl has revealed that some American disciples of the gurus drink their guru's urine believing that it creates divine energies within. Others willingly consume cow's urine, in the belief that the cow goddess will favor their undertakings. As Mastrisciana notes, the most revered Hindu guru of all, Mahatma Gandhi, administered enemas to female devotees. He slept with nude teenage girls to confirm his celibacy, and prescribed cow dung pills for good health. Gandhi also criticized the English colonialists but praised Adolf Hitler and the Nazis.

In yet another excellent guide to the Hindu gurus, *Riders of the Cosmic Circuit*, Christian author and cult expert Tal Brooke, writes that the Enlightened Masters who claim to be nothing less than gods using a physical body as a medium are in reality perfectly possessed by demonic spirits. He says that, in essence, the original human inhabitants of the gurus' bodies no longer even exist. Instead, the gurus are possessed by "a massive, baleful intelligence that is ageless," and, "is extremely powerful and extremely evil." Tal says that the rituals of Hinduism result in "the total desecration, degradation, defamation of a soul during the ritual." He shows clearly that the mega-gurus of the Hindu religion have surrendered themselves to a horrendously evil force.

As Tal states, they "surrender by degradation--eating feces, coitus of dead bodies, cannibalism, human sacrifice ... blowing the lid off of conventional morality." I cannot recommend strong enough that every New Ager in America today should read the revealing books *Riders of the Cosmic Circuit*, by Tal Brooke, and *God's of the New Age*, by Caryl Mastrisciana, if they are to discover the awful truth about Hinduism.

The Teachings of the Hindus

Hinduism teaches transmigration of the soul *(samsara)*. It says that man will proceed through endless cycles of samsara, balancing out his karma on the wheel of life until finally the *atman* (soul) of the individual is absorbed by the Universal Soul *(brahman)*. Hinduism emphasizes *pantheism,* the theory that God is all, that all created matter is God. It also preaches the concept of *maya*, that all of reality is simply an illusion. It is because of this belief in maya that the incredible, hideous poverty of the Indian caste system has been allowed to continue. Hindus have little sympathy for their fellow human beings because, according to the Hindu scriptures (which include the *Rig Veda,* the *Upanishads,* etc.) all of the universe is simply a great cosmic game known as *Lila*. It is matter of dancing atoms endlessly active which resemble the dance of the god Sheva.

Hindus believe in millions of gods, but primarily in a trinity of gods composed of Vishnu, the preserver, Sheva, the destroyer, and Brahma, the creator. Vishnu is said to come in many incarnations. He is the vedic sun god who reincarnates again and again as a Christ figure throughout the history of mankind. There is also a strong belief in the goddess, the female consort of the gods. Hindus have encouraged orgies and temple prostitution as well as sacrifices of human beings and animals. The goddess Kali is presented as a bloodthirsty deity of the most sinister nature. But all of this, says the Hindu, is necessary to fulfill the karma of mankind.

Unable to be Forgiven

The tragedy of Hinduism is that the Hindu can never become a new creation totally forgiven by God in this lifetime. The Christian is assured of eternal salvation through such passages as 2 Cor. 5:17 and John 9:1-3, both of which totally refute the Hindu ideas of karma and reincarnation. For example, in refuting the doctrine of reincarnation, Jesus clearly taught His disciples that a certain blind man's condition was *not* the result of sins committed in a previous existence (see John 9:1-3). And Hebrews 9:27 tells us that man lives but *one* life on planet earth, then there is judgment.

The Christian believes in *grace*, the Hindus fervently believe in and practice *works*. This is the cardinal difference between the two faiths, but there are, of course, many more. Because of their failure to acknowledge Jesus as Lord of all, the Hindu has no way out of this life and therefore becomes a victim of superstition and terror.

Praise God there are many Hindus today discovering the Truth of the Lord Jesus Christ. One such Hindu yogi is Rabi Maharaj. In his Christian book, *Escape to Light*, Rabi tells us of the joy he has known since accepting Jesus as Lord. In an interview, Rabi stated:

> I had never heard in Hinduism that God is a God of love or that God loves me. God is impersonal in Hinduism. He cannot be a God of love because the Hindu god is without essence or quality. The fact that God is a God of love really shook me up, and also that God wants to come into my life. That really kind of knocked me over, especially the fact that Jesus died to forgive me all my sins. In Hinduism, you do the dying for the gods, the gods don't die for you.

I AM

Guy Ballard (1879-1939), leader of the *I AM Ascended Master Religious Activity*, began his group after claiming to come in contact with the Ascended Master Saint Germain, a spirit being who is said to have been one of the most famous occultists of all time when he was in his physical incarnation in 18th century France. Ballard later wrote that while hiking around the area near Mount Shasta in Northern California, he met Saint Germain and was offered a refreshing drink, a creamy liquid, which the spirit being identified as a substance coming from the Universal Supply. Drinking it down, Ballard had a vivid spiritual transformation experience. Saint Germain then offered to be Ballard's guide so that he, Ballard, could assume the role of Messenger of the Ascended Masters.

Ballard's I AM group was extremely popular during the 1930s and 40s. After his death it was led by his wife, Edna. Under the pen name Godfre Ray King, Ballard published his first book, *Unveiled Mysteries*, in 1934. *The Magic Present* followed, as well as a number of other writings.

Ballard's I AM philosophy is in many ways the same as that of the Church Universal and Triumphant. It recommends decreeing, affirmations, and communications with spirits known collectively as the Great White Brotherhood.

After the death of Guy's wife, Edna, a board of directors took over the supervision of I AM. In 1978 the headquarters of I AM was moved to new facilities in Schaumburg, Illinois. The group publishes its materials under the name Saint Germain Press, including a monthly publication, *The Voice of the I AM*.

Reportedly, there are well over 300 I AM centers or sanctuaries in over 20 countries around the world, including centers in Denver, Colorado; Austin, Texas; and Los Angeles, California.

INSIGHT (JOHN-ROGER)

Insight is the brainchild of Roger Hinkins, who changed his name to "John-Roger" after, according to his own account, he became possessed by the spirit of "John the Beloved." Following his possession by "John," Roger Hinkins left his job as a Rosemead, California high school English teacher, began to call himself Dr. John-Roger Hinkins, then later simply John-Roger, and went on to found one of the most powerful of New Age churches and empires, the *Movement of Spiritual Inner Awareness*, or MSIA (pronounced "messiah"). Elsewhere in this book I discuss John-Roger's MSIA group. In this section, I will briefly focus on the organization known as *Insight*, formally *Insight Transformation Seminars*, which is an offshoot of the Movement of Spiritual Inner Awareness.

Insight seminars ostensibly are for the purpose of developing a person's "potential" and "self-worth." They incorporate the mystical teachings of John-Roger, which include his concepts of the Mystical Traveler Consciousness and the metaphysical powers and consciousness which John-Roger believes men can possess and wield. Reportedly, the Insight seminars brought in over $8 million in one recent year, and John-Roger's organization owns many millions of dollars more in real estate and other holdings, including a $6 million building on Los Angeles' Wilshire Boulevard.

Although Insight contends that its teachings are devoid of religious or spiritual intent, cult researchers have found this not to be the case. For example, in an exposé in the *Los Angeles Times* newspaper of August 14, 1988, it was reported that, "Before each session of each Insight training, for example, facilitators and assistants would purify themselves in the training room by 'calling in the light,' reciting 'Father-Mother God, we ask just now to be placed in the Light of the Holy Spirit, through John-Roger, the Mystical Traveler, Preceptor Consciousness, and we ask that only that which is for the highest good to be brought forth.'"

Michael Hess, 40, a former follower of John-Roger, echoing the sentiments of others involved in this cult group, was quoted in the *Los Angeles Times* as stating: "Anyone who got involved quickly learned there was a spiritual side" to the Insight seminars. Insight was into the business of raising cash as well as consciousness. Reportedly, instructors ask for and often get donor checks of $7,000 each from some participants. This is in addition to the standard $450 per person fee.

The shameful thing is that some of the most reputable firms and corporations in America evidently paid John-Roger's group, Insight, millions and millions of dollars to train their employees in his method. Among the corporate clients of Insight have been Abbott Labs, Beth-Israel Hospital, Campbell's Soup, Lockheed, McDonell-Douglas, NBC-TV, Pillsbury, and Rockwell International. Also, taxpayers have regrettably been suckered into paying for Insight training bought by the Social Security Administration, the United States Navy, and many other governmental agencies. Insight seminars are conducted in cities across America from Boston, Philadelphia, and Washington, D.C. on the East coast, to St. Louis and Chicago in the Midwest, Dallas and Houston in Texas, and every major city on the West Coast.

INSTITUTE OF NOETIC SCIENCES

The *Institute of Noetic Sciences* was founded in 1973 by Dr. Edgar D. Mitchell, Apollo 14 astronaut. Its membership is impressive, including Dr. Herbert Benson of Harvard

University, the man whose teachings have promoted meditation throughout America; Dr. Elmer Green of the Menninger Clinic; Dr. Dan Goleman, senior editor of *Psychology
Today* magazine; and others. In addition, Mitchell has been
able to obtain major funding and support for his Institute
from such corporations as Mobil Oil and the Atari Computer
Corporation.

Mitchell's Institute of Noetic Sciences is a promoter of
holistic medicine. Among its projects is Tibetan meditation
in which monks selected by Tibetan Buddhism's Dalai Lama
were studied. The Institute has also promoted the Soviet-
American Exchange Program, and Mitchell has been a
favored speaker at John Denver's Windstar Community in
Colorado.

Mitchell's contention is that man's mind is part of a
"natural force on earth." Using New Age terminology, he
believes that such ESP abilities as telepathy, clairvoyance,
and telekinesis should be explored and developed so that
men can expand their consciousness.

It is a shame that such a prestigious man as Edgar
Mitchell has lent his reputation and has wasted much of his
life on such unscientific, unfounded, and dangerous drivel.
In 1988, the National Research Council of the National
Academy of Sciences released its extensive report on
Enhancing Human Performance. After researching for over
two years and after studying over 130 years of research, the
14 distinguished scientists on a committee appointed by the
National Research Council determined that virtually all
claims by New Agers of the effectiveness of such techniques
as guided imagery, meditation, biofeedback, neurolinguistic
programming, split brain (right brain, left brain) learning,
and similar techniques are totally without foundation and
devoid of proof. Moreover, the committee found "no
scientific justification for the existence of parapsychological
phenomena." This was the most massive and definitive study
ever conducted and the committee spent $500,000 of
taxpayers money to conduct this research. Nevertheless,
such groups as Edgar Mitchell's Institute of Noetic Sciences

continue to promote the dubious advantages of their New Age pseudoscientific techniques.

THE INTERNATIONAL NEW THOUGHT ALLIANCE

The International New Thought Alliance is an association of pastors, teachers, churches, and others who believe in the New Thought philosophy. In essence, New Thought *is* New Age. Perhaps the best-known groups promoting New Thought are Unity Church, the Church of Religious Science, and Christian Science. Among the advocates and disciples of New Thought today are such famous persons as Houston Mayor Kathy Whitmire, Terry Cole-Whittaker, former popular television evangelist, and Norman Cousins, editor of *Saturday Review*.

Many in the New Thought movement have also named the Crystal Cathedral's Robert Schuller as one of their own while Norman Vincent Peale has also been acclaimed as a New Thought man. Schuller has been a guest speaker at the Unity Church's international convention. Meanwhile, Peale admits that he was heavily influenced by New Thought. Referring to Ernest Holmes, the founder of the Church of Religious Science, also known as Science of Mind, Norman Vincent Peale has stated: "Only those who knew me as a boy can fully appreciate what Ernest Holmes did for me. Why, he made me a positive thinker."

Each year the International New Thought Alliance has an annual congress. One has only to attend one of these events to comprehend that "New Thought" is nothing more than a synonym for "New Age." Here, in essence, are the teachings of most teachers of New Thought: (1) God is an impersonal force; (2) God is immanent; God is simply Mind; (3) The universe and everything in it is the very body of God; (4) Thoughts are real things. They are creative. To accomplish miracles or make things happen, man has only to exercise his thought process; (5) Death, evil, illness, disease, are all illusions and can be dispelled through mind powers; (6) God is individualized in humanity; thus, man becomes God; (7) Positive affirmations by an individual can result in perfect health, riches, and prosperity. Therefore, such techniques as positive thinking, visualization, guided imagery, and other mental techniques may be used with great profit; (8) Salvation is universal since each person comes into the world with a divine nature.

JEHOVAH'S WITNESSES

Jehovah's Witnesses is definitely a New Age cult. This church's doctrine is generally right in line with that of other New Age cults and denominations. For example, the belief that Jesus is a created being--just another one of many gods. Indeed, the Jehovah's  Witnesses claim that Jesus is actually Michael the Archangel! Also, check out the Jehovah's Witnesses bible, the New World Translation. In it you will see the revealing and perverted wording in John 1 that "In the beginning was the Word and the Word was with God, and the Word was *a* God." Unlike the King James Version, the word "a" is inserted.

The Jehovah's Witnesses also believe in other heresies shared by their companions in the New Age. First, we see the Jehovah's Witnesses' contention that Jesus is not only a created God, but He is a deity *inferior* to God the Father. Next, the Jehovah's Witnesses believe that unsaved men will not be sent to hell for there is no such place. Instead, to a Jehovah's Witness, hell is merely the grave. When a person dies, he supposedly goes to "hell," or the grave, and at the Last Judgment, the person rises out of an unconscious sleep. Then at the Judgment, the person will either get to live on the new earth or else be annihilated entirely. In effect, the biblical teaching that hell is a place of eternal punishment and torment is dismissed entirely by the Jehovah's Witnesses cult. Moreover, according to the Jehovah's Witnesses, no one can really know whether or not they are saved until *after* the Judgment.

Did Lord Maitreya appear to the Jehovah's Witnesses?

Interestingly enough, many in the New Age are beginning to discover the common ground they have with the Jehovah's Witnesses. For example, in Benjamin Creme's publication, *Share International* (Vol. 7, No. 8, October 1988), we are told:

> Maitreya (Lord Maitreya, the New Age "Christ") has appeared at meetings of Jehovah's Witnesses ... Some Jehovah's Witnesses have had certain experiences as a result of Maitreya's presence among them which have led them to abandon an entrenched "ideological" position.

Benjamin Creme further explains that "Religion, political systems, ideologies, are 'rungs of the ladder' which are necessary in order to 'reach the roof.' Once you have reached the roof you do not need them." In other words, all false religions are being lifted by Satan to "the roof." In this, Creme does not lie, for indeed, the Jehovah's Witnesses and other New Age groups shall all "reach the roof" when they become as One (see Revelation 17 and Revelation 13).

The Jehovah's Witnesses were founded in the late 19th century by a man named Charles T. Russell. Russell had studied the oriental religions and was a confessed believer in pyramidology, expressing frequently his theory that the Great Pyramid contained signs and mysteries direct from God. In their book, *Witnesses of Jehovah*, Leonard and Marjorie Chretian fully expose the unbiblical, cult foundations of Jehovah's Witnesses and its founder, Charles T. Russell. They note that stamped in gold on the front covers of the *Studies and the Scriptures* series of Russell's books is a winged solar disc. The Chretians observe that:

> This symbol originated in ancient Egypt, where it was the quintessential symbol representing Horus, the sun god. The winged disk was used throughout the centuries to represent the supreme god of other pagan cults and societies. It was the symbol for the baal god during Jezebel's reign, as well as the god of the Zoroastrian cult, founded by Zoroaster, the Persian religious prophet whom Russell wrote about with admiration.

Though the Jehovah's Witnesses are not fond of being reminded of it, their founder Russell made a number of false prophecies. In fact, even after his death, his successors continued to make false prophecies. For instance, in 1917 the Jehovah's Witnesses book, *The Finished Mystery*, contained the prophecy that the following year, 1918, would see God destroying all of Christendom except the Jehovah's Witnesses and the world falling into a global anarchy by 1920. Also, it was prophesied that God's Kingdom would be established on earth in 1931. Naturally, none of these events transpired. It was not the first time the Jehovah's Witnesses had inaccurately predicted the Lord's coming. Their publication, *The Watchtower*, had also said that Christ would come in 1874, and that the Church would be caught up to Heaven in 1878.

The New Age Heresies of the Jehovah's Witnesses

In their brochure, *What Do Jehovah's Witnesses Believe?,* the cult itself clearly demonstrates its New Age worldview with the following statements:

> Jehovah's Witnesses believe that God is greater than Jesus ... Thus, we do not believe that Jesus is equal with the Father, as the Trinity doctrine says. Rather, we believe that He was created by God, and that He is subordinate to Him.

> Jesus Christ will not be the only king of God's government. He will have many co-rulers with Him in heaven.

The Jehovah's Witnesses are guilty of many such heresies. For example, the cult teaches that a person is saved through works and not by grace and faith alone; it teaches that God is through with the Jews and with the nation of Israel. The 144,000 mentioned in Revelation 14:1-3 are simply humans who are resurrected to rule with Christ in heaven instead of the 12 tribes of Israel as the Bible clearly reveals.

But none of these heresies are as striking as the Jehovah's Witnesses denial of the majesty of Jesus Christ. Although God's name is indeed Jehovah (see Psalm 83:18), the Holy Bible unquestionably tells us in John 1 that *Jesus is God and was God from the beginning.* What's more, we read in Philippians 2:9-11 that *the name of Jesus is above all other names:*

> Wherefore God also hath highly exalted Him, and given Him a name which is above every name: That at the name of Jesus every knee should bow, of things in heaven, and things in earth, and things under the earth; And that every tongue should confess that Jesus Christ is Lord, to the glory of God the Father.

KEN KEYES COLLEGE

Ken Keyes College is an adult learning institution in Coos Bay, Oregon which promotes the works of bestselling New Age author and speaker Ken Keyes. The College publishes *Ken Keyes College Quarterly* newspaper giving updates of course offerings which emphasize workshops and seminars on such pep-talk topics as "Unconditional Love," "Playful Methods for Creative Living," and "Methods for Awakening." Mainly, these are sugar-coated training sessions for people hungry for self-help, pop psychology fast fixes.

Ken Keyes and his wife, Penny, founders of this institution, are on close terms with the elite of other New Age organizations, such as Jerry Jampolsky *(A Course in Miracles)*, Unity Church, and the various 12-step programs.

Wally Hill, the administrator of the college, says that his "personal growth trip" involved yoga massage, hypnotism, and Reiki natural healing. His boss, Ken Keyes, is author of the million-seller book, *Handbook to Higher Consciousness*, which claims to teach readers how to use meditative, self-talk techniques for self-transformation into the new consciousness paradigm.

Keyes is also author of the influential book, *The Hundredth Monkey*, which many New Age authorities cite as proof of the validity of their theory that society is about to take a *quantum leap* into the New Age--as soon as enough people are into the *new consciousness*. True scientists, however, scoff at Keyes' ideas.

Another Keyes book, *Planethood*, calls for a one world government to insure world disarmament and peace. Keyes is well-known for his advocacy of One Worldism.

KOSMON (OASHPE)

In 1881 Dr. John Ballou Newbrough sat in front of his typewriter as spirits began to dictate to him a new bible, which was published under the name *OASHPE*. Some 1,008 pages in length, *OASHPE* proclaims the arrival of "the New Kosmon Era," a New Age in which man  will be exalted and all of the other gods, including Jesus, will be put away. As Walter Wiers states in the Kosmon book, *Last Battle For Earth,* "It's time for a change of gods. The old gods--Allah, Buddha, Christ, Jehovah, and the others of the East and the Mideast have at last reached the age of retirement."

The book of *OASHPE* itself, on pages 562 through 564, quotes the Kosmon god *Jehoviah* (note the similarity to *Jehovah*) as saying: "When the Gods have fulfilled their time in earth and heaven, behold, I put them away."

According to the spirits who dictated this new bible to him, John Newbrough said that *OASHPE* means: *O* for earth, *AH* for sky, and *SPE* for spirit. He contended that the new bible is "A book of advanced spiritual truth, universal light and knowledge, adapted to this new Kosmon Age." Newbrough maintained that the god Jehoviah "is the father-creator of all gods, goddess, and lords!"

Newbrough taught that the spirit authors of *OASHPE* were nine chief gods, each of whom has ruled the earth during a particular cycle of time. Among these nine chief gods are Sethantes, Su, Apollo, Thor, and Osiris. It is interesting that the OASHPE cult and its bible totally neglect Jesus Christ, yet, they exalt the Greek god Apollo, the Norwegian god Thor, and the Egyptian father god Osiris.

In addition, OASHPE promotes the Great Pyramid of Egypt as a sacred monument and even reveals an astounding story about a submerged continent known as *Pan*. Pan was the Greek horned god of the forest; but to the OASHPE cult, Pan is a continent, later known as Lemuria, located in the Pacific Ocean which was submerged about 24,000 years ago. The similarity between OASHPE's teachings and those of Helena Blavatsky's Theosophy in her books on *The Secret Doctrine* is quite informative.

The OASHPE cult particularly admires the Persian teacher Zarahustra, whom they say was also Zoroaster. They say it was Zoroaster who first gave written revelations of a divine nature to human beings.

OASHPE incorporates just about every New Age doctrine imaginable. This eclectic group, through the Amherst Press, in Amherst, Wisconsin, has put out books dealing with the spirit world and spiritualism, the coming of UFOs, New Age politics, magic, the Green Man (the Green Man was known by the pagans to be Lucifer), and North American Indian religions.

Even though the book of *OASHPE* was published over a century ago in 1882, this cult has not been able to gain a significant following. The Universal Faithists of Kosmon, headquartered in Riverton, Utah, are perhaps the best-known OASHPE group. They publish the *Kosmon Voice* magazine which carries articles promoting vegetarianism, holistic healing, environmentalism, and meditation. Another OASHPE publication is *Search* magazine, distributed by Amherst Press.

The OASHPE cult holds out to men and women the promise that after many cycles, they themselves may become a god of a planet, such as the earth. Kosmon also pretends to answer many of the mysteries of the universe, such mysteries being revealed by spirits in the spiritual realm. According to OASHPE, there are many gods and lords. In fact, there are also countless millions of worlds and each world has its own chief ruler, who is a commissioned god, or a goddess.

OASHPE cultists, who call themselves "Faithists," are found isolated throughout America. I have been able to locate groups in New York, Colorado, Arizona, New Mexico, Utah, California, Georgia, and Wisconsin.

KRISHNAMURTI

Jiddu Krishnamurti was a discovery of Annie Besant, president of the Theosophical Society in the late 19th century and early 1900s. Besant and occultist Charles Leadbeater became enamored of the young man Jiddu Krishnamurti and believed him to be the new avatar, the great World Teacher, the Christ of the New Age.

The *Order of the Star in the East* was formed to promote Krishnamurti as the Christ. But on a tour to America, Krishnamurti bombed out. American theosophists, as well as the news media, noted that this shy young Hindu was totally inept and devoid of spiritual knowledge and understanding.

Dejected and embarrassed, Krishnamurti sailed back to India where, in 1929, he broke away from his sponsors in Theosophy and, in fact, repudiated all connections with organized religions and ideologies. From then on until his death in 1986, Krishnamurti traveled the world, writing and speaking to as many people who continued to believe in him.

Evidently, Krishnamurti did gain significant support in later years. For example, he spoke before the United Nations and was endorsed or lauded by such notables as U.S. Senator Claiborne Pell and noted economist Milton Friedman. Krishnamurti also wrote a number of books and articles which his modern-day followers have collected in the Krishnamurti library and the Krishnamurti Archives. His work in America is carried on by the *Krishnamurti Foundation of America*, headquartered in Ojai, California. Moreover, Krishnamurti's teachings are emphasized at the Oak Grove School, a day-school for elementary students which is a project of the Krishnamurti Foundation.

LAZARIS

Lazaris is a spirit, an entity which Christians easily recognize as a demon but the New Age honors as an all-wise, all-knowing, much reincarnated Master. Jach Pursel is the medium and spirit channeler who has given the new "Lazaris" to the world. Jach Pursel was a regional insurance supervisor in Florida when he began dabbling in meditation. In 1974, he fell asleep during a meditation exercise and suddenly, he and his wife Peny say, an entirely different entity who later identified himself as "Lazaris" suddenly began speaking through Jach's mouth as he lay asleep. Lazaris, who speaks with an unusual Chaucerian Middle-English accent, has now been speaking through Jach Pursel for 15 years. His themes are quite familiar to those in the New Age since they echo other demon spirits channeled by New Age mediums such as Seth and Ramtha.

Lazaris has become quite popular. Jach Pursel, his channeler, has traveled around the United States presenting seminars, workshops, and speeches. I recently received a letter from a businessman in Florida who was absolutely flabbergasted when he attended a recent Chamber of Commerce meeting. He was told that there would be a wonderful motivational speech given. At the podium was Jach Pursel. When Lazaris' voice began to utter words from Jach's mouth and spout a mish-mash of business advice, the man got so disgusted that he abruptly got out of his chair and left the room. Yet later, many businessmen who were in attendance told this Christian man that they were very pleased with what Jach Pursel and Lazaris had to say.

Jach Pursel's ads promise people "a night of magic and miracles" with Lazaris. Brochures say such things as: "Lazaris is stunning. People marvel at the intensity of the love . . . They are in awe of the way Lazaris' love and insight seem literally to dissolve the blockages and resistance and then open the doors to success. Words cannot describe the wonder."

According to the "wisdom" of Lazaris, "You enter your personal New Age when you are ready to know that you create your own reality." Becoming a God, says Lazaris, is taking back the power that you have given someone else (probably meaning Jesus Christ). Lazaris gives this definition of God:

> God is the name given to the creator of all reality or the Source. God is all that is . . . God has been referred to as "the All," the "Is-ness," "All-ness," the "god force," "the god energy."

Lazaris also insists that God is both male and female and that people are just as well off worshipping the goddess as a male god.

LIFESPRING

The *National Law Journal* (August 13, 1984) reported that *"Lifespring,* like other California human potential groups founded in the late 1960s and the early 1970s, mixes Eastern philosophy, psychology, and strict discipline in an effort to get students to reevaluate their belief system. Lifespring has come under intense criticism in recent years from people who claim to have suffered psychotic episodes and from relatives of students who have committed suicide after taking the course."

The same article from the *National Law Journal* reported that a former Lifespring participant had won $800,000 in a suit against the organization. A Philadelphia jury awarded Debra Bingham, 30, the money after they heard testimony that she had attended two Lifespring training courses that led to her being hospitalized for a month in a mental institution for severe depression and suicidal tendencies. The woman had also lost her job as a result of her continuing psychological problems.

Founded in 1974 by John P. Hanley and associates, Lifespring has trained well over 150,000 individuals in its methods. Yet, the group continues to receive negative publicity, being the subject of repeated lawsuits and even the target of a scathing exposé conducted by investigators of ABC's "20/20" television news program.

Lifespring teaches that man is perfect, that "at the essence, or core, of each of us is a perfect, loving, and caring being." Lifespring promises enlightenment. In one advertisement of Lifespring, a man is quoted as saying that if he had gone to Tibet and meditated on a mountain top it would have taken years for enlightenment, but "Lifespring got me there in just five days."

Lifespring also teaches that we ourselves are the creators of our own light. Its instructors say that our own self-esteem and self-worth are paramount and that "self-love is the greatest love." The training involves meditation and the development of mind and psychic powers alien to traditional Christianity. The group's publication, *Lifespring Family News* (Vol. 1, No. 2), bragged, "The seminars make use of the most effective principles, intellectual concepts and techniques of ... parapsychology ... and Eastern disciplines."

Participants in the Lifespring training have reported that they were introduced to the powers of ESP, astral or soul travel, and the occultic concept of the Third Eye. In one instance, participants were told to exchange shoes with other people in order to absorb the vibrations and energies of the other person. Such Hindu doctrines as the chakras, or energy centers and points in the body have been taught as well.

As one Christian investigator has observed, Lifespring is unable to deliver what it promises because man himself is not a god ("For thou being a man makest thyself God."--John 10:33). Lifespring teaches that a person must look inside rather than to Jesus Christ. But in truth, Jesus Christ is the only source from which life springs. He is the fountain of living waters.

LUCIS TRUST

"Seventy years ago, in late 1919, Alice Bailey and the Tibetan, Dwjhal Khul, entered into an extraordinary telepathic collaboration which was to last for 30 years. Twenty-four Alice Bailey books were written and published as a result of their work together. Today these teach-ings are helping to spread the Ageless Wisdom in all parts of the world. They have provided the foundation on which the Lucis Trust was established and inspiration for its service to humanity."

The above statement comes directly from the *Lucis Trust,* jointly headquartered in London, New York, and Geneva. What it tells us is that, in the Lucis Trust view, its founder Alice Bailey and a spirit from beyond whom she called the Tibetan, or Dwjhal Khul, together produced 24 books which are now the core teachings of the Lucis Trust. Certainly the philosophies of the Lucis Trust have spread to "all parts of the world." This is an incredibly important New Age occultic organization. Alice Bailey passed away in the 1970s, but her books, dictated to her by the Tibetan, live on. And they have influenced scores of other New Age organizations and leaders. Other than Alice Bailey (and her spirit guides), the two most important individuals who have influenced the Lucis Trust have been Alice Bailey's husband, Foster Bailey, and the related Mary Bailey.

Today, Perry Coles is president of the Lucis Trust. Until

recently, the Lucis Trust's address was at 866 United Nations Plaza. This organization is closely linked with the United Nations. In fact, it has been placed on the roster of the Economic and Social Council of the United Nations (ECOSOC) to indicate its special consultative status with the United Nations.

Membership of the Lucis Trust evidently includes some astonishingly powerful individuals. In his book, *Secret Societies Take The Offense*, Dr. John Coleman states that the Lucis Trust has over 6,000 active members. They include Robert McNamara, former Secretary of Defense of the United States and head of the World Bank; Donald Regan, former Chief of Staff under President Reagan; Arthur Burns, former Chairman of the Federal Reserve Board; Henry Kissinger, former Secretary of State; David Rockefeller, megabanker and head of Chase Manhattan Bank; James Baker III, current Secretary of State; Paul Volcker, former Chairman of the Federal Reserve Board; James Schlesinger, former Secretary of Defense; Harold Brown, former Secretary of Defense; and George Schultz, former Secretary of State. If this is true, it is quite amazing because the Lucis Trust is patently occultic.

Lucifer the Light Bearer?

The words *Lucis* and *Illuminati* basically mean the same thing. The word "lucis" comes directly from the name Lucifer, which means "light bearer" or "the one who brings light." *Webster's New Twenty-first Century Dictionary* says this: "Lucifer: light bringing, to bear light. Satan, as especially the leader of the revolt of the angels before his fall." Revealingly, when the Lucis Trust first began, founded by Alice Bailey, it was called *Lucifer Publishing!* It was incorporated in 1922, however, under its present name. This organization is registered in Great Britain, Germany, Holland, and Switzerland. In fact, according to its own publications we are told:

The Lucis Trust was incorporated in the United States in 1922. It is officially recognized by the federal government and by various state governments as tax exempt. The Lucis Trust ... is a non-profit world service organization receiving and using monies to promote activities concerned with the establishment of life, human relations, and world cooperation and sharing. The Lucis Trust ... has bank accounts and financial agents in many other countries, including Geneva, Switzerland, where the European headquarters of the work is established. The financial and legal affairs of the Lucis Trust are controlled by an international Board of Trustees, aided by additional trustees and elected officers and members in different countries. Enough men of goodwill working to create the New World Order of brotherhood, cooperation, and life relationship, can defeat the forces of materialism and liberate the sense of shared responsibility for human welfare within the hearts and minds of men.

What we see, then, is that in its own proclamation, the Lucis Trust defines its purpose as that of establishing a "New World Order." To achieve this goal, the Lucis Trust has established subsidiary organizations which include the Arcane School, the Lucis Publishing Companies, World Goodwill, Triangles, Lucis Trust Libraries, and Radio Lucis. Elsewhere in this book we take a look at the Arcane School and World Goodwill.

The Great Invocation

The teachings of the Lucis Trust have been translated into over 50 languages, and the books by Alice Bailey and Dwjhal Khul have been sold in the millions. The Lucis Trust has also published a common prayer, often praised as "the prayer of the New Age." They formally call it *The Great Invocation.*

The Great Invocation is printed and sent out in tens of thousands of copies. Some churches, Protestant and Catholic, use the Great Invocation during worship. Yet, few are aware of the inner meaning, the true occultic nature, of this prayer of the New Age. It literally calls for Satan, or Lucifer, to come forth from his secret place and through death and power establish his kingdom on planet earth.

To illustrate the Satanic nature of the Great Invocation, here are a few brief stanzas, followed by a Christian interpretation of their hidden meanings:

> Let the Lords of Liberation issue forth
> Let the rider from the Secret Place come forth
> And coming, save.
> Come forth, O Mighty One.
>
> Let Light and Love and Power and Death
> Fulfill the purpose of the Coming One.
>
> From the centre where the Will of God is known
> Let purpose guide the little wills of men
> The purpose which the Masters know and serve.
>
> Let the Plan of Love and light work out
> And may it seal the door where evil dwells.
>
> Let Light and Love and Power restore the Plan on Earth.

When we understand New Age doctrines and analyze those doctrines in light of the bible, we can readily explain this invocation:

"Let the Lords of Liberation issue forth": Let the gates of hell be opened and the demons issue forth (see Rev. 6:8, 9:1-11).

"Let the Rider from the Secret Place come forth": Let Satan be loosed from the pit to take peace from the earth, to kill and slaughter, and to gather unsaved souls (see Rev. 6:3-17, 9:11).

"Let Light and Love and Power and Death fulfill the purpose of the Coming One": Let Satan's ploys of "light" and "love" deceive so he can go forth with power to destroy souls.

"From the centre where the Will of God is known": From Shamballa, the mystical, invisible kingdom where the New Age "Christ" and demons reside (i.e., hell), where the will of Satan is known.

"The purpose which the Masters know and serve": The Plan of Satan to ascend unto the heavens and become God, which his demons know and serve.

"Let the Plan of Love and Light work out": Let Satan's Plan to rule the universe and have man worship him as God prevail.

"And may it (The Plan) seal the door where evil dwells": And may Satan's Plan succeed in extinguishing all traces of God and eliminating those who know His Word.

According to Alice Bailey, Christianity is fast becoming outmoded. The true god of this world is a being she refers to as "Sanat Kumara." This is, in fact, the very same deity worshipped by Benjamin Creme and his Tara Center, a cult discussed elsewhere also in this book. It is also the same teaching spread by Theosophy. In fact, both the Lucis Trust and the Tara Center are offshoots of Helena Blavatsky's Theosophy. All three teach that Sanat Kumara, the lord of this world, manifests himself in the mystical kingdom of Shambala. Supposedly, Sanat came from Venus and with him came the Lords of Flame. What is really being referred to, of course, is none other than Lucifer, whom occultism has for centuries claimed came from the planet Venus bringing with him other fire gods and angelic deities of the flame.

Occultism and White Magic

There is much other evidence that this is an occultic organization. For example, there is Alice Bailey's book, *A*

Treatise on White Magic. The Lucis Trust touts this book as providing the 15 rules for magic. It promotes a form of occultism called White Magic and suggests that man, being essentially and inherently divine, can develop all the magical, supernatural powers of a god once he becomes conscious of his divinity and liberates himself from "matter."

The Lucis Trust also promotes the reappearance of the "Christ," but not Jesus Christ. As one of their publications states:

> *The reappearance of the Christ*: Many religions today expect the coming of an Avatar or Savior. The second coming of Christ, as the World Teacher for the Age of Aquarius, is presented in this book as an imminent event, logical and practical in the continuity of divine revelation through the ages. The Christ belongs to all mankind; he can be known and understood as "the same great identity in all the world religions."

In other words, according to the Lucis Trust, the Christ who is to come will be the Messiah expected by Islam, Hinduism, and Buddhism, as well as Christianity.

The Lucis Trust can certainly be given much credit for the current revival of occultism throughout the world. Bailey also provided the foundation for modern *occult astrology*. In her book, *Esoteric Astrology*, she theorizes that "the science of esoteric astrology is . . . the basic occult science of the future."

It is obvious that the future, as presented by the Lucis Trust, has no place for Jesus Christ. Mary Bailey, representing the Arcane School of the Lucis Trust, recently toured the United States and Canada and her meetings were given wide publicity. When asked by one person "Do you think we may see the second coming of Christ," Mrs. Bailey replied, "This event could occur in our time . . . It is unlikely he will be known by the name of Jesus because . . . the Master Jesus and the Christ are in fact two separate identities . . . Jesus is not the Christ."

The Hierarchy and a One World Order

The Lucis Trust is also promoter of the idea that there is a hidden hierarchy that promises to push the world forward into the New Age. This hierarchy is known by various names including the Lords of Compassion, the Society of Illumined Minds, and the Masters of Wisdom. The parallel organization of Lucis Trust, World Goodwill, proposes that these secretive men have been formed into a group called the New Group of World Servers.

The campaign for a One World Order is at the forefront of New Age teachings. In her book *Education for a New Age*, Alice Bailey insists that the age of nations and countries is about over. In the New Age, she maintains, *"World citizenship* should be the goal of the enlightened everywhere and the hallmark of the spiritual man." She states, "We need the political synthesis of a world federation with the World Brain." Moreover, she writes, "In the coming world state, the individual will subordinate his personality to the good of the whole."

The Lucis Trust believes in every type of occult New Age teachings imaginable. For example, reincarnation and communication with spirits are promoted, with Alice Bailey proclaiming, "Death is not a disaster to be feared; the Work of the destroyer is not really cruel or desirable." Alice Bailey has remarked that one of the tasks of the educators of the future will be to teach the meaning of reincarnation and karma, which the Lucis Trust calls the Law of Rebirth. Significantly, in its call for a New World Religion, Alice Bailey writes: "The doctrine of reincarnation will be one of the keynotes of the New World Religion."

Naturally, the Lucis Trust will be a backer of all religions except the one that teaches the exclusivity of Jesus Christ. Thus, Bailey writes: "The great theme of the New World Religion will be the recognition of the many divine approaches ... The platform of the New World Religion will be built by many groups, working under the inspiration of the Christ."

I have yet to visit a well-stocked New Age bookstore that does not carry at least some of the books of Alice Bailey. They include such titles as *The Destiny of the Nations; The Externalization of the Hierarchy; Initiation, Human and Solar; Letters on Occult Meditation; The Reappearance of the Christ;* and *A Treatise on Cosmic Fire.* Also, the Lucis Publishing Company has put out the works of Foster Bailey, which include *Running God's Plan* and a book promoting Freemasonry entitled *The Spirit of Masonry.* Also distributed by Lucis Publishing Company is the revealing book *Toward A World Religion For The New Age,* by Lola A. Davis. The Lucis Trust also publishes the *Beacon* magazine as well as many other special reports and booklets. Their logo is what appears to be an occultic, or satanic, circle enclosing a triangle--which, in occultism, indicates the unholy trinity. Inside also is the Tridentine mark superimposed over a slanted cross.

Because of the deeply esoteric nature of its teachings, I consider the Lucis Trust one of the most dangerous of New Age groups. The complicated and sophisticated books of Alice Bailey ingeniously weave within their pages the most insidious teachings ever developed in the annals of humankind. Yet, the Lucis Trust operates behind the facade of goodwill and love. Unsophisticated seekers, particularly those who have rejected the Bible as the literal Word of God, can easily be sucked into the swirling vortex of Lucis Trust doctrines and philosophies. Even some sincere Christians may initially be lured in by the Lucis Trust's profession of belief that the "Christ" is soon to return.

The Lucis Trust seeks an even wider audience. As far back as October 1982, the *Reader's Digest* published a full-page ad, under the paid sponsorship of the Lucis Trust, which displayed The Great Invocation. In small type at the bottom of the ad the Lucis Trust called on every individual, regardless of faith, to pray the Great Invocation so that the world's savior could come. To the unwary, the Lucis Trust was referring to Jesus; but to the initiated the truth was far more ominous: anyone praying the Lucis Trust's Great

Invocation was simply invoking the *false Messiah*, the beast of Revelation 13 to come forward and seize the throne of world power.

THE MAYAN ORDER

Rose Dawn, The Star Girl, was heard over the powerful radio station XERA in Del Rio, Texas in the mid-1930s. According to a recent story in *Texas Monthly* magazine (February 1990), Rose intrigued listeners by promising them they could master their abilities through the spiritualist powers of "the Mayans." Curious listeners who sent in the requested small fee received a booklet entitled *The Revelation Secret* which told them how they could obtain their desires and develop personal magnetism.

Today, the *Mayan Order* continues, though the Star Girl who founded it has passed away. Now mostly a mail-order course, those who send in their enrollment fcc and pay monthly dues are able to "learn the ancient wisdom of the Mayans as well as esoteric secrets from India, Egypt, and the orient." Recruits must keep the secret teachings confidential. Thus, they are given secret passwords, handgrips, and signs. Only in this way, says the literature of the Mayan Order, can they "succeed in the attainment of that most illusive state--Real Happiness." This elusive state is available to those who join the "Golden Circle of Mayanry" so that they can learn to develop an awareness of their inner self and "the forces within you."

The free-lance writer who wrote the article for the *Texas Monthly* magazine visited the Mayan Order. He found it operating in a two-story, Spanish-style office building bearing a large weathered sign with the words "Mayan

Order." Interestingly, he reported that the Mayan Order continues to use the late, charismatic Rose Dawn, the Star Girl, in letters from beyond sent to interested seekers. "Dear friend," read a recent epistle from the departed Star Girl. "My hand is extended to you in full Mayan Companionship . . . Will you accept it--today?"

MEDITATION GROUP FOR THE NEW AGE

The *Meditation Group for the New Age (MGNA)* is closely linked spiritually with the groups founded by Alice Bailey: the Lucis Trust, World Goodwill, Triangles, and the Arcane School. Headquartered in Ojai, California, at a site the group calls "Meditation Mount," this organization sends out brochures and mailings around the world. In fact, in a recent letter to its followers, MGNA boasted that its literature is now being mailed to 86 different countries. This group has also fostered local meditation groups around the world. Boldly pro-New Age, the Meditation Group for the New Age ends much of its literature with the final word of *Namaskara* which means "I salute the divinity in you." The group also mails out printed copies of *The Great Invocation,* given to Alice Bailey by her spirit guide Djwahl Khul, the Tibetan Master.

MGNA believes the answer to all the world's problems can be found in meditation. Its 10,000 membership actively meditates for world peace.

MESSIANIC CHURCH OF YAHWEH

The Messianic Church of Yahweh (MCY) was a group founded by Randall Baer, a brilliant man who wrote bestselling New Age books on crystal powers and planetary transformation. Randall Baer's MCY was based on the teachings of J. J. Hurtag and his false bible, *The Keys of Enoch,* as well as an eclectic blend of many other New Age and pseudo-Christian cult ideas acquired and applied by Randall Baer. MCY appeared to be biblical, but, in fact, was not. The cult was dissolved by Randall Baer when he converted to Christianity and resolved to do his best to expose the dangers of New Age occultism.

The New Age movement was Randall Baer's entire life and his consuming passion for 15 years. From the time he was a teenager he hungrily immersed himself in New Age occultism. By the age of 30, an uncanny sequence of dramatic events had propelled the brilliant Randall Baer into a meteoric rise to international renown as an expert in "crystal powers" and New Age religion. Randall Baer's work was featured on T.V.'s *20/20.* He was able to write his own ticket on the national lecture circuit. As a famous star on the New Age scene, he was riding high.

But one day, unexpectedly, a dark and hideous force entered Randall Baer's life. Overpowered, he was sucked into an incredible vortex of unimaginable evil and blackness. In desperation Randall cried out, "Jesus, help me!" And from that moment, Randall Baer's life changed. Totally.

Saved from doom only by the grace of God, his testimonial book, *Inside The New Age Nightmare,* is Randall Baer's revealing exposé of what the New Age really stands for. Here is the New Age in all its deception and hidden brutality, including the scheme to usher in an occult "Messiah."

Shockingly, just days before his book was to be released, Randall Baer was found dead. The police report states only that his car veered mysteriously off a 300 foot cliff in Colorado into the rocky valley below. Who killed Randall Baer? We do not know for sure if his death was accidental or by evil design. We do know that if he had lived, he would have been a powerful spokesman for true Christianity and a witness against the New Age deception.

THE MONROE INSTITUTE

Robert A. Monroe was a media executive who in 1958 began having out-of-body experiences, "traveling to locales far removed from the physical and spiritual realities of life." He recorded his experiences in his bestselling book, *Journeys Out of the Body,* and a follow-up book, *Far Journeys.* These books catapulted him to New Age fame and enabled him to found the *Monroe Institute* in Faber, Virginia.

The Monroe Institute offers "a system of planned self-evolution--the extraordinary capacity to transform one's consciousness." One of its programs is called "The Gateway Program." This is a series of taped exercises which progressively move the individual from deep relaxation to the ultimate thresholds of consciousness, using the techniques of deep meditation. This course and others are offered through in-home course work or at the Institute itself.

The Monroe Institute puts out the most glossy and slick publications and advertisements imaginable to lure and attract its audience. Its board of advisors includes an impressive array of engineers, biochemists, physicists, educators, psychologists, and medical doctors. All of these lend an aura of scientific respectability to the Monroe Institute. However, as I noted in the section on the Institute of Noetic Sciences, there is absolutely not one shred of scientific evidence that the techniques employed by such groups as the Monroe Institute are valid and scientific.

MONTESSORI

It's called the *"Montessori Method,"* after its founder, the late Italian educator Dr. Maria Montessori. It's in place across America and even the world as a curriculum for public and private school classrooms. Even some church schools and Sunday school programs have adopted the Montessori Method. Few realize the deep occultic roots of Maria Montessori and her Method.

Some of the awful truth about Montessori was revealed in my book, *Ravaged By the New Age.* Not every school which requires students to fulfill the Montessori curriculum embraces all of the tenets of the Montessori program. Nevertheless, my research indicates that the occultic underpinnings and foundations of the Montessori curriculum are so subtly hidden and so insidiously woven into her writings and techniques that even the most experienced and seasoned Christian educator often can be misled into thinking that the Montessori Method and curriculum are harmless.

However, a look at Montessori herself and the official Montessori curriculum that is promoted by some of the Montessori groups should enlighten any reasonable investigator as to the dubious nature of Montessori. It's all there in the official Montessori curriculum: the Mother Goddess, Earth and nature worship, occult symbols, New Age fantasy tales of Atlantis and Lemuria, Hindu psychology, the Nazi Aryan super race theory, Egyptian mythologies, the Cosmic

Plan, the "perfect human" lie, the Universal Oneness theme.

Maria Montessori: The New Age-Nazi Connection

Who was this Maria Montessori, whose education methods and thinly veiled religious beliefs are being promoted today in over 3,000 public school districts across the U.S.A.? Even some of her staunchest supporters admit that she and Fascist Italy's Benito Mussolini worked closely together in the 1920s and 1930s to bring her teachings to bear throughout Italy. Indeed, dictator Mussolini was at one time the President of the Montessori Society of Italy!

Montessori's fame then spread to Nazi Germany where the Montessori Method found favor with Adolf Hitler's education overlords. Montessori was a great friend of the occultic group, Theosophy. In India, she lived and worked with Theosophy leaders, who also published a number of her works. Hindu leader Gandhi praised her work and her "method." Her system of "Cosmic Education" was especially pleasing to the Hindus and Theosophy.

Today, the Montessori Method of "positive education" is taught at the New Age commune of Elizabeth Clare Prophet, head of the cultic Church Universal and Triumphant. Indeed, Prophet, who believes that her spirit guide, Count Saint Germain, is superior to Jesus, has founded a group called *Montessori International.* Thousands of Montessori schools have sprung up across the U.S.A. and the world, many begun by ardent New Agers and occultists, others by sincere but misguided educators.

Montessori to Bring in World Peace and "A New Type of Man"

The North American Montessori Teachers Association (NAMTA), in affiliation with the Montessori Association

International, glowingly describes the influence of Maria Montessori on the new educational method being prescribed today for so many thousands of schools. This method can help to bring in *world peace*, they claim because, as Montessori herself stated, it will result in "A new type of man, a better humanity." It will also, NAMTA comments, help man succeed in the "global task" of "reconstruction." In a recent NAMTA *Journal*, the educators stated:

> Maria Montessori, along with many other enlightened thinkers of our time, foresaw nothing less than the emergence of a new human culture. This new culture, a global, planetized humanity, would be based on a new consciousness of the unity and interdependence of all being, the interconnectedness of all forms of energy and matter. It is the culture of the present paradigm shift, by which we are beginning to align ourselves to educate the human potential for conscious cooperation with the evolution of life on the planet.

The above statement parrots the typical New Age line with all its talk about "new human culture;" "global, planetized humanity," "new consciousness," "unity," "interdependence of all forms," "energy," "paradigm shift," "human potential," "conscious cooperation," and "evolution."

NAMTA recognizes the New Age religious doctrine of reincarnation--also a principal, guiding belief of their founder, Maria Montessori. The organization encourages teachers and educators to help the "incarnating" child find "her" own place in the cosmos and to adopt the New Age idea of a divine earth. NAMTA also calls on teachers to fulfill the "vision" of founder Montessori:

> Our task as Montessori educators has a new dimension. A first goal has always been to help the child find her own place in the cosmos, which includes

incarnating and being humanized by the micro-culture. In addition, we must aid the child to transcend the micro-culture and to incarnate the globalized/planetized culture without which we as a species will not survive.

Our Montessori legacy is a rich one, for it contains both the vision and the means to implement it. At every developmental level, from toddlerhood on, we teach the needs of people. Cosmic Education is a daily experience as children and adults from many cultural and language groups come together. Within that diversity, we offer a curriculum based on cooperation, interdependence, and respect for all forms of life. We offer a curriculum that honors individual and group differences while emphasizing our essential connectedness to each other and to the Earth. In Maria Montessori's time, hers was a futurist vision. In ours, it is the vision of *now*.

In a recent edition of *Holistic Education Review* was an article entitled "Montessori and Spiritual Education." The author quoted Maria Montessori from her book, *Education For a New World:* "The world was not created for us to enjoy, but we are created to evolve the cosmos." In other words, Montessori believed strongly that man was a part of the cosmos and that all is God. Montessori was, after all, a Theosophist.

Montessori taught that within each child there is *already* a perfectly developed adult human being. This was because of her understanding of the Hindu/Theosophy concept of reincarnation. It was Montessori's contention that a method could be employed in which the spirit of the adult inside the child, derived from a previous incarnation, could develop its latent wisdom received from its many ancient lives. Thus, whenever an educator or a teacher tells me they believe strongly in the Montessori Method, my response has to be: Why do you endorse the most hardcore of occultic concepts?

Some mistakenly believe that they can take only the best of Montessori and discard what is not good. But consider this analogy: Once a capsule of cyanide has been placed in a glass of lemonade, who can remove each and every molecule of the poison? No, the entire glass of lemonade must be dumped down the sink and the glass must be sterilized if it is to be a safe vessel in the future. Likewise, the Montessori Method contains hidden spiritual poisons and toxins which can prove fatal to children.

MORAL REARMAMENT (MRA)

Moral Rearmament was founded by an American, Frank Buchman, around 1922 as the Oxford Group. In 1938 the name was changed to *Moral Rearmament,* or *MRA.* Buchman's Oxford Group received worldwide renown during the 30s until the world's press, including *Time* and *Newsweek* magazines, reported on a speech in which Buchman praised Adolf Hitler and the Nazis for their campaign against the Jews in Germany. Said Buchman, "I thank God for Adolf Hitler." It was also revealed that Buchman traveled to Germany on a secret mission to meet with Heinrich Himmler, head of the Nazi concentration camps.

Neither Buchman's original Oxford Group or today's Moral Rearmament is exclusively Christian. One can be a Hindu, a Moslem, or a Buddhist and be a member. Indeed, founder Buchman is known to have traveled to India where it is believed he worked with Hindu initiates to set up chapters of the Oxford Group. MRA has no churches and no pastors. It is not a denomination, but a worldwide spiritual fellowship. Buchman taught that a man could begin quietly each day with pen and paper and write down the impressions and instructions from "God," whomever that may be for the individual. This was called Quiet Time. Soon, however, reports began to circulate that at Oxford Group chapters in the United States, Great Britain, and elsewhere, people were getting together for Quiet Time parties in which "spooks," or spirits encouraged them to do some quite unorthodox things, including sexual acts outside of marriage. This further weakened the credibility of Buchman's fellowship.

In his excellent book, *More Understanding Alternative Medicine*, Englishman Roy Livesey, a well respected Christian author, tells of his attendance at a Moral Rearmament conference. At the conference were speakers and participants from all the world's religions, but, as Livesey observed, the prevailing message at the MRA conference was that no one should "fall into the trap and seek only one God." Nor, said Livesey, was there any recognition among the participants that Jesus Christ is *the* Way, *the* Truth, *the* Life.

MORMONS (LDS)

The Mormon Church--officially the *Church of Jesus Christ of Latter-day Saints (LDS)*--was founded in the 1830s by American Joseph Smith. Joseph Smith was a Mason and an occultist. It is known that he worked an occultic Jupiter (the Roman god) talisman which he called his "Masonic Jewel." He carried it with him always and it was on his person when he died. Historians of Mormonism have noted that Smith's entire family was deeply involved in the occult. Joseph Smith himself was arrested in 1826 for an occult practice called "glass looking." Smith had claimed that for a fee he could find buried treasure by simply looking through his magical

"Peepstone." The authorities were not amused.

Because of founder Smith's occultism, the entire Mormon faith is thoroughly immersed in disguised satanism and heretical false teachings. For example, here are just a few of the teachings of the Mormon Church: (1) Jesus was married to the sisters of Lazarus and to Mary Magdalene; (2) He converted water to wine at his own wedding; (3) Jesus was begotten in the flesh sexually by God, who is also a fleshly being; (4) Jesus' wives and children were present at his crucifixion; (5) Jesus is the brother of Satan and he became Savior only after His salvation was approved by a vote of the Council of the gods; (6) Men who are Mormons and who follow the Mormon teachings, becoming initiated into a higher state, become gods of their own planets. As gods they may have millions of wives and enjoy endless sex; (7) God Himself was once simply an exalted man. God is not an eternal being. Instead, He worked Himself up to Godhood; (8) Salvation is not possible except through the prophet of the Mormon Church, Joseph Smith; (9) There is a Mother in heaven as well as a Father; (10) The Old and New Testaments of the Holy Bible are flawed, imperfect, and inferior to the works of Joseph Smith, which include *The Book of Mormon,* called "another Testament of Jesus Christ," and *Pearl of Great Price.*

And More Occult Heresies

After reviewing the above list of Mormon heresies, turn to pages 46 through 48 of this book and examine the chart "New Age vs. True Christianity: A Contrast." You will discover that the Mormon Church is *totally* a part of the New Age religion and movement. Of course, the most grievous error of the Mormons is the denial of Jesus Christ. Not only does the Mormon doctrine deny the virgin birth of Jesus, but Mormons insist that Jesus is not unique from other men. Also, it is taught that Jesus' death on the cross did not atone for our sins. Furthermore, Mormonism teaches that all men are potential gods. The Mormon credo is: "As man is, God once was: As God is, man may become."

It would take me hundreds of pages to describe all of the false doctrines and wierd teachings of the Mormon Church. Isn't it amazing, then, that many confused and unknowing Christian pastors and ministry leaders are misled into believing that the Mormon Church is simply another Christian denomination?

New Temple Rituals: Adapting to New Age Unity

Not only are the Mormon rituals and doctrines classic New Age, but the Mormon hierarchy has begun to update its temple rituals and teachings to become more acceptable to society as a whole and to the New Age movement and the emerging one world, unified religion in particular. For example, recently the church dropped its requirement that women must, in the temple ritual, pledge to obey their husbands. The Mormons also eliminated the part of their temple ritual in which a character portraying a non-Mormon "preacher" was paid by Satan to spread false doctrines.

The emerging theme in the Mormon Church today is that salvation through Mormonism is not exclusive. It is clear that the new changes, combined with the bedrock doctrines of Mormonism, bring this heretical church fully into agreement with the overall theology of the New Age Religion. Since the Mormon Church has at least 5,500,000 members worldwide and possibly as many as 8 million, the revisions and new changes in church doctrine and practice are highly significant. If the Mormon Church, at some future moment in time, throws its weight completely behind the New Age, a momentum could be created in which a One World Religion could almost instantly become a reality.

For more information about Mormonism and its satanic character and nature, I recommend the book *The God Makers* by Ed Decker and Dave Hunt. Another excellent book on Mormonism is *Mormonism: Shadow or Reality?* by

Jerald and Sandra Tanner, two former Mormons who are now Christians. Also, interested individuals may contact one of the following ministries:

Ed Decker
Saints Alive in Jesus
P.O. Box 1076
Issaquah, WA 98027

John Smith
Utah Missions
P.O. Box 348
Marlow, OK 73055

MOVEMENT OF SPIRITUAL INNER AWARENESS (MSIA)

It has been called "the Cadillac of cults." Its followers claim that its founder and head is the embodiment of "John the Beloved" and that he has been endowed with a Christ-like power known as the "Mystical Traveler Consciousness." The *Los Angeles Times*, in an exposé of this cult group (August 14, 1988), called it an "international New Age empire." The leader of this cult: John-Roger. His cult: the *Movement of Spiritual Inner Awareness,* or *MSIA* (pronounced "Messiah").

In 1963 MSIA's John-Roger was known as Roger Hinkins, and he was an English teacher at Rosemead High School in California. Then he underwent a kidney stone operation in a Los Angeles hospital. In a freak accident, possibly caused by a sedative overdose, Hinkins went into a nine-day coma.

"When I woke up nine days later," he said, "there was another being in me and he called himself John ... When I opened my eyes, I remember my mother sitting there saying, 'Who are you?' And the voice said, 'I am John.' And she said,

'Is Roger there?' He said, 'Yes, he is in here too.'"

Thus, Roger Hinkins became John-Roger, a man in a physical body possessed by a spirit known as John the Beloved.

Already known as a charismatic man who was a hero to his students, John-Roger began to teach in the homes of friends around Southern California. People seemed to be astounded by his practical advice and spiritual wisdom. Soon he was able to found his "church," the Movement of Spiritual Inner Awareness (MSIA). By the mid-1970s, thousands of people were reading the monthly newsletter of MSIA for which John-Roger charged a yearly fee. They had also begun to listen to audio tapes of John-Roger chanting the "sacred names of God." Some became eligible to become Ministers of Light in the "Melchizedek Priesthood." MSIA was legally incorporated as a church and its ministers began to perform regular ministerial duties such as baptisms and marriages. John-Roger proclaimed that his followers were spreading the Light, a positive energy which Christians, he said, know as the Holy Spirit. John-Roger called himself the Mystical Traveler and soon began to be widely recognized for his wealth and health teachings.

In 1974 John-Roger and MSIA moved into a sumptuous mansion in Los Angeles which he dubbed "The Purple Rose Ashram of the New Age," or PRANA. It is now referred to as the Prana Theological Seminary and College of Philosophy. Teachings of Prana include the dispelling of negative energies and the absorption of the "Mystical Traveler Consciousness." Soon, John-Roger became a national phenomenon and MSIA Light Centers were set up in New York, Boston, Philadelphia, New Jersey, Chicago, and even in Paris and London. Moreover, John-Roger established a subsidiary group, Insight Transformational Seminars, to conduct training sessions for some of America's top corporations. Some 50,000 people have gone through these seminars, it is reported.

Mother Theresa, Bishop Tutu, and more...

John-Roger has been acclaimed by some of America's most well-known celebrities, politicians, and religious clergy. Beginning in 1983, John-Roger's cult foundation began its sponsorship of an annual event called the "International Integrity Awards." Each year John-Roger personally presents the award, and dignitaries have come from all over the world eager to receive it. Among the recipients are Catholic Missionary Mother Theresa, South African Archbishop Desmond Tutu, Los Angeles Mayor Tom Bradley, polio researcher Dr. Jonas Salk, and singer Stevie Wonder. In 1986 Poland's Solidarity leader Lech Welesa attempted to leave Poland to accept one of John-Roger's Integrity awards. When he was prevented from doing so by Poland's communist government, John-Roger's group received worldwide news coverage. At the awards gala, the popular guru

Mother Theresa, a recipient of John-Roger's Integrity Award, shown with the New Age spiritual leader.

John-Roger presents the award winners with leaded-crystal pyramids and checks for $10,000. The celebrity-laden, black tie audience of 1,000 has included actor John Forsythe, Beach Boy Carl Wilson, actresses Teri Garr, Ellen Burstyn and Oscar nominee Sally Kirkland, and consumer advocate Ralph Nader.

Charges of Homosexuality and Brainwashing

More recently, John-Roger ran into some difficulty when disillusioned former cult members went to the news media to protest that John-Roger is not quite the man he appears to be. Some said that he has conducted a campaign of hate and has even encouraged vandalism against those who have left the cult.

The *Los Angeles Times* decided to investigate and eventually ran a series of exposé articles about John-Roger and the cult. A revealing article by *People* magazine followed. In these articles John-Roger was accused of abusing his spiritual authority by brainwashing his followers, seducing young male staffers, and intimidating dissenters. Some dissidents said that John-Roger used hidden listening devices at the organization's Santa Monica headquarters to support his claim of having mind-reading powers. One man, Victor Toso, said that he had been victimized by John-Roger and persuaded to engage in a homosexual relationship. According to Toso, John-Roger uses sex to seal young men into "the Brotherhood." Ex-followers also claim that John-Roger had declared that people who question him had placed themselves under a devil-like spirit power and its field of negativity, known as "the red monk."

In answer to these charges, John-Roger recently conducted a meeting of supporters in which he read passages from the Bible warning them that they would have to give account on the Day of Judgment for every evil word they have spoken.

Though the allegations and charges against John-Roger

rocked the Southern California area in 1988 and vastly damaged his credibility, reportedly his organization continues, though the glory days possibly are over.

THE MYSTERY SCHOOL

The Mystery School, in Pomona, New York, asks its applicants for a year's commitment, during which time the individual will be instructed on the ancient mysteries as they were taught by the pagans in Greece, Turkey, Afghanistan, Ireland, Egypt, France, Scandinavia, and so forth. This is the promise of the brochures published by Jean Houston, the School's founder. Houston was formerly the president of the American Association of Humanistic Psychology, and she is a very popular speaker at New Age conferences throughout the United States. A few years ago she began the Mystery School. Its activities involve classic mythology, Eastern and Oriental religious teachings, and especially the mythologies of the goddess. For example, Houston states that, "Studying and enacting the transformation of a war goddess, Athena ... can give us clues about transforming ourselves and the people who can help green the world."

According to Houston, as of 1989 some 1,200 people from all over the U.S. and the earth have attended the Mystery School course. Houston claims that the Mystery School will enable participants to know "the Source of All Being." In reality, this New Age program will simply divert and keep people away from the only true God there is, Jesus Christ. For those people who are truly interested in the ultimate destination of those who become involved in what has been called "the Ancient Mysteries," all one needs to do is turn to Revelation 17 of their Holy Bible. There they will discover that the last days church of Satan is pictured as a Mystery Woman, the goddess, whose destiny is most pathetic.

NATIVE AMERICAN INDIAN CULTS AND RELIGIONS

The Native American Indian tribes of North America developed religions which were strikingly similar to those of other pagan civilizations around the world. The sight of the Indian Medicine Man dressed with buffalo skins and horns and doing a dance around some totem pole or fire is not a figment of somebody's imagination. That was actually a ritual by many Native American Indian tribes. Today among New Agers, one of the hottest fads is the revival of the spiritualistic system of the Indians.

The Native American Indian religion is a growth industry. New Age groups are proliferating. For example, there is the Bear Tribe Medicine Society, led by founder Sun Bear, its medicine chief. There is the Earth Circle, and the XAT Medicine Society which advertises its goal as the "teaching of the old ways for a New Age." There is also a group known as the White Buffalo Society, which made the news recently when a woman died after she was buried alive in a "soul cleansing" initiation ceremony.

The Native American Indian worshippers have had their religious practices endorsed by Joseph Campbell, best-selling author of *The Power of Myth*, who stated that "We have today to learn to get back into accord with the wisdom of nature and realize again our brotherhood with the animals and with the water and with the sea." Rituals and practices of these cults and groups include Vision Quest, a cultural rite of passage and ceremony in which people spend several days of "earth awareness exercises" so that they can "open their ears and eyes and hearts to Mother Earth." This instruction includes fasting and seeking of guidance of spirits at some sacred mountain or in some other nature setting. Some Native American groups smoke peyote or marijuana to achieve altered states of consciousness. Most also use the sweat lodge for the same purpose, and they dance the Circle Dance, also to gain a higher state of consciousness. Mandalas, talismans and meditation-centering devices are frequently used, medicine wheels are consulted, systems of earth astrology are promoted, environmentalism is pushed, and the smoking of the pipe around the circle is common.

The Great Spirit and The Force Are One

The Native American Indian theology of the "Great Spirit," the all-in-all, fits in quite nicely with the New Age doctrine of an impersonal force as God. Indeed, the Indian medicine men and spiritual leaders preach tolerance and the brotherhood of all creeds and religions, believing that there is only one Ultimate Reality.

The Native American Indian cults and religions rarely include mention of Jesus Christ in their rituals and ceremonies. Yet, there has been a movement among some to "walk the sacred circle with Jesus Christ." Incredibly, Cardinal Frances Arinze, a Vatican official who is head of the Pontifical Council for Interreligious Dialogue, spoke to more than 2,000 Native American Catholics gathered at Northern Dakota State University on August 2-6, 1989, and told the assemblage that, "The Creator has always walked with the American Indian people and their ancestors." Cardinal Arinze urged the Indians to claim their heritage and then he issued this heretical statement: "Christ is found in the traditional sacred ways of Native Americans."

While it is true of course that Jesus Christ can fulfill the needs of people of all cultures, including Native American

Indians, the Catholic Cardinal is totally incorrect in his strange belief that Christ is found in the "traditional sacred ways of American Indians." The traditional sacred ways of Native Americans are undeniably occultic, and the occult world and Jesus are poles apart.

It should not be assumed that the membership of the Native American Indian cults and religions is only Indian. In fact, the vast majority of those who participate in these cult groups are non-Indian Americans, people who are looking for the newest fad in the New Age and think they have found what they are looking for among the witch doctors and medicine men of the Navajo, Cherokee, Choctaw, Sioux, and other peoples. It should also be understood that there are many Native Americans who *are* believers in Jesus Christ and are solid Christians. These Christians are distressed and saddened by the revival of the cult groups and the New Age occultic influences which are sweeping their communities and reservations.

NEW AGE BIBLE AND PHILOSOPHY CENTER

Corinne Heline, who recently passed away, was one of the most brilliant writers of the New Age Movement. Her cardinal work is a set of seven bible commentaries on the New Testament and the Old Testament which are entitled *New Age Bible Interpretation*. These commentaries, which analyze and reinterpret the Holy Bible from an esoteric and occultic viewpoint, were first published in the 1930s and have been popular in New Age and occult circles now for more than half a century. They continue to be sold through the *New Age Bible and Philosophy Center* in Santa Monica, California. The works of Corinne's husband, Theodore Heline, are also offered by this New Age publishing group.

The books of Corinne Heline give us an indication of how broad and far-ranging were her occultic and esoteric interests. Among Corinne Heline's published works are the following books: *Mystery of the Christos; Tarot and the Bible; Mythology and the Bible; Mystic Masonry and the Bible; Occult Anatomy and the Bible; Sacred Science of Numbers; Supreme Initiations of the Blessed Virgin; Color and Music in the New Age; Esoteric Music of Richard Wagner;* and *Mysteries of the Holy Grail.* In all of these works and especially in her *New Age Bible Interpretation*, Corinne Heline enthusiastically endorsed all the various New Age philosophies, including most of the doctrines of Helena Blavatsky's Theosophy group. For example, Heline endorsed Blavatsky's view that man has been spiritually evolving into divinity and that there are seven spiritual races, culminated by the Ayran and the Aquarian.

An interesting feature of Heline's works is her veneration of Mary, Mother of Jesus. Calling her the Blessed Lady, Heline believed that Mary was herself divine. In her *New Age Bible Interpretation*, volume VI, she wrote:

> Mary accompanied the Master on journeyings through towns and villages of the Holy Land. By her divinely awakened powers she, following in her Lord's footsteps, also ministered unto the sorrowing and healed the sick . . . Mary was at this time exquisitely beautiful in appearance--tall and youthfully slender, her long flowing hair forming a bright sheen about her head. Her delicate oval face was illumined by lustrous eyes, through which the powers of her radiant spirit shown like the perpetual light of some heavenly altar flame . . . The processes of time were stilled within her. Her physical body no longer knew the forces of age and disintegration . . .

Since Corinne Heline, like almost all leaders and authorities in the New Age Movement, believed in communication with the spirit world, it is very likely that her description of Mary was received by her in messages from demonic spirits.

NEW AGE CHURCHES

Recently in *The Baptist Standard*, the most widely distributed Baptist publication in the state of Texas, a top official of the Southern Baptist Convention suggested that Baptist churches did not have to worry about losing members to New Age Churches since, "There are no New Age churches." Ironically, the very week that this particular issue of *The Baptist Standard* was published, the *Houston Chronicle* carried a feature story on New Age churches in that city!

There are indeed New Age churches established across America and even the world, and some of these churches are growing astronomically. Their names sometimes have a mystical, esoteric flavor, but often the New Age churches adopt Christian-sounding names. Among the New Age churches you will find the *Church of Amron, Church of Today, Creative Learning Center, Church of the White Eagle Lodge, Healing Light Center, Unity By the Sea, Union Temple of Isis, Collegians International Church, Church of Conscious Harmony, New Lighted Way, Church of the Aquarian Age, the Liberal Catholic Church*, and *Light of Christ Community Church.*

Some of the New Age churches have memberships ranging in the thousands and their numbers are multiplied by the use of local radio and television media. The teachings and spiritual practices, as well as the training of the pastors, ministers, and clergymen of these churches, vary greatly. But it can be said that all embrace the essential New Age doctrines (see pages 47 through 48 of this book).

For example, the *Centre Church of Spiritual Quest*, in Jacksonville, Florida, has as its logo a pyramid and the cross linked together. A recent newsletter of this church publicizes such special events as a meeting to be conducted by "A wonderful extraterrestrial named Terone, who is seven-feet tall and comes from the planet Altar, in the Galaxy Sirius." The Church newsletter also announces past life regression classes, channeling of the spirit Rama, and Reiki healing classes to assist people to attune themselves to "the Universal Life Energy Force."

Meanwhile, in Corpus Christi, Texas, federal judge Philip Schraub is pastor of the *Chapel of Spiritual Light*, a church whose congregation communes with what Schraub called, "The Higher Spiritual Plane." Schraub notes that in his courtroom, it is his job to set bond and pass sentence on drug traffickers and other criminals. He suggests that these are souls "from the lower astral planes"--caught in some unfortunate incarnation in which they are paying back their karmic debts. At the Chapel of Spiritual Light, "Pastor" Schraub teaches about the Great White Brotherhood and assures his parishioners that there is no such thing as "hell, fire, and brimstone."

Jewish New Age Synagogues

Not all New Age churches stress their so-called "Christian" ties. There is also a movement in the Jewish community to establish New Age-oriented synagogues. One such Jewish synagogue is the *Makom Ohr Shalom* in Woodland Hills, California. This synagogue is led by Rabbi Ted Falcon, Ph.D, who bills himself as "a practicing psychotherapist and storyteller who designs metaphors and meditations for personal evolution." In *L.A. Resources* newspaper (Winter issue 1989-90), the Makom Ohr Shalom synagogue advertised that Rabbi Falcon "is well-known for his classes on the Kabbalah (an ancient form of mystical occultism) and mysticism, psychology, and spirituality."

Many of the Jewish New Age synagogues express belief in and worship the Mother Goddess as well as the Father God. They call her the "Goddess of the Sabbat." Such beliefs remind us of the heretical practices engaged in by Ahab and Jezebel in the Bible. Ahab and Jezebel also worshipped the Mother Goddess, whom they believed to be the consort of Baal. Today the New Age synagogues are bringing back this same unholy worship which brought God's wrath down on the people of Israel so many times in the past.

THE NEW AGE SCHOOL

The New Age School is an organization in the state of Iowa which was started by New Age activists. Their goal is to bring people from what they call the "Heartland of America" (Iowa, Minnesota, Wisconsin, Illinois, Indiana, Missouri, Nebraska, and the Dakotas) together to share a common vision. In other words: the New Age vision. Their symbol is the six-pointed star inside a circle, the star being made up of two triangles combined together. Inside is yet another triangle in the shape of a pyramid.

The New Age School offers a variety of courses and also brings New Agers together for periodic celebrations. Among the topics recently offered by the New Age School: "Reincarnation--the Great Reality;" "The Healing Force;" "The Healing Power of Sound and Color;" "Dreams, Visions, Personal Myths;" "Psychic Explorations;" and "Navigating Inner Space and the Heaven Worlds."

Principal teachers of the New Age School include Dr. Marilyn Rossner, Catholic priest John Rossner, and Nan Porter. In addition, New Age authors are brought in from outside the Midwest. A recent outside teacher was Joseph Tilton Pearce, author of *The Magical Child.*

OMEGA INSTITUTE

The Omega Institute is formally called the Omega Institute for Holistic Studies. In its facilities at Rhinebeck, New York, amidst a scenic locale near the Hudson River, Omega operates one of the largest and most well-known training centers for the New Age Movement. Its board of directors includes such New Age notables as Tom Jackson and Ram Dass, and the Omega Institute manages to bring in world-class New Age speakers to conduct seminars and workshops.

The staff at the Omega Institute operate the community all twelve months of the year. Students come in for anywhere from four to 13 weeks to take part in the programs. Catalogs and course brochures are sent out by mail to a substantial mailing list. The training and courses are on a variety of New Age topics. Indeed, almost nothing is excluded from the curriculum. In a recent year, the Omega Institute invited Catholic priest Matthew Fox to teach on "Creation Spirituality," author Michael Harner to speak on the "Shamanic Journey," Englishman Philip Carr-Gomm to speak on "The Druid Path," Native American Indian leader Dennis Banks to speak on "The Sacred Circle," and David Spangler to teach on "Divine Play."

Other well-known New Age leaders who have come to Omega Institute include novelist Joseph Heller, Ninja martial arts teacher Stephen Hayes, self-esteem teachers

Nathaniel and Devers Branden, and humanist Ashley Montagu. Courses are also offered on Zen, Dervish Dancing, Ritual Arts of Tibet, Gaia the Earth Goddess, Emotional Healing for Adult Children of Alcoholics, Tarot Astrology, and the I Ching.

ORDER OF THE GOLDEN DAWN

The Order of the Golden Dawn is an elitist occult society that had its origins in 1887 in England. Over the years its membership has included some of the most renowned men in the world--for example, the Irish poet W. B. Yeats--as well as some very curious characters, such as Arthur Madras, the creator of *Dracula*, and occult author Dr. Israel Regardie.

The current head of The Order of the Golden Dawn (more recently called *The Golden Dawn Society and Temple*) is a man named Christopher Hyatt. Hyatt was interviewed in 1987 by fellow occultist Antero Alli in *Magical Blend* magazine (issue number 16, pp. 20-22). His comments during this interview were quite instructive as to the thinking of both himself and his organization. Complaining that fundamentalists were "digging their heals into the ground" and attempting to "enforce their dogma," Hyatt predicted that the fundamentalist forces will be overcome. There will be a "changing of the guards," he declared.

Exactly how will this "changing of the guards" take place? "I see," he stressed, "that the earth still requires some blood before it is ready to move into new and different areas."

> The Guards of the Ancient era ... the ones dying right now ... are not willing to give up their authority

so easily. I foresee, on a mass scale, that the New Age is not going to come into being as so many people believe and wish to believe. I see it as requiring a heck of a lot of blood, disruption, chaos, and pain for a mass change to occur.

THE PACIFIC INSTITUTE

It was his course on "New Age Thinking for Achieving Your Potential" which made Louis Tice's organization, *The Pacific Institute,* one of the leading lights in the United States among the mind dynamics and psychological motivation seminar companies. However, in the mid-80s, as conservative Christians began to catch on to the dangers of the New Age, the Pacific Institute rethought its marketing strategy. "New Age Thinking for Achieving Your Potential" was retired and a new curriculum, "Investment in Excellence" took its place. Critics noted, however, that the new training series employed most of the same rhetoric, encouraging the belief that through visualization and mantra-like affirmations, people can change their behavior patterns and influence others.

The Pacific Institute insists it has no affiliation with the New Age Movement but its courses suggest otherwise. Although there is no evidence of blatant occultism in the curricula, still one can easily see the definite signs of New Age influence and human potential psychology. In the teaching manual which accompanies the 19-part video presentation of "Investment in Excellence" we immediately see that Unit One has course material on "The Wizard." The course guide explains that:

The session closes with a discussion of the Wizard of Oz--how, through one-time affirmation, through the power of psycho-linguistics, our lives are influenced. We see how powerful 'wizards' determine our behavior. *We also see that we can be our own wizards; how through positive affirmations we can truly be our own person, our own authority...*

Elsewhere in the training guide the student is taught that visualization and imagery can change habits and reduce stress. There is also an emphasis on self-talk, another humanistic psychology technique. The material suggests that self-talk can have a powerful influence on a person: "In effect, it makes you your own prophet." As to whether a person should seek outside of themselves to discover the reality of a transcendent God, the material remarks: "All lasting and meaningful change starts on the inside and works its way out." This is certainly in contradiction with the Bible which tells us that the transformation experience--being born again in the spirit (John 3:3)--is a gift of God, not of our own doing, and that no man can come to the Father except the Holy Spirit draw him.

The psychological techniques employed by the Pacific Institute may not be overtly occultic, but they are of decidedly little worth in enhancing human effectiveness. It is shameful that many of America's top corporations and governmental agencies have paid the Pacific Institute untold millions of dollars to present courses which provide such minimal, if any value. The National Research Council of the National Academy of Sciences, in its prestigious report, *Enhancing Human Performance* (1988), determined that there was *no scientific basis* at all for such concepts as self-talk, visualization, guided imagery, and so-forth.

In addition, employees who are compelled by their employers to attend training courses and seminars on-the-job--whether they come labeled as "New Age" or not--should know that they are *not* required to go to these courses, and the employer cannot retaliate in any way. If the employee believes that such training violates his or her religious beliefs, civil rights or conscience, the employee *cannot* be compelled to attend. The law stands behind the Christian in this matter according to an important ruling of the Equal Employment Opportunity Commission. For more information about this EEOC ruling (refer to: EEOC ruling #N-915.022, February, 1988), write to Coordination and Guidance Services Office, Equal Employment Opportunity Commission, 1801 L Street NW, Washington, D.C., 20507, or phone toll-free 1-800-USA-EEOC.

PEACEVISION

PeaceVision, headquartered in Houston, Texas, is an organization "committed to peace and planetary upliftment and dedicated ... to peace and cooperation on a global scale." This statement comes from PeaceVision itself. This is the group which makes and distributes the popular bumper stickers you have probably seen on dozens of cars

PeaceVision distributes this popular bumper sticker.

which implore us to "Visualize World Peace." PeaceVision also sells and distributes mini-stickers which are in the form of the all-seeing eye with a globe inside and also state "Visualize World Peace." In the New Age theology, it is believed that if enough individuals across the planet visualize world peace simultaneously that the collective thought powers accumulated will cause humanity to take a *quantum leap* into the New Age, supposedly to be an era of global harmony, love, sharing, and peace.

PERELANDRA COMMUNITY

Though it may shock some Christians who admire his books, fantasy writer C.S. Lewis, the late Englishman who wrote *The Chronicles of Narnia* and many other books, is a great hero to New Agers. They view his writings, especially his novels, as the embodiment of New Age teachings on the sacredness of earth and a confirmation of the essential New Age doctrine that "all is one." Especially beloved of New Agers is C.S. Lewis' novel *Perelandra*, which promotes the concept of the entire planet as the "Green Lady." The Green Lady, they say, refers to the Goddess of the pagan mythologies. Indeed, New Agers have even established the *Perelandra Community* based on the writings of C.S. Lewis.

Recently, an interviewer for *New Realities* magazine (May/June 1988) interviewed Machaelle Small Wright, the founder of the Perelandra Community. Located some 60 miles south of Washington, D.C., near the tiny hamlet of Jeffersonton, Virginia, Perelandra sits astride 22 acres of meadows, woods, streams, and gardens. Wright welcomes visitors to the community but one cannot become a resident until Wright is satisfied that the person has read Lewis' novel

Perelandra.

In an article written for the *Virginia Biological Farmer,* Machaelle Small Wright was pictured as a woman who talked to fairies and angels and who believed she could materialize manure out of thin air. Wright also is presented as able to persuade moles and other garden creatures to do her bidding and insects to leave her garden alone. She has authored a "how-to" book entitled *Perelandra Garden Workbook: A Complete Guide to Gardening With Nature Intelligences.*

As Wright describes Perelandra, the name was chosen because of C. S. Lewis' *Perelandra.* For example, the word "perelandra" means "venus, planet of perfection." Among occultists, it is believed that Lucifer, a good being, came from the planet Venus to Earth. The residents of Perelandra believe that Lewis' concepts of good and bad countervailing each other in a harmonious balance is a picture of the real metaphysical world.

Wright and her Perelandra Community are not the only ones to laud C. S. Lewis as a fellow New Ager. The "Books of Light" New Age Bookclub has chosen C. S. Lewis' novels as main selections. One New Age publisher actually named their company *Aslan Publishing,* after the main character, the god-lion Aslan, in C. S. Lewis' *Chronicles of Narnia.*

Jean Houston, of the New Age's The Mystery School, has also highly commended C. S. Lewis' mythological book *Perelandra.* In a recent brochure sent out by The Mystery School she exclaims: "The fictional works of visionary writers like Lewis Carroll *(Alice in Wonderland)* . . . and the fantasies of C. S. Lewis *(Perelandra)* and Madeleine L'Engle *(A Wrinkle in Time)* and many others may serve to inspire our creation of the new myth." In the New Age, the "new myth" is a cult phrase for the New Age kingdom on planet earth.

(Note: Several of his biographers noted that C. S. Lewis was *not* a fundamentalist Christian. He did not believe that the Christian Bible is inerrant or that it is the only set of inspired scriptures. Instead, Lewis expressed the belief that Jesus and

Christianity were the *fulfillment* of all the ancient pagan myths--"the myth that came true." For more information about Lewis' unorthodox views, please see the book, *C. S. Lewis on Scripture,* by Michael J. Christensen (Nashville: Abingdon Press, 1979).

PHILOSOPHICAL RESEARCH SOCIETY

The *Philosophical Research Society* was founded in 1934 by Manley P. Hall, an esoteric occultist and 33rd degree Mason. Hall's book, *The Secret Teachings of All Ages,* is a massive compendium of esoteric philosophies and occult doctrines over the ages. He has authored many other works which are of intense interest to intellectually-minded New Agers, occultists, and researchers of comparative religions. The Philosophical Research Society has its headquarters in Los Angeles, California, with offices, a book store, and an auditorium where numerous lectures are regularly presented on a variety of topics.

The Society also publishes a great number of books including reprints of rare esoteric manuscripts and books. Subject matter includes esoteric astrology, angels and spirits, Cabala and Tarot, magic, reincarnation, karma, and death, the oriental religions, and medieval alchemy. Manley P. Hall also has written a book greatly admired by fellow Masons entitled *Lost Keys of Freemasonry.* Although brief, this book is very revealing of the true teachings of the Masonic Lodge.

RAMTHA

JZ Knight is perhaps the best-known of all New Age spirit channelers. Her contention is that a 35,000-year old warrior/spirit named *Ramtha* began coming to her in 1978 and became her teacher. At the time, Knight was a housewife in Washington state who had been dabbling with a number of occultic methods, including pyramid power. After Ramtha came into her life, JZ Knight became famed throughout the New Age world. She traveled from city to city charging hundreds of dollars to the individuals who came to hear Ramtha speak from her mouth.

Ramtha, whose voice is very stilted and foreign, spouts much the same occultic gibberish as other spirit guides. Through JZ Knight, Ramtha tells his followers that "Love" is everything, that they are themselves divine, and that even Lucifer is a divine entity. Typically, Knight introduces Ramtha by going into a semiconscious state, shaking, then going limp. Suddenly, she becomes animated again as Ramtha. JZ then walks through the audience speaking in Ramtha's low, rhythmic voice, spouting great "wisdom."

JZ Knight has certainly enriched herself through the teachings of Ramtha. According to news reports (for example see *Newsweek*, December 15, 1986), she has been able to buy a large ranch in Washington state and stock it complete with Arabian thoroughbred horses. Visitors report that they are shocked to find that her horses live in an utter state of luxury: Indeed, crystal chandeliers hang from the rafters of the stable.

It hasn't hurt JZ Knight's reputation that such celebrities as Linda Evans, of TV's *Dynasty* fame, frequently travel to see her in Washington and seek advice from Ramtha. Reporters who have attended sessions in which JZ Knight channeled Ramtha say that people cry, sob, and a few of them have flung themselves at JZ Knight's feet. Some begin to jerk their bodies, others break out in uncontrollable laughter. Such devoteés are brisk buyers of Ramtha's teachings in the form of audiotapes, videos, and books.

THE REORGANIZED CHURCH OF JESUS CHRIST OF LATTER-DAY SAINTS (RLDS)

The Reorganized Church of Jesus Christ of Latter-day Saints (RLDS) is the second largest Mormon sect. When the founder of Mormonism, Joseph Smith, was killed in Carthage, Illinois, most of the members left with Brigham Young and settled in Utah to found what has become the main group of Mormons. A smaller group, claiming to be "The True Church," continued with Joseph Smith's son Joseph III as their prophet. This group continues to the present time as the RLDS with sons in the family replacing the elder Smiths.

The RLDS fully believes that *The Book of Mormon* is the Word of God and accepts many of the occult practices of its larger cousin in Salt Lake City. There are several traditional Mormon doctrines that the RLDS has rejected, such as baptism for the dead and the multiple god theory. However, over the years, the RLDS has adopted fresh new doctrines which are even more stunning in their occultic foundations. In the 1970s the then prophet of the RLDS church, W. Wallace Smith, proclaimed that he had received prophecies which directed the church's mission in certain new directions. Consequently, the RLDS began to associate with and support such groups as the liberal, feminist National Organization for Women (NOW) and the World Council of Churches. The RLDS hierarchy became involved in the peace movement. Some in the RLDS structure began to promote gay rights, abortion rights, and other liberal and socialistic causes.

Though some of the membership were unhappy with these goings-on, most kept quiet because they believed that W. Wallace Smith was called of God to be the prophet, seer, and revelator of the Church. In 1984 the new prophet/head of the RLDS, Wallace B. Smith, son of W. Wallace, received his famous revelation declaring that women could be ordained into the RLDS priesthood. Prophet Wallace also put out the word that a temple that had been in the works for many years and which was to be constructed in Independence, Missouri, where the headquarters of the RLDS is located, shall be dedicated to the purpose of peace.

The RLDS temple under construction has a spiral design much like the famed Babylonian ziggaraut which the Bible calls the Tower of Babel. Indeed, prophet Wallace B. Smith, speaking of the temple design, has stated: "The design gives the impression of seeking to link that which is earthbound with the creator who is beyond our reach." (*Saints Herald,* October 1988). The new spiral tower temple will be 340 feet high, 26 stories tall in all, and will be the center of what the RLDS calls "the coming Theocratic Democracy."

The reorganized Mormon church has congregations throughout the United States and the world, and is especially strong in Third World nations.

ROSICRUCIANS

There are dozens, maybe more, of groups which call themselves *Rosicrucians*. Generally, though their organizational structure and beliefs may vary somewhat, the basic theology and teachings of all these groups is remarkably similar. The best known Rosicrucian society is the group known simply as "the Rosicrucians," or formally as the *Ancient and Mystical Order Rosae Crucis*, whose Supreme Grand Lodge is in San Jose, California. This group goes by its initials, *A.M.O.R.C.* The AMORC declares itself to be the only authorized ancient fraternity of Rosicrucians perpetuating the true traditions of the original society.

The Rosicrucians say that theirs is an illustrious historical order and that such men as English mathematician Isaac Newton, French composer Claude Debussy, English philosopher Frances Bacon, and American statesman Benjamin Franklin were all Rosicrucians. There is some evidence that this is true. History records that Rosicrucianism originated from Freemasonry orders and spread throughout Europe in the 17th century, attracting many influential proponents. The first American Rosicrucian chapter appears to have been founded in Pennsylvania in 1694, while the AMORC group was evidently formed by Harvey Spencer Lewis (1883-1939), a writer and occultist from New York City, in 1915. Immediately, the group's publication, *The American Rosae Crucis*, began distribution and in 1917 the first national convention was held. The AMORC order spread rapidly thereafter.

Two other important Rosicrucian groups in America are the *Rosicrucian Fellowship*, founded by Max Heindel in 1913 and now headquartered in Oceanside, California, and the *Fraternitas Rosae Crucis*, founded in 1858 by Pascal B. Randolph. The latter group grew rapidly in numbers about the turn of the century as a man named R. Swimburne Clymer established its headquarters in Quakertown, Pennsylvania. The present Grand Master is his son, Emerson.

What the Rosicrucians Believe

Rosicrucianism is basically a religious sect which claims it is not religious. Members believe that Jesus was "one of earth's greatest teachers" along with Mohammed, Buddha, Plato, the Hindu gods, and many others. To the Rosicrucians, Christ was not a person but a spirit who took possession of the physical body of Jesus. They say that every man actually possesses the Christ spirit but it must be awakened by good deeds and behavior. In other words, we ourselves accomplish our own salvation through works. The blood atonement of Jesus is said to be an invention of Christianity.

Spirit beings are viewed by the Rosicrucians as good and they are heartily welcomed, especially those who claim to be members of the Great White Brotherhood and the Ascended Masters. Like other New Agers, the Rosicrucians profess a belief in reincarnation, emphasize the "perennial philosophy" and the "ancient wisdom," especially of the Egyptian era, and predict that mankind is moving into the New Age.

The AMORC order of Rosicrucianism, in San Jose, California, operates a unique museum which contains many artifacts and art items from Egypt and the Middle East. It also operates a vast publishing empire and attracts thousands of new recruits through polished ads placed in a number of secular and occult magazines. Answer the ad of AMORC and the group will send you a sophisticated, slick publication called *Mastery of Life* which assures you that by joining AMORC and by paying its fees and annual dues, you will be initiated into the greatest mysteries of the universe.

St. James's Church, London

One of the most famous churches in the world is *St. James's Church*, Piccadilly, in London. Once upon a time, the gospel truth of Jesus Christ and His Word were preached from the pulpit of this grand church structure. But no more. Today, the church has become thoroughly New Age and is permeated with witchcraft. Satan reigns at St. James's, Piccadilly. Behind the main altar of St. James's, to the left is a huge, sculpted black bird, to the right a rainbow is the focal point. Incense fills the air.

A recent *Spring Programme* of concerts, workshops, and seminars offered at St. James's Church stated: "St. James's is dedicated to New Age thinking: ideas which provide creative and spiritual alternatives to currently accepted Western thought."

Among the courses offered were: "Druidism: Its Relevance Today;" "What on Earth is the New Age?;" "What is the New Age Christ?;" "Ley Lines, Art, and Healing the Earth;" "Extra Sensory Perception;" "Models of God for an Ecological and Nuclear Age;" "Dancing the Aramaic Jesus and Creation Spirituality;" "Sacred Dance;" "Wesak-The Buddha's Birthday;" "Sacred Dance and Meditation During New Moons;" "Yoga Meditation;" "Rainbow Economics;" and "Mysticism and Social Action."

Music concerts at St. James's also reflect the new occultic orientation. For example, on April 27, 1989 there was held an "Inti-Raymi Festival of the Sun" at which the participants celebrated Mother Earth's cycle of fertility and rebirth. The ancient Incan religion--worship of the sun god-- was also celebrated.

The Bible clearly prophesies that many churches will, in the last days, preach another gospel. As Paul told the Galatians: "But though we, or an angel from heaven, preach any other gospel unto you than that which we have preached unto you, *let him be accursed*" (Gal. 1:8). Paul also warned that: "In the latter times some shall depart from the faith, giving heed to seducing spirits, and doctrines of devils" (I Tim. 4:1).

In a book and on Britain's BBC-TV, Donald Reeves, pastor of St. James's, made no secret of his contempt for those who preach that Jesus alone saves. "My conversion to Christianity," said Reeves, "had nothing to do with the

Bible, nor the person of Jesus Christ . . . I do not believe that it matters. It is impossible to say, as some evangelists do, with St. Paul, that Jesus Christ is the same yesterday, today and forever!"

Regardless, Reeves insists that he is a "Christian" and that his New Age offerings at St. James's are "Christian." His followers likewise claim Jesus as Master and Christianity as their chosen "faith."

In contrast to Reeve's assertion that he was converted without Jesus' saving grace, we read in Acts 4:12: "Neither is there salvation in any other: for there is none other name under heaven given among men, whereby we must be saved."

ST. JOHN THE DIVINE CATHEDRAL

St. John the Divine Cathedral in New York City is America's largest. It is also a New Age church, although officially it is affiliated with the Episcopal Church. Headed by pastor James P. Morton, this New Age cathedral achieved notoriety in recent years by temporarily displaying a life-sized crucifix with a shapely, female Christ with breasts bared. St. John's called the statue "Christa." The cathedral also has reportedly housed a Buddha statue.

David Spangler, a dedicated Luciferian who teaches that Lucifer is the same force as Christ, was invited to perform a Eucharist at St. John the Divine. Episcopal priest Morton has also endorsed the Earth Religion, contending that Mother Earth is sacred, and he has conducted Native American Indian religious ceremonies.

St. John the Divine Cathedral is closely connected with another New Age group called *Lindisfarne*, and the *Temple of Understanding*, yet another New Age-oriented organization, is headquartered at St. John the Divine Cathedral.

SANAT KUMARA

Sanat Kumara is simply another name for Satan. Indeed, notice that the name "Sanat" is simply the same as "Satan" with the letters slightly scrambled. New Agers leaders such as Benjamin Creme, David Spangler, Alice Bailey, and Helena Blavatsky have all recognized the spirit being known as Sanat Kumara as their supreme deity. For example, according to Alice Bailey of the Lucis Trust, Sanat Kumara is the New Age "God," the "Ancient of Days," and the "One Initiator Whose Star Shown Forth." New Age teachers say that Sanat Kumara came to our planet from Venus and took up residence in the mystical land of Shamballa in the mountains somewhere in Tibet. Benjamin Creme has written:

> In this coming age, many people will see God as Sanat Kumara. They will come before Sanat Kumara and take the Third Initiation ... When you take the Third Initiation you see God as Sanat Kumara, the Lord of the World, who is a real physical being in etheric matter on Shamballa.

There are several New Age "Sanat" groups. In addition to the organizations of Creme and Bailey, another New Age group that embraces Sanat Kumara is an organization which calls itself the *University of the Twelve Rays of the Grand*

Central Sun, located in Charlotte, North Carolina. This group has proclaimed that Sanat Kumara is the one known in The Bible as "the Ancient One of Days, Yahweh, Jehovah, the I AM THAT I AM." The group also maintains that Sanat is "the Light of the Great Central Sun, the Buddha of the Far East, the Lord Maitreya, and the Christ." The phrase "Great Central Sun" is common among New Agers. In occultism, the ultimate deity is actually Lucifer, who is known to the ancient pagans and to modern occultists alike as the Sun God.

SCHOOL OF SACRED ARTS

The *School of Sacred Arts,* founded by Elaine Moore Hirsh, has dedicated itself to teaching, preserving, and perpetuating sacred art traditions from around the world. The school, located in New York City, mails out brochures with pictures of both Jesus and Buddha. Its faculty includes experts on art from about every religion imaginable, including Islam, Tibetan Buddhism, Eastern Orthodox, Hebrew, Hindu, and Ancient Egyptian. Elaine Hirsh believes that "Sacred art is a means of expressing the holy." She says that the artists and scholars of the School of Sacred Art "have come together under one roof to share our secret traditions and spiritual strengths ... We share a common goal." This organization is helping to promote a unified world religious system in which every man worships his own choice of god or goddess, though its statement of purpose does not specifically express this.

SCIENTOLOGY (DIANETICS)

"Scientology is a religion by its basic tenets, practice, historical background, and by the definition of the word religion itself. It is recognized as such by courts and country after country around the world..." This is a statement taken directly from a *Church of Scientology* advertising supplement in the *Los Angeles Times* newspaper in 1990. Scientology is one of the best known of all New Age groups. Millions of people have read L. Ron Hubbard's #1 New York Times bestseller *Dianetics*, subtitled *The Modern Science of Mental Health*. A long string of celebrities have testified that they have been favorably influenced by Scientology. Their numbers include Grammy award winner musician Chick Corea, Elvis Presley's former wife, actress Priscilla Presley, and actors John Travolta and Sonny Bono.

Since its inception over 35 years ago, the Church of Scientology has grown from one church in the United States to over 700 churches, missions, and groups in more than 65 countries around the world. It bills itself as "The fastest growing religion in the world" and boasts that it has millions of members on six continents. Scientology is aggressively seeking new members, spending millions of dollars annually in advertising through TV and print media.

What is "Dianetics?"

In addition to *Dianetics*, the late L. Ron Hubbard authored 22 other national bestsellers, many of them science fiction novels related to the teachings of the Church of Scientology. Scientology defines "Dianetics" as "*dia*, the Greek word for "through," and *nous*, the Greek word for "soul." They say that Dianetics is "what the soul is doing to the body" and characterize it as "the analysis, control, and development of human thought."

There is evidence that L. Ron Hubbard was at one time closely linked with British satanist Aleister Crowley, who worshipped Horus the war god and Nuit, the Egyptian mother goddess, the same goddess known to the Hindus as Kali and to the Greeks at Ephesus as Diana. There are also strong indications that the word "dianetics" in reality has its origins in the worship of the goddess *Diana*. When the Apostle Paul was at Ephesus he confronted merchants who were making money from the sale of souvenirs and paraphernalia to worshippers of the goddess. They were enraged because Paul was persuading so many of the followers of Diana to convert to Christianity. Moreover, today in witchcraft, Diana is commonly worshipped. The suggestion, then, is that L. Ron Hubbard's Dianetics is simply some type of sophisticated, scientific-sounding jargon that reflects the hidden worship of the goddess Diana.

In an expose' book co-authored by his own son, L. Ron Hubbard, Jr., and entitled *L. Ron Hubbard: Madman or Messiah?*, an eye-witness account is given of a young woman scientology recruit who was disciplined by the cult after she supposedly violated one of the cult's rules. According to the book, the young woman was taken to the bowels of the ship *Apollo* owned by Hubbard's Scientology and forced to undergo the following ritual to atone for her "indiscretion:"

> The ceremonies were done below deck . . . There a large idol of (Mother Goddess) Kali had been erected . . . It looked very solid and real and was painted gold. The only light . . . down in the bowels of the ship was the flickering of a few candles . . .

> She was brought forward and led to Kali . . . Then, following the orders relayed from L. Ron Hubbard, she bowed down and chanted to the idol, admitting her "evil intentions" . . . and dipped her hands in blood (or a solution which was a very good imitation), and smeared it onto the idol, after which chicken bones were strung around her neck.

She came out of there in shock and was overcome with grief for some 48 hours.

Beliefs of Scientology

Whether or not Dianetics is based on the worship of the goddess Diana, it is certainly true that the practice of Scientology and its methods puts a person in grave spiritual danger. L. Ron Hubbard once bragged that Scientology was the "herald of a New Age." He called it the "road to freedom." But, in fact, this is yet another variation of the overall New Age World Religion which will put its followers in complete bondage to demonic forces. Scientology teaches that man is basically good, that the cause of all his problems lies in past experiences during previous incarnations. Through the techniques of Scientology, especially the auditing of one's past lives and the process of reaching "clear" by use of the E-meter, or electropsychometer (a kind of lie detector which monitors stress), the individual can supposedly achieve a form of salvation. Scientology also teaches the same spiritual race theories as do other New Agers, although different names are used for the various race strata. Quoted below, from Scientology's own literature, are other beliefs of this New Age religion:

There are gods above all other gods, and gods beyond the gods of the universes.

Hell is a total myth--a vicious lie.

The Christ legend was implanted a million years ago.

Personal salvation is freedom from the cycle of birth and death (reincarnation).

The above quotes indicate the unchristian nature of Scientology. Scientology is extremely critical of Christianity

Scientology founder L. Ron Hubbard.

and Christ. According to Scientology doctrine, the highest spiritual race of mankind today is the "Thetan." An Operating Thetan (OT) is a person who is "above clear" and is god-like. But Scientology teaches that "Neither Lord Buddha or Jesus Christ were OT's." Of course, this is in great variance to the Holy Bible which tells us that Christ is "... the image of the invisible God ... For by Him were all things created, that are in heaven, and that are in earth, visible and invisible ... All things were created by Him, and for Him: And He is before all things, and by Him all things consist" (Col. 1:15-17, and see Heb. 1:13).

Scientology also teaches that life is simply "a game," a game in which everyone can win. The Church encourages a number of occult practices including astral travel, or out-of-body experiences, as well as the belief that a person can discover past-life experiences. Through its techniques, Scientology says that it can help the person to deal with the problems of the past and the present so that the god-like Thetan spirit of the person can express itself. Like many other New Age cult groups, Scientology rarely talks about the nature of God Himself. The Church's focus is on individual self-improvement and the creation of a planet which Scientology proposes could become free from environmental problems, war, drugs and crimes if only people were to avail themselves of Scientology's benefits.

To discover more about Scientology, I recommend you

consult one or more of the many books which have come out over the years exposing this group. These books include *The Hidden Side of Scientology*, by Omar V. Garrison; *The Bare-Face Messiah*, by Russell Miller; *A Piece of Blue Sky: Scientology, Dianetics, and L. Ron Hubbard Exposed*, by John Atack; and *L. Ron Hubbard: Messiah or Madman?*, by L. Ron Hubbard, Jr. and Bent Coryden.

SELF-REALIZATION FELLOWSHIP

Those who are naive enough to believe that *yoga* is simply a series of physical exercises much like calisthenics have obviously not studied the Hindu religion. The late Paramahansa Yogananda, founder of the *Self-Realization Fellowship*, specializes in imparting to his followers "the ancient philosophy of yoga." Yogananda makes it very clear that in his Hindu religion yoga is a spiritual philosophy and a part of the religious process. Yogananda teaches a form of yoga called *Kriya Yoga*. In Kriya Yoga a person uses their own mental processes to supposedly experience God directly through occult meditation.

Yogananda is the bestselling author of the book *Autobiography of a Yogi*. His group operates Self-Realization Fellowship meditation centers around the United States and abroad where students meet for worship services and to practice the meditation techniques learned in lessons available by mail. The Mother Center, as Self-Realization calls it, the international headquarters, is in Los Angeles. An American woman re-named Sri Daya Mata, whose title is "The Reverend Mother," is president. In India, a related group is known as the Yogoda Satsanga Society. The logo for the group is a lotus flower with a star inside a circle.

Paramahansa Yogananda emphasized that each person is God and that the way to godhood is to realize or awaken to this truth. Thus, the name "self-realization." He wrote that, "Only spiritual consciousness--realization of God's presence in oneself and in every living being--can save the world." Yogananda also tried to explain away Jesus Christ's words in John 14:6 when Christ testified, "I am the Way, the Truth, and the Life: No man cometh unto the Father, but by me." According to Yogananda, Jesus never meant that he was the *only* Son of God, but that no man can realize his own godhood until he has first manifested the "Christ Consciousness." Jesus was not any more special than you or I, says Yogananda. He was simply a man who achieved oneness with the Christ Consciousness, so much that his own ego was dissolved.

The answer to self-realization lies in the principal of reincarnation, writes Yogananda: "The truth is that man reincarnates on earth until he has consciously regained his status as a son of God."

According to the literature published by the Self-Realization Fellowship, Sri Daya Mata, its president, is the spiritual successor of Yogananda. She spent more than 20 years of day-to-day association with her guru master Yogananda. Like her mentor, she believes that the words in Psalm 46:10: "Be still and know that I am God" apply to the individual. These are not words from God, but are words we must incorporate into our own consciousness so that each person can say "I am God."

During his lifetime, Paramahansa Yogananda was one of the most well-known gurus. He came to America as early as 1920 and in the mid-20s filled halls in Los Angeles, Boston, and elsewhere almost to capacity as he addressed such groups as the International Congress of Religious Liberals. Yogananda died in 1952.

SETH

Psychologist Jane Roberts first met the spirit *Seth* when she began experimenting with a Ouija board. The date was December 8, 1963. Roberts had decided to do a book on extra-sensory perception (ESP). She decided to obtain a Ouija board so she could sort of "do it  yourself" and see if the spirits of the beyond could really be communicated with.

On a snowy winter evening she and her husband, Rob, began to move the pointer around on the Ouija board. "Do you have a message for us?" Rob asked. "Consciousness is like a flower with many petals," replied the pointer. Fascinated by the seeming ability of the Ouija's pointer to provide answers, Rob and Jane quickly asked, "By what name do you prefer to be called?" The answer: "To God, all names are his names."

From that occultic beginning, Jane Roberts went on to conduct over 500 sessions with Seth. Eventually, the spirit Seth literally would take over her body and control her physical responses during the sessions.

When Jane Roberts first published her books, beginning with *Seth Speaks* and including *The Seth Material*, they were an overnight sensation among those interested in medium-istic activities, the supernatural, paranormal behavior, and the New Age movement. Jane Roberts continued to write more books, including *The Education of Oversoul Seven; The Nature of Personal Reality; Psychic Politics; The Unknown Reality: A Seth Book; The God of Jane;* and *Seth: Dreams and Projection of Consciousness.*

Soon, those who had read the Seth books began to meet at local homes around the United States and overseas, devouring Seth's works much as a Bible study group in a conservative protestant church would the Bible. What Seth taught them was vintage New Age material. For example, the channel spirit entity told psychic/medium Jane Roberts:

It is natural to be bisexual.
Evil and destruction do not exist.
We create our own reality.
There is no authority superior to the guidance of a person's inner self.

Seth's teachings also include admonitions that meditation and contact with spirit beings are very important to one's spiritual development. Moreover, Seth taught that it was natural to be gay, whether homosexual or lesbian. And he suggested that New Age doctrines and philosophies were on target. Finally, he affirmed the New Age belief in reincarnation, claiming that he himself had lived many lives. For example, Seth claims to have lived in the body of a Mr. Frank Withers, who died in Elmira, New York in 1942.

Today, advocates of Seth continue to meet in local homes, but a number of formal centers have also been established in the United States. Psychic Jane Roberts is

Jane Roberts channeling the spirit "Seth."

now deceased. Still, the teachings she gave the world through Seth continue their dynamism.

Seth Conferences

In Austin, Texas, each year Seth disciples from around the globe meet annually to fellowship and study Seth's teachings in depth. In 1988 the seminars during this annual convention included the channelling of "Abraham," by Esther Hicks, a spirit channeler, and seminars entitled "The Nature and Value of Dreams;" "God Concept;" and "Getting What You Want." Perhaps the most interesting seminar, however, was one conducted by a Mr. Toni Kosydar, a former high school coach from Reno, Nevada. Kosydar, believe it or not, taught the conferees how to *speak in tongues*. Indeed, he taught them how to *sing* in tongues. Here is how a conference brochure described the course, *What is Sumari, and How Did it Come About?*, to be taught by Toni Kosydar:

> Toni will speak on how Jane Roberts came to sing in Sumari and what the experience meant to her--and could mean to us. Jane: "I heard a babel of voices in strange languages. I didn't know what I was supposed to do with them, but I knew that something was expected of me. Suddenly I chanted the words in a loud, ringing voice: 'Sumari, Ispania, Wena nefarie, Dena dena nefarie, Lona Lona Lona Sumari.' Then, in whisper, someone else said in my voice, 'I am Sumari. You are Sumari. It is your family name. Throughout the ages you have been Sumari. I am acquainting you with your heritage.' At the same time a delicious warmth filled my body. It came like a glow, from inside, radiating outward."

The brochure went on to explain that this is what was called "speaking in tongues." It explained that: "The Sumari language is not an language in the ordinary sense. Its importance lies in its sounds, not in its written patterns. The sounds do things. The meaning is apart from the power of the sounds."

During the conference, Toni Kosydar demonstrated how a person could create and then interpret the Sumari songs that involve speaking in tongues. In addition, he also taught the group how they could all sing in tongues and dance at the same time in a form of holy dancing.

The Seth World Conference in Austin is only one of a number of activities conducted by Seth around the nation. Through the Seth Centers, one can purchase audio tapes by Roberts and also the Seth video, which demonstrates Seth speaking through Jane Roberts. The Seth Centers provide consultations, perform past life regressions so that people can learn what kind of lives they lived in previous incarnations, and distribute metaphysical material. The use of dreams and their interpretations is also important in the Seth material.

SHARE INTERNATIONAL

"Lord Maitreya, the Christ is back," says Benjamin Creme, co-leader of *Share International*, and he is going to put an end to the inequality of economic distribution in the world. That is the message of *Share International*, a magazine published by the foundation of the same name which has administrative offices in London and Los Angeles. The directors of Share International are Peter Liefhebber, a Dutch journalist who Share International says is "concerned with the creation of a new world economic order," and Benjamin Creme, a British artist and occult author. Their contention is that a spirit entity named Lord Maitreya has manifested himself on earth, in the physical flesh, and now lives in a Pakistani community in a suburb of London, England. Soon the Christ will reveal himself and inspire all of humanity with the will to end mass hunger and abolish threat of war. To accomplish this, the rich must share with the poor and the world's resources must be redistributed equally to all. Share International is basically a subsidiary or an adjunct to the Tara Center, a cultic group which we will study later in this book.

THE SILVA METHOD

It used to be called "Silva Mind Control," but the term "mind control" had many negative connotations and so José Silva, the Laredo, Texas, hypnotist who founded *The Silva Method,* astutely decided to change the name a few years ago. Silva, who claims that he is still a believer in the Roman Catholic Church in which he was raised, nevertheless advocates a number of occultic practices and teachings to those who undertake the Silva Method. Admittedly this is a popular course. It was estimated some five years ago that about six million people in more than 70 countries had taken the 48-hour-long course. Hundreds of thousands of these individuals were so pleased that they went on to take advanced courses in the Silva Method.

The Silva Method promises to put the person into contact with a spirit guide who can stay with the individual and become a life-long companion. So for those who wish to conjure up through visualization and occult meditation a demonic spirit from the deep and befriend that spirit for an eternity, Silva is just the thing. Silva proposes that by use of the visualization and meditation process it recommends, it can teach the individual to develop capability at the *delta* level of mind consciousness. At this level, so the claim goes, the person becomes cosmically conscious and is capable of "Christ awareness."

Silva has also endorsed a faddish but very unscientific left brain, right brain theory of pop-psychology. The notion is that the right brain is the creative, intuitive, spiritual and emotional side of a person's personality while the left side is more mathematical, logical, commonsense, and rational. Silva and other New Age theorists propose that an individual's right brain, his or her spiritual side, can be developed, resulting in spiritual growth. Again, I wish to emphasize that the United States Government, through the National Research Council of the National Academy of Sciences, thoroughly researched all the claims of the right brain, left brain theorists and found them severely wanting. Indeed, although man certainly does physically have left and right brain hemispheres, there is no evidence whatsoever to indicate that one side or the other has the different functions-- for example, rational, logical, inquisitive, spiritual, creative, etc.--as proposed by quack-psychology. Nevertheless, because the theory has caught on in the public imagination, Silva and other groups continue to use it and benefit.

You can contact Marilyn Monroe...or Thomas Jefferson!

The Silva Method entices recruits into paying and attending their courses by promising to develop ESP, clairvoyant powers. Some who have graduated from the course have claimed that they were able to visualize such famous personages as Shakespeare, King Henry VIII, Marilyn Monroe, Elvis Presley, George Washington, Thomas Jefferson, and John Wayne, among others. Some individuals have even said that they were able to engage in "sex relationships" with the departed spirits. One Silva graduate related that during his visualizing of a certain well-known author who had passed away some years before, a spirit who had been the critic of that author in real life suddenly came on the scene and the two spirits began to fiercely debate the author's works.

Although the Silva Method would no doubt deny its occultic basis, nevertheless, there is little attempt by its teachers to cover up the fact that the Silva Method employs techniques and ideas closely related to hypnosis, yoga, and Transcendental Meditation. What they do not admit is that there is grave danger to those who summon up demonic spirits from the depths of their own imaginations. In her bestselling book, *The Beautiful Side of Evil*, Christian author Johanna Michaelson told of her experiences with the Silva Method. The teacher and guide whom she visualized was "Jesus," but it turned out that this was a false Jesus, another Jesus (see 2 Cor. 11:4, and Gal. 1). Eventually, the Jesus who had at first seemed so loving, soothing, and kind revealed his true self. To her horror, Johanna discovered that the "Jesus" she had been visualizing and worshipping was a demonic spirit who attempted to frighten her into submission by changing into the form of a vicious werewolf! Only by turning away from everything she had learned in Silva and turning to the *real Jesus* was Johanna Michaelson able to overcome this astonishingly evil presence.

SIRIUS COMMUNITY

The star known as Sirius is visible in the skies over America only during the winter months. The Sirius star was honored by many ancient religions. It was considered sacred to the Egyptians who worshipped the goddess Isis. Likewise, the ancient Hindus and especially the Dogon tribe of Africa venerated Sirius. Throughout the centuries Sirius has been recognized by most occultists and esoteric teachers as the location where Lucifer and his hierarchy dwell. In Christian terminology, Sirius is simply a secretive codeword for "hell."

The New Age community called *Sirius* is named after the star. However, the leaders of the Sirius Community say that their star is "the source of love and wisdom for the planet." There is no reference to Lucifer or Satan in this group's literature. Sirius Community was begun in 1978 on 86 acres of land by former members of the Findhorn Community in Scotland. Today there is only a small group of New Agers at Sirius, but there are many associate members across the country and the world. The community practices group meditation and believes in atunement to nature and in the interconnectedness of all things. Recently, an issue of the *Sirius Journal*, the newsletter of the Sirius Community, pictured a man dressed as the pied piper leading children through the woods during May Day festivities in the community. How appropriate for a community which claims to be a "center of light and positive vision and service to the world" but in reality is yet another vehicle being used by the Adversary today.

SOCIETY OF CRYSTAL SKULLS, INTERNATIONAL

Are crystal skulls "now coming forth to assist in creating Planetary Peace and to announce a Golden Age?" Do crystal skulls contain "the untold secrets of the Universe and life itself?" Are crystal skulls "the most powerful tools that exist for expanding the mind?" These are the astonishing assertions of the *Society of Crystal Skulls, International (SCSI)*, an organization founded in New York and California in the 1940s by Frank R. "Nick" Nocerino.

A number of crystal skulls have been discovered around the world by archaeologists and anthropologists. They believe that the pagans carved these crystal skulls to facilitate worship of the spirit world and to placate demonic forces. Today, those in the New Age and the occultic and esoteric societies do not always fully agree with the scientific community on the origins of these skulls. Some maintain that the skulls were brought here by UFO aliens. Others have proposed even more bizarre origins for the crystal skulls that have been found.

Frank Nocerino has studied metaphysical matters for over 40 years and has lectured extensively on crystal skulls. He and his group maintain that the skulls may include images of UFOs and that inside the skulls one can find holographic pictures. They also suggest that the skulls may actually be "ancient computers" and that if they can be reactivated, the skulls can "help usher in the manifestation of the Aquarian Age." Many in the New Age also believe that the crystal skulls have esoteric healing powers and can be used as a medium to contact and communicate with spirits.

Frank Nocerino, head of this Society, is presented as an authority in what the Society terms "psychic and hypnotic sciences." He has also made the news by assisting in the investigation of houses supposedly haunted by ghosts and poltergeists. The Society of Crystal Skulls, International is located in Pinole, California. The society distributes literature and especially the book *Mysteries of the Crystal Skulls Revealed*. The group also offers a video, in which Nick Nocerino introduces viewers to crystals, entitled *Your Personal Journey in The Crystal Skulls.*

SPIRITUALISM

It is a bestselling book published by a major New York publisher. Its shocking title is *The Dead Are Alive: They Can and Do Communicate With You.* The book's author is Harold Sherman, a psychic and spirit medium who also wrote a companion book, *You Live After Death.* Harold Sherman is only one of many who practice *Spiritualism*, but the unfortunate thing about Sherman's book is that it is endorsed by a well-known Christian authority: Dr. Norman Vincent Peale. On the cover of Sherman's book is this blurb by Peale: "A masterpiece! Could be the greatest of all of Sherman's great books. I hope it will be widely read."

Norman Vincent Peale is not the only person to endorse spiritualism. Although the Bible expressly prohibits communication with the spirit world (for example see Deut. 18), in recent years more and more so-called "Christian" authorities are admitting their involvement in what is called *necromancy*, communication with demonic spirits.

Bestselling books have been written advocating spiritualism. Perhaps the best-known author is Ruth Montgomery, a former journalist who supposedly conjured up the late Arthur Ford from the spirit world and later developed contact with a number of other spirits. In such books as *The Walk-Ins* and *Strangers Among Us,* Montgomery insisted that the spirit world is benign and is actively promoting the good of the living. Another who admits to contact with the spirit world is Bernie S. Siegel, M.D., who wrote the bestseller *Love, Medicine, and Miracles.* Dr. Siegel says that the name of his spirit guide is "George."

Although almost every New Age leader readily admits that his or her guidance comes directly from the spirit world, there has been for many years a spiritualist association of churches in the United States and abroad. The *National Spiritualist Association of the U.S.A.* was organized in Chicago in 1893 and has held annual conventions almost every year since. It is not, however, the only spiritualist association. Also there are many independent spiritualist congregations. In a recent issue of *The Messenger*, called "a magazine about, by, and for Spiritualists," a number of churches were listed, including the First Psychic Spiritualist Church of Brightmore, Detroit, Michigan; the Church of Spiritual Love, Deerfield, Florida; Believers Circle, Bakersfield, California; and the Spiritual Church of Harmony, Peoria, Illinois.

Spiritualists do not believe in a personal God, but instead affirm a belief in "Infinite Intelligence." They believe that the individual spirit continues after death and that departed individuals can therefore be contacted and communicated with. They also insist that these contacts can be scientifically proven. They believe that the highest morality is contained in the Golden Rule and that individuals have no responsibility to obey a personal God but instead must obey "Nature's physical and moral laws." In essence, spiritualists believe that men are good, that there is no original sin, nor was there a fall from grace. They deny that man needs salvation through Jesus Christ, and they reject the biblical doctrine of eternal punishment in hell for unbelievers who reject the one true God.

Spiritualist churches have worship services in which they invoke the spirits to give them spiritual understanding and show them the way to peace and happiness. They have readings also. One reading from the *Spiritualist Manual* declares: "How great the power of spirits! A host of invisible intelligences, exalted and wise, surround us everywhere."

In meetings, the church's leader calls on the spirits to come forth to be received with joy and thanksgiving. It has also been reported that in a number of spiritualist churches, members of the congregation participate in what can only be described as "mind-sex" with spirits. This is done through a form of visualization, imagery, and fantasizing.

Unfortunately, men and women who have recently lost loved ones and are in an understandably hurting state of mourning are often quite vulnerable to the promises of spiritualist charlatans. Such charlatans claim that departed loved ones can be contacted in the spirit world through the ceremonies, invocations, and rituals of the spiritualist churches. Many bereaved persons have been conned out of great sums of money by such flim-flams.

SRI AUROBINDO

Hindu guru *Sri Aurobindo*, now deceased, developed a large following of devoteés from the United States, Canada, Europe, and his native India. In the section on *Auroville*, I discussed the founding of that Hindu ashram community by Aurobindo and his female companion and co-teacher, The Mother.

In the United States, several groups continue to promote the teachings of Aurobindo. One such group is the Sri Aurobindo Association, in High Falls, New York. This group publishes a periodic newsletter/magazine called *Collaboration*. In addition, the group holds an annual meeting at which a number of authors and teachers of Aurobindo are brought in to conduct seminars. For example, last year, seminars and workshops were conducted on such topics as *Tai Chi; Sri Aurobindo's Yoga; Health and Healing in the Yoga; Parenting in the Yoga; Dreams and Visions; African Dance;* and *Astrology as a Tool of Awareness.* It is plain to see that the interests of the modern-day followers of Aurobindo is quite varied. Indeed, there were also workshops on square dancing, chanting, and meditation.

Like all Hindu yoga groups, Sri Aurobindo followers believe strongly in the laws of karma and rebirth as taught in the Hindu scriptures. They are also believers in the mother goddess and in the universal force which all New Agers contend is "God." They also feel strongly about the sacred word "aum." All are deeply connected to the memory of Sri Aurobindo and perceive themselves as disciples of The Mother as well.

In addition to the Sri Aurobindo Association, there are a number of other related groups. There is for example, Sabitri House in Crestone, Colorado, which inspires to become a community on the order of Auroville. One of the supporters of Sri Aurobindo is Maurice Strong and his wife Hanne. They are, in fact, the chief officers of the Sri Aurobindo learning center in Baca Bluffs, Crestone, Colorado. Strong is an extremely rich man who has definite connections with what some would call the Illuminati; for example, David Rockefeller, the Rothschilds, and others of the money elite. (For more information about this group, whom I call the "Lords of Money," see my book *MILLENNIUM: Peace, Promises, And They Day They Take Our Money Away*).

Other Sri Aurobindo centers are located in San Francisco, California; Culver City, California; Sacramento, California; and New Delhi, India. In addition, a number of Sri Aurobindo disciples make a pilgrimage each year to Auroville in south India for the international meeting of the group.

SRI CHINMOY

Olympic champion sprinter Carl Lewis gives *Sri Chinmoy* credit for inspiring him to break world records as an athlete. Well-known guitarist John McLaughlin adoringly calls Sri Chinmoy "a divine being." Such laudatory compliments are not unusual for the Hindu guru Sri Chinmoy. This is a man who has talked with the Pope and is well-known at the United Nations, where he regularly conducts meditation for U.N. officials. In 1990 Sri Chinmoy was invited to the Soviet Union where he met privately with President Mikhail Gorbachev and gave the Russian leader a book of "love poems" written by Chinmoy.

Sri Chinmoy came to the United States in 1964. He now operates centers in the United States, Canada, Europe, and Australia. He teaches the Hindu spiritual doctrine of yoga, advocating that his followers can become united with "the Supreme," his name for God, by practicing Hatha Yoga, meditation, and vegetarianism, and by total devotion and surrender to their guru. Naturally, for those who are his own students, Chinmoy is the guru who demands unswerving devotion.

THE STELLE GROUP

The Stelle Group became famed throughout the New Age Movement in the 1960s after its leader, Richard Kieninger (a.k.a. Eklal Kueshana) wrote the bestselling book, *The Ultimate Frontier.* Kieninger claimed in the book that he had been initiated by the Ascended Masters in a ritualistic ceremony in which a cutting was made on his body, leaving a mysterious "mark." Kieninger is no longer with the group; he left after a dispute over finances and amidst allegations of misconduct.

The Stelle Group is a community in Stelle, Illinois which professes belief in "mystic Brotherhoods" from the spirit world. The group owns 200 acres of farmland and offers developed lots to prospective residents. It also offers a Home Study Course, presents guest lectures and seminars, makes a reading room available, and publishes a quarterly journal, *The Philosopher's Stone*. The latter publication features articles on such topics as metaphysics, health, prosperity, self-reliance, and personal growth.

SUFI MOSLEMS

Sufism is a form of Islamic belief which deviates from orthodox Islam and adopts almost all of the primary teachings of the New Age Religion. The word *Sufi* has a number of meanings but essentially means "purity," as in pure wool. There are as many as 70 orders of Sufi Moslems around the world. But in the United States the principal Sufi order is the *Sufi Islamia Ruhaniat Society* in San Francisco, California. This society was established by American Samuel L. Lewis (known among the Sufis by the name of Murshid Sufi Ahmed Murad Chisti). Lewis founded the Sufi choir and also began an organization called *The Dances of Universal Peace*, in which Sufis dance to symbolize their message of the brotherhood of all humanity. Dancing also serves the purpose of bringing the dancers into a state of altered consciousness as they whirl, howl, and whip themselves into a frenzy.

Fundamentalist Moslems have almost nothing in common with the Sufi Moslems. The Sufis do not believe that Allah and Muhammad are the only way. They teach that the only holy book is "the sacred manuscript of nature." Furthermore, among their tenets is the idea that there is only one religion and that is the religion of the individual soul; the Sufis say there is only one truth, "the true knowledge of our own being." Moreover, there is only one path, the path to human perfection. The object of the Sufi movement, according to its leaders, is "to realize and spread the knowledge of unity." They also say that they wish to bring the world's two opposite poles, East and West, together to establish a universal brotherhood without national or racial boundaries.

Interestingly enough, one of the top Sufi leaders has said that he began his order when Mary, the mother of Jesus, appeared to him as a spirit and directed him to do so. This is just one indication of the universalism of the Sufis and their acceptance and tolerance of any and all beliefs. The Sufis also revere Jesus Christ and the Bible, but they do not regard Jesus as the only way to salvation nor the Bible as the only set of sacred scriptures. It is entirely possible that you may come across a Sufi Moslem who insists that his faith is perfectly compatible with Christianity. In such an instance, you must be ready to discuss with the person the Truth: that Jesus Christ is uniquely God, that the authority of the Holy Bible is assured, and that man cannot find peace and grace except through Christ alone.

SWEDENBORGIANISM

Emmanuel Swedenborg (1688-1772) was a brilliant scholar widely recognized in his time for his expertise in geology and mineralogy. He was acclaimed as a university professor, was a member of the Swedish parliament, and was recognized for his research on metallurgy and crystals. However, later in life he became fascinated with esoteric writings and occult literature.

Emmanuel Swedenborg sought and acquired such occultic abilities as astral travel (spirit travel to other worlds to communicate with spirit entities). He practiced automatic handwriting and consulted mediums. He wrote commentaries on the Bible from an occult/esoteric perspective. Bible prophesy especially fascinated Swedenborg. Many say that Swedenborg can rightly be called the "Father of Spiritualism."

Possibly the best known Swedenborg group is the *Church of the New Jerusalem*. Generally, Swedenborgians believe that Swedenborg's writings were divinely inspired. Among their teachings: that there is a state, much like the Catholic's purgatory, where after death the individual goes to prepare for heaven or hell. Another teaching is that Jesus did not shed His blood for our sins but simply died on the cross after "a life of service." Moreover, the Holy Spirit is not a personality, say the Swedenborgians, and Jesus Christ is not wholly God, for God is a force that can be called the "Divine Essence."

Like their founder, Emmanuel Swedenborg, modern-day Swedenborgians believe that the Old Testament is of little value. They are also opposed to almost anything written by the Apostle Paul.

With all of these heresies and despite their strong and fervent belief in communication with the spirit world, the Church of the New Jerusalem has been fully accepted for membership in both the National of Churches (NCC) and the World Council of Churches (WCC). Maybe this has a lot to say about the NCC and WCC. In a recent issue of *Chrysalis*, a journal of the Swedenborg Foundation, a Swedenborg group in New York City, we find articles on reincarnation, the I Ching, and other occultic subjects. Because of their endorsement of the Swedenborgians, what does this tell us about *whom* the NCC and WCC serve?

TARA CENTER

The headline from one of the sensationalist weekly tabloids trumpeted: "Mystic Heals Thousands Then Vanishes into Thin Air!" In the article itself, the author announced:

> Jesus Christ has returned to earth amidst sweeping reports of miraculous mass healings and strange religious events. Jesus is said to have recently appeared before 6,000 worshippers at the Church of Bethlehem near Nairobi, Kenya. He addressed the crowd in perfect Swahili--the local language--and is said to have healed 20 cripples, then vanished into thin air, according to a report in the *Kenya Times*.

According to the Tara Center of North Hollywood, California, and London, this is only one of the many reports that have begun to flood the world indicating that the "Christ" is back. The leader of the Tara Center, Benjamin Creme, claims that Christ has returned but that his real name is "Lord Maitreya." The mystical Maitreya is the one whom worshippers in Kenya believed was Jesus Christ, says Creme. In addition, the Tara Center has maintained that, actually, Maitreya is the reincarnation of Mother Mary, the mother of Jesus.

Evidently, Creme and his Tara Center either have a lot of money to waste or they are sincere in their beliefs, or both, because their announcements that the Christ is back have been published as full-page ads in such major newspapers as *The London Times, USA Today, The Los Angeles Times, The New York Times*, and as many as 16 other major newspapers across the world. Similar ads have been placed in the *Reader's Digest.*

In an issue of *The Emergence* (October 1990), a news tabloid published by the Tara Center, the headline blared, "He's back!" The fine print said that:

He has been expected for generations by all the major religions. Christians know Him as the Christ, and expect His eminent return. The Jews await Him as the Messiah; the Hindus look for the coming of Krishna; Buddhists expect Maitreya Buddha; the Muslims anticipate the Imam Mahdi. The names may be different but they all designate the same One: The World Teacher whose personal name is Maitreya. He returns now, at the beginning of the Age of Aquarius, as the teacher and guide for those of every religion and those of no religion.

It is Creme's contention that this Christ descended from the mythical land of Shamballa above the mountains of Tibet. Then, assuming the body of a Pakistani, he traveled to London where he has since taken up residence in a poverty-stricken suburb populated by local Pakistanis. Creme's group has a number of times declared that "within a few months," Lord Maitreya will reveal himself to the world, appearing magically on television screens across the globe and declaring himself as the Christ of the new Aquarian Age. This is the event that Creme calls the "Day of Declaration." Creme says that all peoples will understand Maitreya's voice telepathically in their own language and that this will fulfill the Bible prophecy that the eyes of all in the world will see Him (Christ) simultaneously. Unfortunately, Mr. Creme has not read his Bible very closely. According to I Thessalonians, Jesus Christ will return to earth *in* the air, not *on* the air.

Creme's failed prophesies of the imminent return of Maitreya do not seem to have dented the reputation of either this articulate Englishman or his occultic group, the Tara Center. In recent years the group has escalated its activities.

I had the opportunity to debate Mr. Creme on a radio talk show in the state of Texas. Though Creme spoke persuasively about his Lord Maitreya, each time he made a statement that conflicted with the Bible, I quickly brought it to the attention of the audience. Following one exchange, in which Creme politely called me an idiot for believing that Jesus, instead of Maitreya, was the real Christ, I calmly referred Creme to I John 2:22 which states: "Who is a liar but he that denieth that Jesus is the Christ? He is antichrist, that denieth Father and the Son." In other words, I let Creme and his followers know right on the air that their master was none other than Satan himself and that anyone who confesses that Jesus is not *the* Christ is of the antichrist.

After about an hour of these exchanges, Benjamin Creme became so angry and agitated with me that he angrily bellowed out, "You . . . you . . . you're just like all those other Christian fundamentalists. You have no intelligence of your own. All you can do is refer back to the Bible." To which I immediately responded, "Praise God, why should I attempt to use my own intelligence when the greatest intelligence of the universe, God Almighty, wrote this Book?"

Creme has traveled the United States and Europe as well as mainland China, Australia, New Zealand, and other nations, stumping for his Lord Maitreya. His group, the Tara Center, has also established a number of "Transmission Meditation" groups. These consist of smaller local groups who hold meetings at which the followers of Maitreya gather and meditate. Most visualize the return of the Lord Maitreya and recite and chant the Great Invocation of Alice Bailey and the Lucis Trust. The Tara Center also publishes newsletters and books. Creme has authored such books as *Maitreya's Messages* and *The Reappearance of the Christ.*

Benjamin Creme has said that he first came to know of the Lord Maitreya as the Christ when certain "Space Brothers" beamed a light into Creme's mind and told him that he was to become the messenger, sort of a "John the Baptist" type forerunner, for the New Age Christ, the Lord Maitreya.

Does Creme's Lord Maitreya really exist or is he simply a figment of the imagination? If he does exist, could Lord Maitreya be the antichrist, the man with the number 666 whose hideous activities are described in Revelation 13?

Personally, I doubt very seriously that this Lord Maitreya will turn out to be the antichrist. Jesus Himself in Matthew 24 warned that in the last days many false christs would come. Maitreya is simply one of the many christs who have been introduced by various New Age leaders. The acceptance by so many of these false christs should remind Christians everywhere that those who truly trust in Jesus Christ are a decided minority in the world. Moreover, Maitreya and the other false Christs serve as a constant reminder to us that these may indeed be the last days.

THE TEMPLE OF SET

When a strange man named Anton LaVey burst on the public scene in the 1960s and announced that the Church of Satan, of which he was the high priest, was founded on May Eve (Walpurgis Night, a holy day for satanists), 1966, most people were  shocked. Could it be that there was actually a Church of Satan operating in America? The answer was most decidedly *yes*. LaVey and his Church of Satan received an inordinate amount of publicity in the first few years of its existence, culminating in the bestseller book by LaVey entitled *The Satanic Bible* and a popular movie, "Rosemary's Baby."

In 1975, Dr. Michael Aquino and his wife Lilith resigned from the Church of Satan and established their own group, *The Temple of Set*. Set is an ancient Egyptian destroyer-type god, whose name is actually a synonym for Satan. Aquino, a Lt. Colonel in the U.S. Army, evidently believes his to be a more sophisticated form of satanism. He has incorporated his knowledge in a book, *The Coming Forth By Night*, and also publishes a newsletter, *The Scroll of Set.*

The several hundred members of this group are scattered about the United States. The Temple of Set itself was first established in San Francisco, but Aquino was soon reassigned by the Army to St. Louis, Missouri. He has now split with Lilith and his marital status is unknown.

There have been many rumors circulated about Michael Aquino and the Temple of Set. At one time he was under investigation for the molestation of young children in satanic rituals. However, the charges were dropped by police and Aquino vehemently denied the allegations, claiming to be a victim of harassment by officials opposed to his religious beliefs.

Aquino maintains that Satan is more an energy force than a person. As a guest on the "Oprah Winfrey Show" and a number of other television programs, Aquino has insisted that his church group is not involved in any child sacrifices or similar satanic practices. Indeed, he adamantly denied that such incidents are even occurring.

Reportedly, Aquino once traveled to Germany where he obtained the use of an arcane medieval castle which was once used by Hitler's concentration camp master, the bloody Heinrich Himmler. At this same castle where Himmler's SS Gestapo troops were initiated in dark occult ceremonies, it is said that Aquino and associates performed a black mass ritual.

An interesting aside of the Aquino saga is that in a recent issue of *The Scroll of Set*, Aquino presented information about his friendship with the late entertainer Sammy Davis, Jr., including the revelation that Davis had been a member in good standing of the Church of Satan during his lifetime. Aquino's account is for the most part confirmed by the late entertainer's own autobiographies.

THEOSOPHY

Theosophy is truly *the* cardinal religious organization of the New Age. Founded by Helena P. Blavatsky (1831-1891), a Russian woman mystic, Theosophy is the original fount from which hundreds of other New Age cults, religions, and organizations have sprung. Blavatsky was a powerfully persuasive advocate of a conglomeration of religious teach-ings, which included Hinduism, Buddhism, Egyptian and Greek mythologies, Satanism, spiritualism, and Freemasonry. All these she intricately combined into a series of books which together became known as *The Secret Doctrine.*

Blavatsky and Her Spiritual Superiors

Blavatsky claimed that her first book, *Isis Unveiled*, was written while she was in Tibet where she made contacts with disembodied higher spiritual beings whom she called "Mahatmas," or "Great Spirits." So taken was Helena Blavatsky with these spirit entities that she actually set up an altar to them in her home.

Helena Blavatsky was said to be a worker of supernatural miracles. On one occasion she reportedly commanded red roses to rain down from the ceiling of the room after a skeptical guest made light of her highly touted miraculous abilities.

For a number of years, Blavatsky resided in India. While there, she became advisor to a number of Indian personages, one of whom was to later become the most famous Hindu leader on planet earth. That man was Mahatmi Gandhi. In his own autobiography, Gandhi stated that as a young man, uncertain about his Hindu religious heritage, he decided to study Christianity to decide if he might convert to Jesus Christ. Hearing of the renowned Blavatsky, and mistaking her for a Christian, he went to see her and inquired about Christianity. Blavatsky bluntly told the young seeker that Hinduism is superior to Christianity and that he should therefore remain a Hindu. Impressed by her charisma and authoritative nature, Gandhi promptly abandoned his study of Christianity and Jesus.

Elvis and Theosophy

A number of renowned people have fallen victim to the evil powers inherent in studying Helena Blavatsky's *Secret Doctrine*. General Abner Doubleday, inventor of the modern American pastime and sport of baseball, was once the president of the Theosophical Society of America. Famed inventor Thomas Edison, father of the electric light, was also a theosophist. And amazingly, singer Elvis Presley, world-acclaimed "King" of rock 'n' roll, evidently became a Blavatsky fan. On one occasion during a live concert, Elvis, who biographers say possessed a personal library amply stocked with occultic books, actually read on-stage from Blavatsky's books.

A number of other famous historical figures were

Helena Blavatsky, often called the "Mother of the New Age."

theosophists, including Nichola Tesla, who devised our present-day electrical generating systems, acclaimed writers George Bernard Shaw and William Butler Yeats, and India's late Prime Minister Jawaharlal Nehru. Like their mentor Blavatsky, all these initiates fervently believed that they were part of a universal brotherhood of illumined souls who are in close communication with leagues of "gods," lesser deities, and angels *(devas)*.

Theosophy in 60 Countries

In a recent interview by the *Chicago Tribune,* Dorothy Abbenhouse, the current president of the Theosophical Society of America, stated:

> There are nearly 30,000 theosophists in 60 countries; 5,500 of them in the United States ... The largest concentration is in India, where adherents number 10,000.

According to Abbenhouse, Theosophy "is not *a* religion. It *is* religion." She further stated: "Its (Theosophy's) concepts and philosophies form the basis for every religion in the world," and she noted that Theosophy promotes various beliefs and philosophies ranging from Hinduism and Tibetan Buddhism to Shamanism (sorcery) and holistic health.

Theosophy has its international headquarters in Madras, India. Since 1926, its U.S. headquarters has been in Wheaton, Illinois on 44 acres of wooded land. There a visitor will find the 15,000-volume Olcott Library and Research Center, with one of the most complete collections available anywhere of occultic, mystical, and Eastern religious literature.

Theosophy carries on an extensive publishing operation (including audiotapes, books, and videos) through the Theosophical Publishing House and the Quest Books imprint. Much of this material focuses on metaphysics and esoteric doctrines. Shirley Nicholson, editor of Quest Books, has boasted, "The Secret Doctrine (of Theosophy founder Helena Blavatsky) is the basis of the New Age."

The Teachings of Theosophy

The word *theosophy* comes from the Greek word "theosophia," meaning "the wisdom of God," or "divine wisdom." Theosophists claim that their doctrine is the *real* Christianity, but in fact, they vehemently renounce almost every tenet of traditional Biblical Christianity. The "Christianity" of Theosophy is closely akin to gnosticism, a body of esoteric beliefs which the Apostle Paul and other New Testament writers uniformly exposed as unholy and erroneous.

Though today's Theosophy teachers rarely bring up the subject, the idea of a New Age "Christ" or "Messiah" was originally the brainchild of Annie Besant, an Englishwoman who became the leader of this group after the death of founder Helena Blavatsky. While living in India, Mrs. Besant, who had abandoned her husband to immerse herself in Theosophy, became entranced by a young Indian boy named Jiddu Krishnamurti. First, she adopted him as her son. Later, in 1925, Besant announced that Krishnamurti was the reincarnated "Christ" for the New Age.

Besant's claim startled the worldwide followers of Theosophy, but most were willing to go along. However, the shy and unassuming young Krishnamurti flopped badly during what was supposed to be a triumphal tour of the United States. Embarrassed over his incompetence, his followers began to cast doubt on Besant's claims that he was indeed the avatar or "Christ" on whom they were waiting.

Finally, in 1931, a dejected Krishnamurti himself abruptly renounced his title of "Christ" and subsequently became an independent guru and "philosopher," a real comedown from his former highly touted and exalted status as "chosen Christ of the world."

The Secret Doctrine

Those who read and study Helena Blavatsky's two volumes of *The Secret Doctrine* and her huge volume *Isis Unveiled* are led into a system of beliefs some call the "Perennial Philosophy" or the "Ancient Wisdom." This system teaches that there are seven levels in the universe. We live on the physical level, or plane. There is also the astral plane, the mental plane, and, highest, the divine plane. Each person, through evolution, is said to be progressing or evolving through successive planes toward godhood, which is taught to be union with the absolute, the hazy all-is-all "god." God to Theosophy is the entire galaxy and universe.

Through Blavatsky's works, Theosophy also teaches a spiritual and physical race theory. The theory holds that humanity is composed of "root races," some inferior, others superior. One such race was that of the Atlanteans who supposedly lived on the mythological continent of *Atlantis*. Some 15,000 years ago, Atlantis was destroyed, Blavatsky's spirit guides told her. In the wake of this destruction, the *Aryan* race became the premier super-race. Through a process of reincarnation, karma, gnosis, and enlightenment, men and women can successfully evolve and effect blissful union with divinity.

If you'll recall Hitler's strange beliefs from studying history, you'll remember that the German dictator held these very same concepts regarding a race of Aryan supermen. In fact, Hitler was a devoteé of Blavatsky's *Secret Doctrine*, which he learned as a result of his early membership in an occultic society named the Thule Society.

The various spirit beings, Theosophy propounds, are led by a superior deity identified as the "Lord of the World." The "Master Jesus" works for this shadowy deity in the spirit world. According to Blavatsky, the Great Seal, or symbol of the Lord of the World includes a combination of symbols, such as the Egyptian ankh, a swastika, the Hindu word *Om*, and two interlocking triangles (the Jewish Star of David). These are said to signify the universalist nature of

Theosophy and its appeal to a multitude of persons with a pantheistic variety of deities, doctrines and beliefs.

In Theosophy, any and all gods are accepted *except* the personal God and the true Jesus of the Old and New Testaments.

Theosophy and its Imitators

Theosophy has spun off or inspired a number of other New Age cults, groups, and religions, including the Lucis Trust, the Church Universal and Triumphant, the Liberal Catholic Church, and the I AM movement. From her grave, the influence of the determined and diabolical Helena P. Blavatsky is still being felt. I have personally had letters from her modern-day fans and admirers who insist that Blavatsky's spirit will someday reincarnate into the body of a man. That man, they say, shall become the one whom the Christians will call the "Antichrist." My response, of course, is that this is quite impossible. Heb. 9:27 clearly explains where the souls of men and women go after death of the physical body. There *will* be an antichrist (see Rev. 13), but he will *not* be Blavatsky reincarnated.

TRANSCENDENTAL MEDITATION (TM)

Through his "Vedic Science," Maharishi Mahesh Yogi says, mankind can create a heaven on earth. To prove this, the Maharishi is spending millions of dollars to build 20 "Heavenly Communities" throughout Canada and the

United States. The residents of these communities will be followers of Maharishi and practitioners of his form of Hindu meditation, popularly known as *Transcendental Meditation,* or TM. The Maharishi is quite a colorful character with his robes and his long scraggly beard and hair. His official address is the Maharishi World Capital of the Age of Enlightenment in Maharishi Nadar, India. But in the United States he bought up a failed college in the state of Iowa and renamed it Maharishi International University (MIU). His group also has centers in almost every large city in America and his followers can be quite fanatical about the benefits of Hindu meditation.

The TM technique is actually no different than any other Hindu occult meditation. The Maharishi has done his best to disguise this fact. He has called it the "Science of Creative Intelligence," and has been able to get many schools to adopt TM as an official course. However, the United States Court of Appeals, sitting in Philadelphia, affirmed an earlier decision of a Federal District Court that declared TM to be religious in nature. Thus, it must be barred from classrooms. In the case of *Malnak v. Maharishi Mahesh Yogi,* October 19, 1977, the presiding judge ruled that TM was an inseparable part of the Hindu tradition and that because of its religious foundations, TM's presence in the public schools violated the establishment clause in the First Amendment to the United States Constitution. Nevertheless, some schools and public learning institutions supported by taxpayer monies continue to offer TM to their students.

Those who undergo TM training believe that they will gain the benefits of creativity, clear thinking, and--in the minds of many--self-divinity. There is absolutely no proof whatsoever to justify these claims. In fact, the scientific evidence available indicates that the regular practice of TM *diminishes* creative thinking and undermines sound, rational processes of the human mind. In reality, TM is simply a religious ritual in which the person prostrates himself or herself to a Hindu guru, chanting a mantra, or word, which in most cases is the name of a Hindu deity.

UFO CULTS AND SOCIETIES

"UFOs Here Now on Special Mission!" This was the headline of an ad recently in *Sun*, a weekly tabloid. The ad offered a book, *Extraterrestrials in Biblical Prophecy*, which says that space visitors are coming to warn the occupants of the earth that there are terrible events soon to transpire and that the world is headed for a spiritual crisis. Unlike the old days when UFOs and flying saucers were considered mechanical objects flown to planet earth by aliens from outer space, today's UFO cults and societies are promoting a *religion* and a *theology*. Regrettably, in most cases, this religion and theology is classic *New Age*.

The evidence that New Age powers have taken over most of the UFO cults and societies is staggering. In *UFO Universe* magazine (Summer 1989), New Age psychic and spirit channeler Brad Steiger wrote an article entitled "UFO Contactees--Herald of the New Age." Steiger contends that the UFOs are seeking to bring "God" physically to this planet and they are offering mankind a "space age theology." He goes on to say: "The UFO contactees may be evolving prototypes of a future evangelism. They may be the heralds of a New Age religion, a blending of technology and traditional religious concepts."

According to Steiger, space vehicles may not be from outer space at all. Instead, they could be evidence of a new consciousness, a new awareness, and a higher state--or frequency--of vibrations. Indeed, the UFOs may actually be god-like presences who are channeling messages to men which, Steiger suggests, "May be the scriptures and theological treatises of the New Age." The same thesis has been suggested in articles in magazines as varied as *Omni, ReVision,* and the *Reader's Digest.*

Even the names of the new UFO cult groups reflect New Age and occultic influences. For example, there is the *Ashtar Command,* which describes itself as an "extraterrestrial communications network." Ashtar (or *Ishtar*) was a name of the goddess who originated in the mystery religion of Babylon (see Revelation 17). The Ashtar Command not only provides its followers information on UFOs and extraterrestrials, but also discusses the benefits of crystals, gemstones, and certain holistic health herbal preparations. One of the latter is called a "New Age Elixir."

Perhaps the best known recent instance of abduction by UFOs is that of Whitley Strieber whose book, *Communion*, became the number one bestselling non-fiction book in the United States. Strieber said that he was abducted by beings who traveled about in a crystal-like, pyramid-shaped spacecraft. The leader of these UFO beings was a "woman," whom Strieber described as resembling "Ishtar, the ancient Babylonian goddess." One can easily recognize the many New Age influences in Strieber's account--for example, the images of the pyramid, crystal, and mother goddess of Babylon.

UFOs Say A World Government is Coming

Many of the individuals who are members of the UFO cults and societies report that they have made contact with the UFO aliens and that these strange beings are bringing a spiritual message to mankind. That message is that mankind must come together as one. There must be a *world government*. Then all of humanity can join the greater galactic federation of planets. Some of the contactees say that the UFO aliens have threatened that if mankind does not voluntarily come together great havoc and destruction will be rained on planet earth. The UFO aliens also tell contactees that Christianity is not the only way, that Jesus is not really God, that all men are evolving into divine beings, and that all religions must be merged into one. Only then will there be peace, love, and fraternity.

There is no doubt that the UFO cults and societies are finding more and more adherents. And there is also no doubt that demonic beings are behind most of the UFO reports. It

The alien pictured on the cover of Whitley Strieber's bestselling Communion. Other UFO contactees report experiences with similar creatures.

appears that the UFOs being sighted are apparitions-- thought forms projected into men's minds by demonic forces. The people seeing the UFOs and conversing with their occupants are quite often very sincere and intelligent people. It cannot be denied that many did experience something. That "something" usually conveys unbiblical and unholy messages, so we can easily discern the source. However, there is no proof whatsoever that the UFOs and the extraterrestrials are actually composed of physical matter. All the evidence is to the contrary.

The UFO phenomenon is primarily a spiritual and mental occurrence. I believe that it is very possible that the current rash of reports of UFO sightings and abductions is simply another part of the prophetic puzzle for today. It is a sign that men and women everywhere have forsaken the true God and have opened up their minds to dark influences.

UNARIUS

"Yes, Napoleon is alive and well, now reincarnated in the present 20th century to tell the incredible story of his life and death." This comes from the colorful catalog of books, tapes, and videos offered by the New Age cult group *Unarius*. I find Unarius the most fascinating and intriguing-- as well as one of the most occultic--of New Age groups. Its founders, Ruth and Ernest Norman, are unbelievable, outrageous and almost comical characters.

Ruth Norman, who dresses up in the most stunning of costumes as a star goddess from another galaxy, makes preposterous claims. For example, she says that she is in reality Uriel, the Solar Logos, who has come to earth to bring man the "Christ Consciousness." To do this, Uriel has supposedly incarnated into the body of Ruth Norman. Mrs. Norman also says, however, that in a previous life she was Mary of Bethany, 13th disciple to Jesus of Nazareth. She and her husband's group, Unarius, offer the most fantastic of books to their audience. One is entitled *The Confessions of I, Bonaparte*. In the book Napoleon Bonaparte, the once

Ruth Norman of Unarius with her royal scepter and regal attire.

Emperor of France whom Unarius claims is now a member of the Universal Brotherhood and a god-like spirit being, says that Ruth Norman--Uriel--is his spiritual mentor.

Unarius also offers the book entitled *The Apology of John the Baptist.* It gives "an account of the tragedy of John and his inordinate desire to advance Jesus as the Jewish Messiah." According to this blasphemous book, the late John the Baptist, now a spirit, confesses his sins in worshipping Jesus and admits that he was insane at the time. Unarius also publishes a book called *The True Life Of Jesus Of Nazareth,* a nonsensical book which Unarius advertises as a book which "slashes through 2000 years of Christian fanaticism." According to Norman, the book "Exposes for all time the great hypocrisy of the Christian religion as a culmination in a villainous plot, contrived by the archvillian, Saul of Tarsus (Paul), and his cohort, Judas Iscariot."

It would be easy to dismiss the dozens of books and products offered by Unarius as absurd examples of fruitcake zaniness, but evidently, judging from the sophisticated catalogs and the vast quantity of publications of the group, Unarius holds a lot of influence among some New Agers. The anti-Christian campaign by Unarius provides graphic and uncontestable proof that the occult world is deadly serious about the destruction of biblical Christianity.

THE UNIFICATION CHURCH (REV. SUN MYUNG MOON)

The Unification Church, popularly known as the "Moonies," has a notorious reputation. Its founder, Rev. Sun Myung Moon of Korea, did time in federal prison for tax manipulation. He became famous in the 70s for conducting mass marriages of over 1,000 couples at once. For these marriages, Moon himself personally selected the bride and bridegroom for each other. Moon's theology as taught by the Unification Church is quite unique. He has published a book, *Divine Principle*, which teaches that Jesus, as well as Adam and Eve, failed to do what God desired. Jesus failed in His mission, says Moon. He was supposed to marry and bear perfect children but was killed before he could accomplish His given tasks. Because of Jesus' failure, Moon has said that a "Lord of the Second Advent" must now come on the world scene. It is he who shall provide for the salvation of the world that Jesus could not achieve. Moreover, Moon intimates that this new Christ will hail from South Korea. Many of his followers believe that Moon refers to himself as that messiah.

Moon teaches a theological concept called *Godism*, the idea that all men are universally evolving into perfection. According to the Moonies, the God of Judaism, Mormonism, Hinduism, Buddhism, and all others is one and the same. Godism is also said to be a formula for ushering in the kingdom of God on earth by human effort. Thus, Moon's philosophies--and his abundant supply of money and financial largesse--have appealed to a number of Christian ministries, evangelists, and leaders who are themselves involved in a heretical movement called the Kingdom Now or Dominion Theology.

Moon's Reincarnated Son

A recent stir was caused when it was exposed that Moon's Unification Theological Seminary had begun to teach that a young man from Zimbabwe was Moon's reincarnated son. Moon's son, Jin, had been killed in a car crash in 1984 at age 17. But now, Moon believes that he has come back from the dead in the body of a visiting church member from Zimbabwe. An official of Moon's church seemed highly pleased with the news accounts of the reincarnation of Moon's son in the body of this Zimbabwean. Frederick Sontag, editorial director of Paragon House, a Moon-financed publishing company, remarked of the reincarnation account, "This has been revitalizing...a sort of calling back of spiritualism... Its really been a great phenomenon." (*Washington Post*, March 30, 1988)

Rev. Moon has created a number of front organizations to promote his doctrines and personal goals. One such group is CAUSA, a political arm.

Moon's Unification Church has few members today, yet his great personal wealth makes him a force to contend with. His goal is said to be that of establishing a super race, a new international family of perfect people. It is clear to see that Moon's theology is classic New Age occultism.

UNITARIAN-UNIVERSALIST CHURCH

In 1959 when the Unitarian Church merged with the Universalist Church to form the *Unitarian-Universalist Association*, it became a case of the blind leading the blind into the ditch. Together, these churches consist of members who have turned their face away from the truth of Holy Scripture. The Unitarian-Universalists have as their goal the promotion of harmony and unity among all religious faiths, Christian or otherwise. Unfortunately, in their desire to promote unity, this church has renounced almost every facet of historical biblical Christianity. Falsely claiming to believe in both Christ and the Bible, the Unitarian-Universalist Association makes light of the virgin birth; they also reject the Trinity and the doctrine of salvation through Jesus Christ alone. They profess that Jesus Christ is little more than a wonderful teacher, and assert that the Bible is only one of many sacred writings available from all the great religions. Naturally, for such a liberal body, concepts such as heaven and hell are considered ridiculous and the Christian doctrine that Jesus Christ died on the cross for our sins is scoffed at and summarily dismissed.

Until recently when the New Age fad caught on with the masses, the Unitarian-Universalist Church was in a tailspin in terms of membership, with its ranks steadily declining. However, in recent years, mainly due to the fact that this group is fully in concord with most of the doctrinal foundations of the New Age Religion, membership has increased slightly. According to the Rev. William F. Schultz, president of the liberal, 190,000 member denomination, membership increased some 1.4 percent in 1989.

UNITY CHURCH

Unity Church is aptly named. One researcher has said that this is a group which embraces practically everything and rejects nothing. Actually this is not correct. Unity Church, also variously called the Unity School of Christianity, the Unity School of Positive Christianity, or the Unity School of Practical Christianity, is willing to accept any and all beliefs *except* fundamentalist Christianity. Such doctrines as the atonement of Jesus Christ on the cross, the inerrancy of the Bible, judgment of a righteous, personal God, and so many other unshakable convictions that Christians have held since our Lord and Savior died on the cross for us--all of these are considered unsophisticated, uncouth, and even ridiculous according to many ministers and members of Unity churches.

Unity's doctrines and teachings are greatly similar to those of Christian Science and the Church of Religious Science. All three are connected with the New Thought movement. When Charles and Myrtle Filmore founded Unity in 1889 their intent was to formalize the teachings of such men as Phineas Parkhurst Quimby, a quack mental healer whose teachings were extremely popular in the latter part of the 19th century.

Unity also borrows heavily from the Hindu teachings of such gurus as Swami Vivekananda, an Indian Hindu leader who achieved a measure of popularity as he came to America and preached the unity of all religions under the umbrella of Hindu superiority. Unity, therefore, embraces such concepts as reincarnation and the existence of many sacred books in addition to the Bible. Like the Hindus, Unity preaches that "God" is not personal but is simply "love," a type of force or energy which permeates the universe. Instead of worshipping Jesus Christ, Unity proposes that we seek our own "Christ Consciousness." In the Unity theology, evil and sin are illusions. As Myrtle Filmore taught, "I am a child of God; therefore, I do not inherit sickness." To eradicate physical ills and mental sickness and to attract happiness, all a person needs to do is to tap into, or become attuned, aligned, or united with the "Divine Mind."

Unity is one of the fastest growing New Age church systems. It is especially seductive because it preaches a Jesus of love and harmony. Rarely do those who attend Unity Churches consult God's Word. If they did, beginning with Genesis and continuing on to the book of Revelation, no doubt the Holy Spirit would convict them and they would quickly discard the heretical teachings of Unity.

URANTIA

I have discovered that *Urantia* is easily among the most deceptive of the New Age cult groups. It is deceptive because it offers mankind another Jesus, a false Jesus. As many as one million people or more have in one way or another been impacted so far by the teachings of Urantia, and the cult group is growing astronomically in numbers each day. It operates through a number of cooperating groups with a variety of names. The Jesusonian Foundation, Boulder, Colorado, is one group. Another is the Urantia Brotherhood and yet a third is the Urantia Foundation. There are also separate "societies," each composed of ten or more people, throughout the United States. The followers of Urantia are also now cooperating with those involved in the *Course in Miracles* cult, and Urantia is reaching out its tentacles to unite many other New Age and apostate Christian groups and churches as well.

Founded in 1955, with its beginnings in Chicago, Illinois, Urantia teaches that traditional--that is biblical--Christianity is in error because it has made these two great mistakes: "First, biblical Christianity teaches that Jesus was the sacrificed Son who would satisfy the Father's stern justice and appease the divine wrath," and second, "Christianity wrongly organizes the Christian teaching so completely about the *person* of Jesus." We readily see, then, that Urantia, although it claims to be a new revelation of Jesus, is a false religion hostile to and in direct competition with true Christianity.

Urantia has chapters, or societies, forming all over the United States. This New Age organization has its own bible, *The Urantia Book*, a 2,097-page behemoth supposedly given by divine inspiration. In this book, disciples learn that they can invite "Thought Adjusters" (Christians know them as demons) to dwell within. These Thought Adjusters allow the individual's Higher Self to experience "the presence of God." Men should be thankful, says *The Urantia Book*, "that the Thought Adjusters *condescend* to offer themselves for actual existence in the minds of material creatures." Lowly humans are indeed blessed that the higher spirit beings are ready "to consummate a probationary union with the animal-origin beings of earth."

The Urantia Book teaches that the indwelling of these spirits should cast out fear and uncertainty. When such negative thoughts enter a person's mind, they should immediately look to "Satania" for relief:

> When the clouds gather overhead, your faith should accept the fact of the presence of the indwelling Adjusters ... Look beyond the mists of mortal uncertainty into the clear shining of the sun of eternal righteousness on the beckoning heights of the mansion worlds of Satania.

Urantia students obviously believe "Satania" to be heaven and the Thought Adjusters to be angelic presences. I have no doubt that many who study *The Urantia Book* truly believe they are doing right. Tragically, the power of Satan has so engulfed the minds of these men and women that they cannot discern the truth.

VALLEY OF THE SUN
(DICK SUTPHEN)

Richard (Dick) Sutphen, founder and head of the *Valley of the Sun*, is definitely one of the major stars in the New Age firmament. A man of entrancing charismatic persona who possesses intellect and wit, Sutphen has established an impressive series of training programs and seminars and is publisher of a number of New Age books, tapes, and videos. Sutphen, an activist against fundamentalist Christianity, once suggested that the New Age had a great advantage because it could change and redefine its terms at ease. At one time Sutphen established a newsletter, the principal function of which was to attack fundamentalist Christian teachers opposed to the New Age Movement.

Sutphen specializes in subliminal message tapes, hypnosis, and occultic New Age symbols. He has advocated meditation, automatic writing, and use of the pendulum, and is an astute believer in traditional metaphysical concepts of reincarnation, karma, and the unity of all religious beliefs. Sutphen is especially well-known for his self-help tapes which promise the individual that he or she can attain any one of a number of personal goals such as high energy, personality transformation, getting by on less sleep, personal power, monetary success, physical healing, psychic ability, and so forth.

WINDSTAR FOUNDATION (JOHN DENVER)

John Denver and his friend, Thomas Crum, inaugurated the *Windstar Foundation* in 1976. Denver is the singer and actor ("Oh God!") who rose to prominence on the back of the nature and environmental lyrics of such songs as "Rocky Mountain High" and "Sunshine on My Shoulder." Through his Windstar Foundation, John Denver has been able to promote his favorite pet philosophies--that the earth is a sacred being and that man must organize into a one world community. Windstar is located on about 1,000 acres in the Rocky Mountains of Colorado, not far from Aspen. Many famous New Agers and occult teachers have trekked to Windstar for symposia and conferences. Among the speakers have been actor Dennis Weaver, management author Dr. Ken Blanchard, Soviet apologist Vladimir Posner, World Futurist Barbara Marx Hubbard, self-help psychologist Leo Buscaglia, Atlanta politician Andrew Young, Cable News Network founder Ted Turner, J. Peter Grace of the Sovereign Military Order of Malta (Knights of Malta) and head of W. R. Grace Corporation, and many, many more.

One of John Denver's newsmaker projects has been to promote his plans to fly on a Soviet space mission. Because he has been a big mover in the world peace movement and has promoted Soviet Union propaganda so often, Denver may very well be selected for a future Soviet space flight. In 1988, wire reports stated that Denver was allowed to give a briefing at NASA headquarters on his plans to fly on a Soviet space mission. According to the reports, some NASA astronauts became very angry because they were required to attend the briefing which they correctly perceived as a bunch of pro-Soviet propaganda. The *Houston Chronicle* reported that one veteran astronaut angrily condemned the September 6, 1988 briefing as a "waste of time and an insult to the astronauts who had better things to do."

Meanwhile, NASA, whose top officials have also invited such New Age leaders as est's Werner Erhard to address high level managers and astronauts, has agreed to team up with the United Nations, Amway Corporation, and John Denver's Windstar Foundation for the cause of "environmental protection and awareness." Amway, in its *Amagram* of May, 1990, bragged of its sponsorship of the project.

WORLD GOODWILL

World Goodwill is an organization closely linked with the Lucis Trust and the Arcane School. Founded by Alice Bailey, whose teachings and works came directly from the demon world through her spirit guide, Dwjhal Khul, the Tibetan Master, World Goodwill is headquartered in New York City. World Goodwill works very closely with the United Nations and its leadership is active not only in New York City but also in London and Geneva. The group publishes a number of reports and conducts symposia and conferences related to its goals which are completely consistent with those of the Lucis Trust.

World Goodwill proposes that there is an unidentified and unnamed group of men existing in the world today who are working together, networking toward the goal of fulfilling the occult Plan of creating a One World Order. Members of this secretive group, which World Goodwill calls the *New Group of World Servers*, are supposedly working in the highest levels of government, finance, education, religion, and other fields to advance the inte-gration of the nations, the unification of all religions, and to inaugurate a New International Economic Order (NIEO).

WORLDWIDE CHURCH OF GOD

The *Worldwide Church of God (WCOG)* was founded by radio evangelist Herbert W. Armstrong in 1934. Armstrong also established Ambassador College and set up a network of churches. For years his *Plain Truth* magazine was read regularly by millions. After Armstrong passed away, the church's membership declined, and today the WCOG operates with decidedly less impact and influence. Significantly, the new leadership of the Worldwide Church of God (WCOG) drastically revised the church's teachings. Many objectionable books by Herbert W. Armstrong were removed from circulation.

A number of countercult authorities believe that its new doctrine places the WCOG in the mainstream of the Christian establishment. As a result, they no longer categorize WCOG as a cult or false religion. However, at least one group insists that the changes in doctrine are cosmetic, for public consumption only, and claims that the aberrant teachings of Armstrong have not been fully renounced.

With the announced changes in doctrine has come a severe rift in church membership. A number of church pastors, remaining faithful to the teachings of founder Herbert W. Armstrong, have split off. These factions continue to promote Armstrongism. Therefore, it is important we examine the key false teachings and doctrines of the *original* Worldwide Church of God.

(1) Like other New Age religious teachers, Herbert W. Armstrong preached that man's destiny is to become divine like God Himself. In his book, *The Incredible Human Potential,* Armstrong stated: "God's purpose in creating man is to reproduce Himself-- with such perfect spiritual character as only God possesses."

(2) Jesus Christ in John 3:3 reveals to us that to receive salvation a man must be born again, becoming a new creature in spirit. Armstrong's contrary teaching is that God does not or cannot instantaneously create a new spirit in a person. In *The Incredible Human Potential*, Armstrong writes: "Such perfect spiritual and holy character cannot be created by fiat. It must

be developed, and that requires time and experience."
In other words, salvation is not the immediate work
of God, a gift to the person who cries out to the
Lord and repents, but is a *process* of *work*s.

(3)   Armstrong taught that Jesus alone of all humans
has so far been saved. He wrote: "Jesus was the
first human ever to achieve it--to be perfected,
finished as a perfect character." (see *Why Were You
Born?*, pages 11-14). Here again we find the New
Age doctrine that Jesus did not come in the flesh as
God, but instead had to earn his salvation through
works. How different is this teaching than the
instruction we find in the Bible. For example, John
8:46 tells us that Jesus alone was born without sin
and lived a sinless life. John 1 clearly tells us that
Jesus was not a created being but has always been
God. Blasphemously, Herbert W. Armstrong also
wrote that the teaching that Jesus came in the flesh
as God is a "Satan-inspired doctrine." Armstrong
maintained that anyone who taught that Jesus was
other than a normal human being when he was born
is "of the antichrist."

(4)   Also, like all other New Agers, Herbert W.
Armstrong's version of the Worldwide Church of
God claims that all of mankind collectively is
becoming God. In *Why Were You Born?* (pages 21,
22) Armstrong stated that at the time of the
resurrection, "We shall then be born of God--we shall
then *be* God!"

(5)   Herbert W. Armstrong taught that the wicked
will not suffer eternal punishment but, instead, will
be annihilated.

(6)   According to Armstrong, the modern nation of
Israel has no place in Bible prophecy and has been

written off by God. Today, Israel is actually Britain and the United States.

(7) In the original Worldwide Church of God theology, the Holy Spirit is not a person, but should more properly be translated as an "It."

(8) The Armstrong group says that Jesus Himself had to be "born again." At his resurrection, Jesus became born again and took on a spirit body.

(9) According to Armstrong's Worldwide Church of God, God the Father is not all-knowing but He continues His learning process. Even though there will be billions of gods, each of whom will continue to learn, God the Father will stay ahead of the other gods because He had a head start.

This is only a sampling of some of the more ridiculous and unholy doctrines of the Armstrong version of the Worldwide Church of God. Though it comes seductively wrapped with prophetic garb and sets itself apart from other New Age groups, with its own unique brand of morality and its strong belief in the Old Testament commandments and other legalistic requirements, any Christian who buys into the teachings of Armstrong's WCOG is treading on dangerous territory.

It is a wonderful thing if the new leadership of the Worldwide Church of God has truly turned from these heretical teachings. However, caution is in order. I recommend that Christians who are considering joining this church fully examine its current teachings in light of the Scriptures.

References and Bibliography

A Course in Miracles (Tiburon, California: Foundation for Inner Peace, 1975).

Adler, Margot. *Drawing Down the Moon* (Boston: Beacon Press, 1979).

Ahern, Geoffrey. *Sun at Midnight: The Rudolf Steiner Movement and the Western Esoteric Tradition* (Wellingborough, England: The Aquarian Press, 1984).

Algeo, John. "Will the Real H. P. Blavatsky Please Stand Up?," *The Quest* magazine, Autumn 1988.

Allan, John, *et. al. A Book of Beliefs* (England: Lion Books, 1981).

Armstrong, Herbert W. *The Incredible Human Potential* (Pasadena, California: Worldwide Church of God, 1978).

Atwater, P.M.H. "Perelandra: Cooperating and Co-Creating with Nature," *New Realities* magazine, May/June 1988.

Auroville International Information, 1988 Yearbook.

Bailey, Alice. *Education in the New Age* (New York: Lucis Trust Publishing, 1948).

Bailey, Alice. *Reappearance of the Christ* (New York: Lucis Trust Publishing, 1948).

Bailey, Alice. *The Unfinished Autobiography* (New York: Lucis Trust Publishing, 1951).

Bailey, Foster. *The Spirit of Masonry* (New York: Lucis Trust Publishing, 1957).

Blavatsky, H.P. *The Keys to Theosophy* (Pasadena, California: Theosophical University Press, original ed. 1889).

Blavatsky, H.P. *The Secret Doctrine* (Pasadena, California: Theosophical University Press, original ed. 1888).

Bloomfield, Harold H. *et. al. TM (Transcendental Meditation): Discovering Inner Energy and Overcoming Stress* (New York: Dell Books, 1975).

Boa, Kenneth. *Cults, World Religions, and You* (Wheaton, Illinois: Victor Books, 1977).

Book of The Goddess, The. Edited by Carl Olson (New York: Crossroad Publishing, 1986).

Burns, Cathy, *Hidden Secrets of Masonry* (distributed by Living Truth Publishers, Austin, Texas, 1990).

Cady, H. Emilie. *Lessons in Truth: A Course of Twelve Lessons in Practical Christianity* (Kansas City, Missouri: Unity School of Christianity, 1934).

CAUSA Lecture Manual (New York: CAUSA Institute, 1st ed. 1985).

Choices and Connections '88-'89 (Boulder, Colorado: Human Potential Resources, Inc.).

Chretian, Leonard and Marjorie. *Witnesses of Jehovah: A Shocking Exposé of What Jehovah's Witnesses Really Believe* (Eugene, Oregon: Harvest House Publishers).

Chrysalis, Journal of the Swedenborg Foundation (Vol. II, Issue #3, Autumn 1987).

Clement, Shirley and Virginia Field. *Beginning the Search* (Virginia Beach, Virginia: A.R.E. Press, 1978).

Corydon, Brent and L. Ron Hubbard, Jr. *L. Ron Hubbard: Messiah or Madman?* (Seacacus, New Jersey: Lyle Stuart, Inc., 1987).

Creme, Benjamin. *Maitreya's Mission* (Amsterdam: Share International, 1986).

Creme, Benjamin. *Messages From Maitreya the Christ* (Los Angeles: Tara Center, 1980).

Cumby, Constance. *The Hidden Dangers of The Rainbow* (Lafayette, Louisiana: Huntington House Publishers, 1983).

Dager, Albert. *Are You In A Cult?*, booklet, (Seattle, Washington: Media Spotlight, 1987).

Decker, Ed and Dave Hunt. *The God Makers* (Eugene, Oregon: Harvest House, 1984).

"Eckankar: A Hard Look at a New Religion," special report by Spiritual Counterfeits Project, Berkeley, California.

Epperson, A. Ralph. *The New World Order* (Tucson, Arizona: Publius Press, 1990).

"Erhard's Forum: Est Meets the Eighties," *Newsweek* magazine, April 1, 1985.

Enroth, Ronald. "Any Preventive for the Cults?" *Christian Herald*, circa 1979.

Enroth, Ronald. "How Can You Reach a Cultist?" *Moody Monthly*, Nov. 1987.

Enroth, Ronald. *The Lure of the Cults* (Chappaqua, New York: Christian Herald Books, 1979).

Entwhile, Basil and John Roots. *Moral Rearmament: What Is It?* (Los Angeles: Pace Publications, 1967).

Ferguson, Marilyn. *The Aquarian Conspiracy* (Los Angeles: J. P. Tarcher, Inc., 1980).

Fox, Matthew. *Manifesto for a Global Civilization* (Santa Fe, New Mexico: Bear & Company).

Fox, Matthew. *Original Blessing: A Primer in Creation Spirituality* (Santa Fe, New Mexico: Bear & Company, 1983).

Freeman, James D. *The Story of Unity* (Unity Village, Missouri: Unity Books, rev. ed. 1978).

Garside, Arthur. *The New Age Testament of Light*, (Takapuna, Auckland, New Zealand: New Age Light, 1978).

Geisler, Norman. *False Gods of Our Time* (Eugene, Oregon: Harvest House Publishers, 1985).

Gumprecht, Jane, M.D. *New Age Health Care: Holy or Holistic?* (Orange, California: Promise Publishing, 1988).

"Guns, Bomb Shelters of Sect Worry Neighbors," *The Plain Dealer* (Cleveland, Ohio), Dec. 15, 1989.

Halverson, Dean. "A Course in Miracles: Seeing Yourself as Sinless," *SCP Journal*, Vol. 7, No. 1, 1987.

Halverson, Dean. "A Matter of Course: Conversation with Kenneth Wapnick," *SCP Journal*, Vol. 7, No. 1, 1987.

Heline, Corinne. *New Age Bible Interpretation* (Vols. I-VII) (Santa Monica, California: New Age Bible and Philosophy Center).

Hunt, Dave. *America: The Sorcerer's Apprentice* (Eugene, Oregon: Harvest House Publishers, 1988).

Hunt, Dave. *The Cult Explosion* (Eugene, Oregon: Harvest House Publishers, 1980).

Hyatt, Christopher, interviewed by Antero Ali, "Undoing Yourself," *Magical Blend* magazine, issue #16, 1987.

Ingenito, Marcia. *National New Age Yellow Pages*, First annual 1987 edition (Fullerton, California, 1987).

Irving, Carl. "Cult Recruiters on Campus Gather the Lonely, Insecure," *The Press Enterprise* (Riverside County, California), Mar. 8, 1990.

Isikoff, Michael. "Theological Uproar in Unification Church: Rev. Moon Recognizes Zimbabwean as His Reincarnated Son," *Washington Post*, March 30, 1988.

Johnston, David and Bob Sipchen. "John-Roger. The Story Behind the Remarkable Journey from Rosemead Teacher to Spiritual Leader of a New Age Empire," *Los Angeles Times* (Orange County edition), Aug. 14, 1988, part VI, and Aug. 15, 1988, part V.

Kiefer, Gene. "A Course in Miracles," article in *Critique* magazine #30, 1989.

Kirban, Salem. *Armstrong's Church of God* (Huntingdon Valley, Pennsylvania: Salem Kirban, Inc., 1981).

Koch, Kurt. *Occult ABC* (distributed by Kregel Publishing, Grand Rapids, Michigan, 1978/reprinted 1988).

Kosmon Voice 114 (OAHSPE), Vol. 13:4, August-September 1990.

Kueshana, Eklal (Richard Kieninger), *The Ultimate Frontier* (Chicago: The Stelle Group, 1970).

Larson, Bob. *Larson's New Book of Cults* (Wheaton, Illinois: Tyndale House Publishers, Inc., 1989).

Larson, Bob. *Straight Answers on the New Age* (Nashville: Thomas Nelson, 1989).

LaVey, Anton. *The Satanic Bible* (New York: Avon Books, 1969).

Mac Laine, Shirley, *Out on a Limb* (New York: Bantam Books, 1983).

MacPherson, Pauline Griego. *Can The Elect Be Deceived?* (Denver, Colorado: Bold Truth Press, Inc., 1986).

Matheisen, Michael and "God." *The New American Bible: Ecology of Mind,* (Santa Cruz, California: New Millennium Press, 1987).

Marrs, Texe. *Dark Secrets of the New Age* (Westchester, Illinois: Good News Publishers, 1987).

Marrs, Texe. *Millennium: Peace, Promises, and the Day They Take Our Money Away* (Austin, Texas: Living Truth Publishers, 1990).

Marrs, Texe. *Mystery Mark of the New Age* (Westchester, Illinois: Good News Publishers, 1988).

Marrs, Texe. *Ravaged by the New Age* (Austin, Texas: Living Truth Publishers, 1989).

Marrs, Wanda. *New Age Lies to Women* (Austin, Texas: Living Truth Publishers, 1989).

Martin, Walter. *Kingdom of the Cults* (Minneapolis, Minnesota: Bethany House Publishers, rev. ed. 1985).

McIntosh, Christopher. *The Rosicrucians: The History and Mythology of an Occult Order* (Wellingborough, England: Crucible Books, rev. ed. 1987).

McLaughlin, Corinne, and Gordon Davidson. *Builders of The Dawn* (Walpole, New Hampshire: Stillpoint Publishing, 1985).

Melton, J. Gordon. *Encyclopedic Handbook of Cults in America* (New York: Garland Publishing, Inc., 1986).

Michaelson, Johanna. *Like Lambs to the Slaughter* (Eugene, Oregon: Harvest House Publishers, 1989).

Miller, Edith Starr (Lady Queensborough), *Occult Theocrasy, Vol. 1* (Hawthorne, California: The Christian Book Club of America, 1933/ reprinted 1968).

Montessori, Maria. *Education for A New World* (Madras, India: Kalekshetra Publications, 1948).

Montessori, Maria. *The Three Lords of Ascent* (Madras, India: Kalekshetra Publications, 1948).

Montessori, Maria. *To Educate the Human Potential* (Madras, India: Kalekshetra Publications, 1948).

NAMTA Services Handbook 88-89. (North American Montessori Teachers' Association in affiliation with Association Montessori Internationale).

OAHSPE: A New Bible (New York and London: OAHSPE Publishing Association, 1882).

Palzere, Jane and Anna C. Brown, *The Jesus Letters* (Newington, Connecticut: Janna Press, 1979).

Perry, Robert. *An Introduction to A Course in Miracles* (Fullerton, California: Miracle Distribution Center, 1987).

Plummer, William. "Turmoil in a California Camelot," *People Weekly,* July 1, 1985, pp. 75-77).

Price, John Randolph. *The Planetary Commission* (Austin, Texas: Quartus Books, 1984).

Price, John Randolph. *The Superbeings* (Austin, Texas: Quartus Books, 1981).

Prophet, Mark F. and Elizabeth Clare. *Lord of the Seven Rays: Mirror of Consciousness* (Livingston, Montana: Summit University Press, 1986).

"Psychiatric Disturbances Associated With Erhard Seminars Training: A Report of Cases," by Leonard L. Glass, M.D., Michael A. Kirsch, M.D., and F.M. Parris, M.D., *American Journal of Psychiatry,* March 1977.

"Religion: The Freedom to be Strange," *Time* magazine (March 28, 1977).

Resources 1990 (special edition published by *New Age Journal* magazine).

Ridenour, Fritz. *So What's The Difference?* (Ventura, California: Regal, 1967).

Roberts, Jane. *Seth Speaks* (New York: Prentice-Hall, 1972).

Roberts, Jane. *The Seth Material* (New York: Bantam, Books, 1970).

Rosicrucian Manual (San Jose, California: Supreme Grand Lodge of AMORC, 25th ed., 1978)

Rosten, Jack. *Religions in America* (New York: Simon & Schuster, 1963).

Ruckman, Peter S. *Five Heresies Examined* (Pensacola, Florida: Bible Baptist Bookstore, 1982).

Safran, Claire. "Today's Cults Want You," *Womans Day* magazine, July 10, 1990.

Salvatore, Diane. "The New Victims of Cults." *Ladies Home Journal,* August, 1987.

Schucman, Helen. *A Course in Miracles* (Foundation for Inner Peace, 1975).

Search Magazine (OAHSPE), Winter 1980-1981.

Sinclair, Sir John R. *The Alice Bailey Inheritance* (Wellingborough, Northhamptonshire, England: Turnstone Press, Ltd., 1984).

Siinger, Margaret Thaler. "Coming Out of the Cults," *Psychology Today,* Jan. 1979.

Skutch, Robert. "The Incredible Untold Story Behind 'A Course in Miracles,'" parts 1 and 2, *New Realities* magazine, July/August 1984, and *New Realities,* September/October 1984.

Sparks, Jack. *The Mind Benders* (Nashville: Thomas Nelson, 1979).

Spiritualist Manual, (Milwaukee, Wisconsin: National Spiritualist Association of Churches, revised 1955).

Starhawk, Miriam. "Witchcraft and the Religion of the Great Goddess," *Yoga Journal*, May/June 1986.

Streiber, Whitley. *Communion* (New York: Beechtree Books/William Morrow, 1987).

Swedenborg, Emmanuel. *The Doctrine of the New Jerusalem* (New York: Swedenborg Foundation, 1950).

Szymczak, Patricia. "Theosophists Study Religion and More," *Chicago Tribune*, March 10, 1989, Sec. 2.

Testimony of the Reverend Sun Myung Moon at The Hearing on Religion Freedom, Tues., June 26, 1984, U.S. Senate, Washington, D.C.

The Aquarian Gospel of Jesus the Christ, by "Levi" (Marina Del Rey, California: DeVorss & Co., Publishers, 1907/11th printing 1987).

"The Cult of Death," *Newsweek* magazine, Dec. 4, 1978.

The New Age Catalog, by the editors of *Body Mind Spirit* magazine (New York: Doubleday/Dolphin, 1988).

The New Group of World Servers (New York: World Goodwill).

"The Strange World of est," special report by Spiritual Counterfeits Project, Berkeley, California.

Tice, Louis: *New Age Thinking For Achieving Your Potential* (Seattle, Washington: The Pacific Institute, 1980).

Tucker, Ruth A. *Another Gospel* (Grand Rapids, Michigan: Zondervan, 1989).

Twitchell, Paul. *The Precepts of Eckankar* (Menlo Park, California: Eckankar, 1981).

Watkins, Susan. *Conversations with Seth: The Story of Jane Robert's ESP Class*, 2 Vols. (New York: Prentice Hall, 1980 and 1981).

Westen, Robin. *Channelers: A New Age Directory* (New York: Putnam/ Perigee Books, 1988).

Whalen, William J. *Christianity and American Freemasonry* (Huntingdon, Indiana: Our Sunday Visitor Publishing, rev. ed. 1987).

White, John. "A Course in Miracles: An Interview with Judith Skutch," *Science of Mind* magazine, March 1986.

Wiers, Walter. *Last Battle For Earth (OAHSPE)* (Los Angeles: Walter Wiers, 1978).

Yogi, Maharishi Mahesh. *Inauguration of the Dawn of Enlightenment* (Fairfield, Indiana: Maharishi International University Press, 1975).

Zuromski, Paul, editor, *The New Age Catalog* (New York: Island, 1988).

Index

FOR OUR NEWSLETTER

Texe Marrs offers a free newsletter about Bible prophecy and world events, the New Age Movement, cults, and the occult challenge to Christianity. If you would like to receive a free subscription to this newsletter, please write to:

Living Truth Ministries
1708 Patterson Road
Austin, Texas 78733

ABOUT THE AUTHOR

Well-known author of the #1 national Christian bestseller, *Dark Secrets of The New Age*, **Texe Marrs** has also written 35 other books for such major publishers as Simon & Schuster, John Wiley, Prentice Hall/Arco, Stein & Day, and Dow Jones-Irwin. His books have sold over one million copies.

Texe Marrs was assistant professor of aerospace studies, teaching American defense policy, strategic weapons systems, and related subjects at the University of Texas at Austin from 1977 to 1982. He has also taught international affairs, political science, and psychology for two other universities. A graduate Summa Cum Laude from Park College, Kansas City, Missouri he earned his Master's degree at North Carolina State University.

As a career USAF officer (now retired), he commanded communications-electronics and engineering units. He holds a number of military decorations including the Vietnam Service Medal, and served in Germany, Italy, and throughout Asia.

President of Living Truth Ministries in Austin, Texas, Texe Marrs is a frequent guest on radio and TV talk shows throughout the U.S.A. and Canada. His monthly newsletter, *Flashpoint*, is distributed around the world.